Spiro Zavos played hı[illegible]gby at primary school when he was 5 yea[illegible]ıd has played, watched and written about the ga[illegible] with a passion ever since. After gaining degrees from the University of Wellington and the Catholic University of America, Washington D.C., he worked on the wharves, in wool sheds, in an insurance company and in schools as a teacher before becoming a journalist. He wrote for *The Dominion* and *The Sunday Times* in New Zealand and in the last decade has contributed to *Metro*. Since 1979, he has been an editorial writer on *The Sydney Morning Herald* where in 1991 he began writing a popular rugby column. His other books include *The Real Muldoon*, *Faith of Our Fathers* and *After the Final Whistle*.

the Gold & the Black

SPIRO ZAVOS

THE RUGBY BATTLES FOR THE BLEDISLOE CUP

NEW ZEALAND VS AUSTRALIA 1903–94

ALLEN & UNWIN

For Zolton Zavos and Zachary Zavos

First published in 1995
Allen & Unwin Pty Ltd
9 Atchison Street, St Leonards, NSW 2065 Australia

National Library of Australia
Cataloguing-in-Publication entry:

Zavos, Spiro, 1937– .
The gold and the black: the rugby battles for the Bledisloe Cup.

ISBN 1 86373 904 1.

1. Wallabies (Rugby team). 2. All Blacks (Rugby team). 3. Bledisloe Cup (Rugby tournament). 4. Rugby football - Tournaments - Australia. 5. Rugby football - Tournaments - New Zealand. I. Title.

796.33365

Set in 10/12 pt Palatino by DOCUPRO, Sydney
Printed by McPherson's Printing Group, Maryborough

10 9 8 7 6 5 4 3 2 1

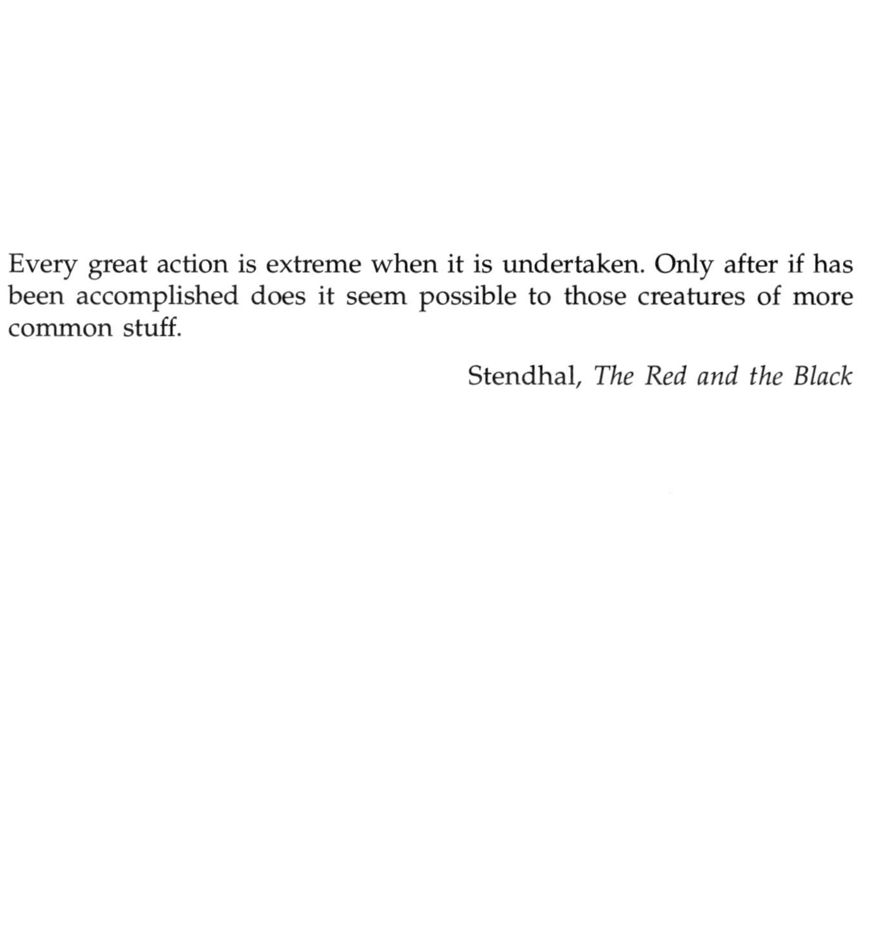

Every great action is extreme when it is undertaken. Only after if has been accomplished does it seem possible to those creatures of more common stuff.

Stendhal, *The Red and the Black*

Contents

Gregan's Tackle

It was the tackle of the century—Gregan's Tackle

The front page of the *Sydney Morning Herald* on Thursday 18 August 1994 carried one of the most dramatic photographs of a rugby match ever taken. The match was the 1994 Bledisloe Cup battle, the 98th Rugby Union Test between the two countries. It was won by the Wallabies 20–16, in a contest that provided a memorable finish that no writer of schoolboy stories could ever dare to present to readers and hope to retain credibility as an author of rattling good yarns. This was the match that will be remembered 100 years on as 'The Test that was won by Gregan's Tackle'.

The headline above the *Herald*'s photograph, which was taken with only four minutes of the Test to go, was a triumphant, nationalistic shout of pleasure: GOTCHA! THE ALL BLACK THAT DIDN'T GET AWAY. The photograph shows a focused, calm-faced All Blacks winger, Jeff Wilson, his brain not yet registering the disaster that has happened to him, diving for the tryline with both feet off the ground, the force of the dive making his blonde hair stand literally on end—and the ball is spilling centimetres away from his left hand. His right hand is stretching and tensing in what is an instinctive, unavailing grab to bring in the ball floating away from him like a fabulous gleaming spheroid. The ball, in this frozen fraction of time, is still tantalisingly close. Still reachable perhaps. Over his right shoulder, about 20 metres back in the distance, can be seen the blurred features of Sean Fitzpatrick, the All Blacks hooker and captain, running up in support as ever, his arms held high to pump the air into his aching lungs, his face with the hint of a smile beginning to form. Have some phrases of a victory speech come into his mind? For the matchwinning try is surely about to be scored, he believes.

Over the other shoulder of the diving Wilson is to be seen the face, inscrutable as a Japanese mask, of the All Blacks halfback, Graeme Bachop, who is running beside his captain. And standing less than a metre away from Wilson, unmarked, is the All Blacks fullback, Shane Howarth. If the ball somehow spills back across to him, or just spills back anywhere nearby, it is the simplest of exercises for Howarth to pick it up and score.

Howarth's feet are forced into the turf of the Sydney Football Stadium like the hooves of a quarter horse trying to stop and then turn. He is leaning back, bracing himself for the dash, in any direction—if the ball is spilled from the grasp of Wilson. The message of despair has not yet passed right through the nerves and sinews of his body. But his fists are clenched. His mouth has the bared-teeth tightness of the grin of death. For his eyes are looking directly at the ball which is floating away from his diving team-mate—floating away and with it the glory of an improbable New Zealand victory.

No Wallabies are visible in the photograph. For at this point in the play the Wallabies are beaten in every aspect of the Test except on the scoreboard. The number of All Blacks streaming up in support of Wilson reflects the dominance the New Zealanders are exerting in this late, but not too late, stage in the match. Over Howarth's tensed right thigh can be seen the blobs of the boots of David Wilson, the Wallaby flanker, lying prone and defeated on the ground, one of the four Wallabies whom Jeff Wilson has beaten with swerves and sidesteps in his dash to the tryline. The right arm and left leg, only, of George Gregan are visible. His tackle on Jeff Wilson has been made from behind, rather than from the side. And because of this miracle of timing and positioning he has hit the diving winger on the back, with great force. A tackle from the side might not have come up on Wilson so unexpectedly. It might, too, have jolted Wilson's left arm more securely around the ball rather than propelling it from his grasp. The power in the Gregan tackle has come from the impetus generated by a strongly planted left leg. Gregan's arms encircle the waist of the All Blacks winger. The fingers on his right hand are spread out as if grasping, searching for that elusive prize, the ball. And the ball is floating away . . . floating away, along with the marvellous tackle, into the collective memory of the thousands of people who watched the Test live or the millions who saw it on television in many countries around the globe. For every person involved, players and spectators, this moment, frozen in the hundreds of black and white dots of a newspaper photograph, will always be the infinity of 'Gregan's Tackle'.

Time, though, in reality, never actually stops. Many things were happening in those seconds just before and just after the photograph was taken. The modern rugby player takes in many facts in millifractions of a second. He puts them through his brain which, in turn, works out messages that are sent to the extremities of the body. Jeff Wilson says he was aware of George Gregan bearing down on him. He believed that he was short of the tryline. So, instead of tucking the ball under his arms to protect it from the impact of the tackle, he decided to stretch out and thump it across the tryline. But as he was extending his arms, at the precise moment when his control over the ball was at its most precarious, he was whacked from behind by Gregan.

The tackle was a carefully calculated one, too. In the Test against Manu Samoa, ten days earlier, Gregan had been confronted with a similar tackle—also at the Randwick end of the Sydney Football Stadium but on the other side of the field. Gregan made that tackle by going in hard for the ribs, using the theory that the shock to the body from such a jarring, painful tackle could cause the player to involuntarily spill the ball. So, as he was coming across the field towards the corner and trying to line up Wilson as he wove in and away from defenders like a skier on a brilliant run through the gates, the memory of the tackle he'd made against Manu Samoa came into his mind. Cornerflagging, but too far away from the ball to make a play, Phil Kearns, the Wallaby hooker and captain and one of the match's vibrant players, was praying to himself: 'Make the tackle George, make the tackle'. Just as Wilson was reaching out for his moment of glory, the tackle was made. It was hard and it was accurate. Wilson's back was hit by Gregan's shoulders. Gregan's arms clamped on to Wilson's rib cage. And, just as theory suggested could happen, the ball flew out in front of the two falling players.

The *Herald*'s photographer, Tim Clayton, one of the leading sports photographers in the world, had four cameras set up to record just this type of incident. And the *Herald* on the back page of its sports section, the day after the Test, published the next photograph in the sequence. It showed Wilson reaching despairingly for the ball, the fingers of his left hand spread out to maximise their reach. Gregan's arms are wrapped around him. The effort of the tackle contorts his face in a grimace. Shane Howarth is leaping up, but the clenched fists and the downturned gape of his mouth indicate that the realisation of the missed try has hit him. In the distance the Wallaby flanker David Wilson is finally sitting up after his missed tackle on Jeff Wilson that had resulted in him lying frustrated and seemingly vanquished on the ground. His eyes seem to be focused on the shining ball which is standing upright, as if being prepared for a kick at goal, over the tryline.

This photograph illustrates the terrible irony for Jeff Wilson. If he had held on to the ball, tucked it firmly in his arms, hunched his shoulders, stiffened his body to absorb the tackle he knew was coming—he would surely have fallen across the line and scored. That quickness of mind and reflexes that allowed the All Blacks winger to make such a dazzling and effective run to the tryline had, in effect, worked against him actually scoring the try.

Wilson's rugbiography prepared for media use during the Bledisloe Cup Test was as follows:

JEFF WILSON (Otago). Winger. Age 20. 1.81m. 91kg. Promotion officer. Tests: 2. Natural athlete who represented New Zealand both at rugby and cricket while a teenager. Scored a hat-trick of tries in spectacular Test debut against Scotland last year. Nicknamed Goldie.

The 'natural athlete' description is an understatement. As a schoolboy in Invercargill, a city at the southern tip of the South Island where the winds blow in from the South Pole, Wilson once scored 66 points in a rugby match, with nine tries and 15 successful kicks at goal. A year or so later, only months out of school, he went in to bat for New Zealand at number eight in a one-day International against Australia. New Zealand needed a virtually impossible 48, with only a few overs left and with seven wickets down. In 28 balls Wilson scored an unbeaten 44 and the series was squared two matches all. His favourite movie, understandably, is *Field of Dreams*.

What the biographical notes didn't acknowledge, though, was that the brilliant young player was coming into the Sydney Test in controversial circumstances. His second Test against England at Twickenham, towards the end of 1993, had been unsuccessful. The pressure of being the frontline goalkicker had overcome him and he missed penalties that are expected to be kicked in a Test. These misses were part of the reason why the All Blacks lost the English Test. The next two Tests, against France in 1994, were lost too. Wilson had been injured early in the season and was unable to retain his position in the All Blacks. The veteran winger, John Kirwan, scorer of the most tries by a New Zealand Test player, was recalled. Two Tests were won against the South Africans and the final Test drawn, with the All Blacks playing in a lacklustre manner in the backs. Wilson was recalled to the All Blacks for the Bledisloe Cup Test. A disappointed John Kirwan gave a press conference claiming that the All Blacks coach and chairman of selectors, Laurie Mains, had 'lost the plot'.

Gregan's prepared rugbiography for use by the media in articles previewing the 1994 Bledisloe Cup Test read:

GEORGE GREGAN (ACT). Halfback. Age 21. 1.71m. 76kg. Student. Tests: 3.

As with the Wilson rugbiography, the bare details of Gregan's rugby career masked a complex story of a player thrust into a critical position for the Wallabies. When he ran on to the field for the Bledisloe Cup Test his credibility as the long-term successor of Nick Farr-Jones, the former inspirational captain and one of rugby's finest halfbacks, was not yet established. In his first outing, against Italy earlier in the 1994 season, Gregan had looked slightly too frail for Test rugby. The big Italian forwards threw him away when chasing after balls spilled by the Wallaby pack. He came off the field with a leg injury towards the end of the Test and it was noticeable that when Peter Slattery, the long-term understudy to Farr-Jones, replaced him the Wallabies looked a more composed side under the Italian pressure. The Australian selectors stayed with Gregan for the next Tests, however. The influence of Glen Ella, the backs coach for the Wallabies and one of the fabulous trio of Ella brothers, Australia's equivalent of New Zealand's Going brothers, was crucial here. At Sevens tournaments, and with the Australian Colts, Ella had seen elements in Gregan's play that shouted out his quality to him as a future Test player of genius. Selectors, those who have played a bit, tend to look for players who play much as *they* did in their prime. What Ella saw was the fourth Ella. Gregan was composed under pressure, graceful, dashing, prepared to take on the defence to break the line, and was 'a really tough character with a good pass'. These qualities came through, as if on cue, in Gregan's third Test against Manu Samoa when the Wallabies, playing glorious running rugby, scored their largest Test win, 73–3.

The final confirmation of Gregan's talents came ten days later in the Test against the All Blacks. Peter Fenton, a well-known rugby identity in Sydney, a former representative coach, theorist, commentator and poet of the game, was enraptured by the way Gregan played: 'Hasn't Australia been lucky with great halfbacks in the 1960s, '70s and '80s, with Catchpole, Hipwell and Farr-Jones? Now this kid could be the halfback of the 1990s.' And Vic and Chris Bear, from the Sydney rugby heartland of Gordon, wrote to the *Herald* that after watching the courageous display by the Wallabies in holding off the storming All Blacks as they tried to win the Test by running the ball from behind their own tryline, 'by George Gregan' their household felt that the young halfback was perhaps a reincarnation of Banjo Paterson's Reverend Mullineux, who:

> Tackles his man like a bulldog ant—
> Fetches him over too!
> Didn't the public cheer and shout
> Watchin' him chuckin' big blokes about . . .
> Flinging him down like an empty sack,
> Right on our goal-line too?

Like Jeff Wilson, George Gregan's journey to fame had its unlikely elements. He was born in Zambia, the child of an Australian pharmacist, John, and a Zimbabwean, Jenny. The couple met when they were working and studying in London. They named their son George Musarurwa Gregan, his given names being taken from his grandfather. Years later, Gregan's parents found out that Musarurwa means 'the chosen one'. His Zimbabwean grandfather played soccer for Rhodesia against South Africa in 1936. George originally thought he might make his mark in sport as a cricket player. As a schoolboy he was an opening batsman who always had plenty of time to play the ball. But, after representing the Australian Capital Territory at an interstate cricket tournament in Perth and returning a lacklustre set of figures, he took up an Australian Institute of Sport rugby scholarship. The next year, he was chosen for the Australian Colts where Glen Ella saw him play.

The shattering conjunction of George Gregan and Jeff Wilson in the tackle that was seen around the world had a metaphorical resonance with the way in which Tests between Australia and New Zealand have unfolded in the 1990s. Jeff Wilson: the golden boy, the inheritor of the mystique of the All Blacks, one of the most successful international teams in the history of organised sport. And Gregan: the epitome of the resurgent Wallabies, a team establishing itself since the 1980s as a predominant power in world rugby after decades of losing. And Gregan coming out on top, literally and metaphorically. After decades of Bledisloe Cup Tests being contests of black on gold, they had become on more occasions than New Zealanders can accept gold on black contests.

From the 1991 World Cup year on, the Wallabies have gained a small—but significant—advantage over the All Blacks. The fact is that the Tests that needed to be won in the 1990s have been won by the Wallabies. It is as if luck, too, aided by play of the highest skill and organisation, had decided to help the Australians. At Sydney in 1991 a freakish bounce which popped the ball into the arms of the flying Wallaby chaser, Rob Egerton, turned the Test Australia's way; at Dublin some months later in the Rugby World Cup semi-final two lightning strikes of genius by David Campese, one resulting in a try to the great winger and the other to Tim Horan, won the match for the Wallabies; in 1992 a John Kirwan fumble with the ball centimetres from the Australian tryline denied the All Blacks both a try and a commanding lead in the first of a Bledisloe Cup series which was finally won by Australia by two Tests to one. And then the Test of 'The tackle that won the Bledisloe Cup'.

At the 1991 Test at Auckland, in the mud and with a ball with seams as wavering as a drunken tart's stockings, Michael Lynagh had a chance to draw the Test with a shot at goal but the crazed ball drifted to the left of the posts. The All Blacks won the third Test at Sydney in 1992, when the series was dead. And at Dunedin, in the only Bledisloe Cup Test in 1993, the All Blacks before a chanting, screaming crowd won the Ambush Test quite comfortably.

On the afternoon before the 1994 Test Phil Kearns gave a captain's press conference to the media. The history of the previous 97 Tests between New Zealand and Australia showed a three-to-one winning ratio in favour of the All Blacks. But this was past history, Kearns claimed. 'When I first played the All Blacks', he conceded in a reference to the 1989 Test at Auckland when he was promoted from the Randwick second grade team to the front row of the Wallabies, 'there was a certain fear about playing them. And I don't think that now there is quite as much fear. During the second Test of the 1990 series in Auckland, a few of us started to get the feeling that we could beat these guys if we played really well. Although we lost that Test, we started to believe that these guys were beatable—they are not invincible as we probably thought they were. Then in the next Test we went out there, defeated them, and that took away a little more of the All Black aura.'

But it was not always like this for Australian rugby teams.

STRONG STOMACHS, HEAVY MUSCLE

Rugby Union grew in popularity in the last decades of the 19th century. Touring, in a period when travel was hazardous and rarely a pleasant experience, was the lifeblood of the new sport. The tour became a characteristic aspect of rugby culture, and being selected to the contingent making a tour became a fetish with players. That obsession remains to this day. There was money to be made then, or thought to be there for the picking, from gate takings. In the discussion about professionalism and rugby in the modern era the diehards forget, or do not care to remember, that in the 19th century rugby was permeated with professionalism. Gate receipts were often shared between the host side and the tourists. There was an inducement in this for teams to be successful and popular. At the end of their careers famous players were often rewarded with 'presentations' that set them up for life. Billy Wallace, the famous New Zealand fullback and member of the first All Blacks side that played Australia in 1903, was presented with a purse of 400 sovereigns, a huge amount of money, to assist him in establishing his own iron foundry when he retired in 1908.

But the real dynamic behind the touring syndrome came from the origins of rugby itself. Dr Arnold, the famous and enlightened headmaster of Rugby School, was a compulsive touring man. As soon as school term finished, sometimes on the very day the boys left to go home, Dr Arnold was out of the school gates himself for a tour on the Continent or a brisk walk of several weeks through England's Lakes District. There was a sense, for him, that touring was next to godliness. This message was inculcated into his boys. The tour, with its demands on the courage and physical resources of the participants, with its possibilities of new experiences and of spreading the word—that of God and the Empire—fitted in, too, with Dr Arnold's ideal of muscular Christianity. When the Christian element was bleached from rugby, the element of the muscular missionary remained.

Those early rugby players needed the courage of missionaries, too. Even as late as 1932, when sea transport had become a sophisticated mode of travelling, the All Blacks were so shaken up on a stormy crossing of the Tasman, with the ship bucking in the tossing, spuming waves for several days, that they abandoned the New Zealand touring ritual of having a shakedown run 'to get their land legs back'. This decision was so remarkable that it was commented upon in the Sydney press.

But there was nothing new or remarkable, in fact, about the difficult crossing. The *Sydney Mail*, a well-written weekly journal produced for the newly rich graziers of New South Wales, covered the first tour of a New South Wales rugby team to New Zealand in 1882 with a series of articles by its correspondent, U. Donohue. His first despatch opened with this memorable account of the departure, the passage across the Tasman Sea, the arrival at Auckland and the first match against a New Zealand team by an Australian rugby team:

> The wharf itself disappeared: new lights broke from new points: the old ones went out; the screw began its monotonous motion, the fog horn made night hideous with its roar, the voice of the captain on the quarter-deck was heard to give the occasional order, and the first football team that has ventured to leave New South Wales for New Zealand was actually on its way down the harbour . . . A miserable day followed, many being the vacant seats at the dinner table. Here let me mention the remarkable performance of one of the team who was ill in so gentlemanly a manner that he was heard all over the ship, but who, whether it was his University training, or his natural British bulldog pluck, or both together, would not give in to old Neptune, but went down to dinner only to return to deck and shriek over the side . . .
>
> Ere the portmanteaus were able to leave the big steamer two customs officials in red-braided clothes opened them and everything in them, tearing the covers of parcels that have been given in care of the members of the team to be taken to New Zealand. However, they found nothing contraband save and except a tiny little revolver which a heroic Woollahra man had brought to overawe the Maoris, who he had heard were not satisfied about Te Whiti's arrest, and might possibly break out . . . The

stern duty of practising was attended to as on the previous day, but with a marked improvement in form. Invitations to a rat hunt in the afternoon were accepted by some. At this humane pastime a dog called Peter carried off first prize killing three rats in 16 seconds . . .

Saturday was fine and the morning was principally taken with sitting for photographs which were capitally taken by Messrs Hemas and Hanna. A light luncheon was eaten at 12, a glass of beer being allowed each man at this as at ordinary meals. All the pipes were put away, and the team dressed and mustered in the sitting-room to be inspected and to hear a lecture from Captain Raper, who assigned to them their places on the field, and said that he felt sure that they would return victorious despite the splendid physique of their antagonists, who averaged a stone heavier than they. A four-horse drag took the team to the convincing ground, and the Auckland team followed immediately behind in another . . .

Mr Henderson captained the Auckland team, and played nine forwards and two halfbacks. Mr Raper, the Sydney captain, played six forwards, two wings, three quarter-backs, three half-backs, and one back. The effect was soon seen in the complete overmatching of the six light Sydney men by their nine heavier opponents, who, when they got the ball, waited till all were together, then broke through by sheer weight, coming on the Sydney quarters before they could get away with the ball . . .

After an early breakfast on the following morning the two teams found themselves on the steamer, *Rose Casey*, on the invitation of Mr Wickens, the owner. The *Rose Casey* carried the players to the much-photographed Kawau, the island-home of the celebrated Premier, Sir George Grey, who met them on the pier, escorted them to his house just at the end of it . . . During the day's outing the astonishing feat of devouring 48 dozen eggs, besides fish, bacon, steamed vegetables, and other solid food, washed down with champagne or beer, was performed by the party of not more than 40 men in two meals.

In 1884 a rugby team from New Zealand crossed the Tasman to further develop the touring culture. This team, too, created a New Zealand dominance over the Australian rivals that was from time to time disrupted by very good Australian sides—like the superb 1929 Wallabies—but was only seriously challenged on a continuing series-by-series basis in the 1980s. This 1884 New Zealand team wore dark blue jerseys with a gold fernleaf on the left breast, with dark shorts and stockings. It played eight matches in New South Wales, winning all of them and scoring 167 points to 17 in the process. In the last match of the tour against what was considered to be a crack New South Wales side, wearing green jerseys with Southern Cross stars, a team especially selected from the 'best men' from all the Sydney clubs, the New Zealanders won 16–0: three goals and a try to nothing. At halftime a large section of the crowd went round the ground to the

SCENES AT THE FOOTBALL MATCH—NEW SOUTH WALES V. NEW ZEALAND.

end nearest the New South Wales tryline, a gesture that was understandable given the superiority of the New Zealanders. (The same practice happens now at Eden Park when Auckland are playing.) A match report of that last game of the 1884 tour of New South Wales said that the sight of spectators trailing around the ground in doeful Indian file to the end the New Zealanders were about to attack was 'disheartening, to say the least of it' for the local champions.

At the end of the tour the Sydney newspapers engaged in some deep contemplation about the rugby superiority of the 'Maorilanders'. The *Sydney Sportsman*, in its 4 June 1884 edition, argued that climate and physique were the crucial factors, with both these elements telling against the Australian players: 'Our winters are too mild and too short to admit of our players acquiring the proficiency attained in colder countries'. To the extent that the drier Australian winters encouraged a game played more in the backs than in the forwards, there was something in this theory. The New Zealanders, too, were 'a fine body of men, well-built, and with their muscular powers fully developed . . . By their side the New South Wales players appeared to be very light, and although it was felt that they would show fight, none believed in their coming off victorious'. Here is an early elaboration of the theme of the inherent invincibility and size of New Zealand rugby players. The fact was that the New Zealanders then, and especially when they became known as All Blacks, were often men from the farming districts. This source of brawny, hard, relentless, stoical and determined players reached its epitome in Colin 'Pinetree' Meads and the legend that he got fit for rugby by running around his farm in gumboots carrying a sheep under each arm. The farmer–All Black–forward pattern prevailed up to the 1980s. The fact that few of the All Blacks forwards now come from farms—Richard Loe is an exception—probably accounts for the fact that New Zealand packs in recent times have been no tougher than their opponents.

Ten days after the earlier cogitations about the New Zealanders and their fitness for rugby, the Sydney *Telegraph* chewed over the implications of the game. 'The humiliation of defeat after defeat', the newspaper argued, 'is somewhat softened by the recollection that Rugby football is the game of New Zealand as cricket is the game of Australia.' The writer then drew from the game a profound insight on the value of a flier on the side of the scrum: 'I wish to draw attention to the following facts: that this New Zealand team had heavy forwards, and yet the lightest forward, Lecky, was one of the best . . . of 21 tries gained by forwards in the eight matches most of them were got by passing rushes in the forwards'.

This (correct) emphasis on the big—but fast and skilful—pack was with New Zealand rugby from the beginning. Auckland in 1882, for instance, opted to play with nine forwards, one of them a 'wing forward'. Yet as late as the 1980s, Bob Dwyer, the Wallaby coach, hoped for 40 per cent possession against the All Blacks in order to give his brilliant backs a chance of winning the match. New Zealand rugby has always known that forwards, rather than backs, win matches. Ninety-five years after the Sydney *Telegraph* pointed to the usefulness, the necessity in fact, of a fast forward like the ubiquitous Lecky, the Sydney University flier, Andy Stewart, was selected to play on the side of the scrum for the Wallabies in the one-off Bledisloe Cup Test of 1979. Stewart's contribution in getting to the breakdowns in the play, securing the fractured ball, making the tackles out wide when the All Blacks created overlaps, in risking life and limb by lying on the ball to stop the All Blacks from rucking it—in playing, in other words, like a traditional New Zealand openside flanker—played a large part in an historic victory. Alan Jones's obsession with a big pack in the 1980s, bringing in Topo Rodriquez from the Argentinian Pumas to give muscle to the front row and bringing back Stephen Cutler from the rugby scrapheap to give height to the pack, completed—finally—the Australian conversion to belief in forward power. It's hardly accidental that the 1980s and 1990s have been the golden era of Australian rugby.

THE NEW ZEALAND SYSTEM

The point that the Sydney journalists missed with their concentration on the size of the New Zealanders as the reason behind their success was that the New Zealand team played to a system that was based on a deep understanding of the fundamentals of the rugby game. The New Zealand method, too, was inflamed by a passion for rugby. An editorial in the *New Zealand Mail* of 23 May 1884, farewelling the New Zealand team, alluded to this when it noted that 'the whole colony will watch its progress. Football has risen in favor with the public, as it has become more and more a game of skill . . . In Wellington, where cricket is at a low ebb, there are no less than 300 enthusiastic footballers, and any number of boys growing up with a love for the game . . . Certainly the game as now played by the chief provincial teams is far more skilful and scientific than it was five or six years ago . . .'

The most detailed explanation of 'the New Zealand method' in this early era was given in *The Complete Rugby Footballer* (Methuen, 1906), a 270-page coaching book written in three weeks by Billy Stead and Dave Gallaher, both captains and outstanding players on the 1905–06 All Blacks tour of the United Kingdom. The treatise is Aristotelian in its rigorous pursuit of rugby logic and best practice:

> Each side, and each player on the side, must have their recognised ruses. A ruse can seldom be tried more than once in a game, but every ruse has, as it were, a double edge. When you have cut with it one way, you can turn round and cut with the other. You gain by the mystery you create and nothing has such a demoralising effect on a side as being beaten by these feints . . . In New Zealand, a back is allowed to stop a rush by throwing himself on the ball, but doing nothing more than that. If he does not get up immediately, he is penalised. We find that lying on the ball, as practised in Britain, slows down the game a great deal, particularly when the referee merely gives a scrum . . .
>
> What we call a loose ruck . . . represents a disordered state occurring, for example, when an opponent has slipped in trying to block a forward rush. In such a case, it has been our policy to enter this ruck with the particular object of heeling out the ball. Our backs are all ready to strike if we can do so, and when the ball is duly heeled out, the scrum-half sets them going, not the least important consideration being that we are a man to the good numerically . . .

> Our principle is that every forward should be a potential back, and in the team that toured Britain there was not a man in the pack who could not have fulfilled the duties of a back if emergency had demanded.

THE MAORI PLAYER

Dave Gallaher was born in Belfast, Northern Ireland, and came to New Zealand as a youngster with his parents. He was a charismatic captain and deep thinker about rugby. On match days he made players spend an hour on their own to 'rest and contemplate the game ahead'. He was killed while serving in the trenches in Belgium in 1917. Billy Stead, like Gallaher, was soon recognised in New Zealand rugby as one of the 'immortals' of the game. A halfback who was 'fast . . . quick to see an opening, his defence par excellence', he never lost a match in 42 appearances for the All Blacks. He was a member of the first New Zealand Maori team to tour Australia, in 1910.

The point about Gallaher and Stead is that they represent how inclusive New Zealand rugby was from its earliest times. This applied particularly in the recognition of the panache, flair, exuberance and deep interest in tactics and strategy that Maori players brought to rugby. The Maori notion of community, the tribal instinct, was suited to a game where the object is for 14 players to create a metre of space for the 15th player to have a clear run through the opposition's defences to the tryline. The Maori temperament and psychology was suited to a team game. For example, while numerous Maoris have played for the All Blacks, it was only in the early 1990s that Adam Parore became the first Maori to play that highly individualistic game, cricket.

The concept of *mana*, the exhibition of bravery and leadership and a significant Maori ideal, had great scope in the rugby game and great Maori players and thinkers with *mana* quickly emerged. The leader of the 1893 New Zealand team to Australia, for instance, was Tom Ellison, schooled at Te Aute, the famous Maori college in Hawkes Bay. A lawyer, captain, tactician, administrator and author, Ellison devised the diamond scrum, the 2–3–2 formation, which modern administrators could consider reintroducing in a 14–man team if they want to speed up rugby and eliminate collapsing scrums from the game. And the All Blacks famous all black uniform of black jersey, silver fern on the breast and black stockings was devised by Ellison. In subsequent modifications, a white collar was added to the jersey and white rings on the stockings. Ellison's book, *The Art of Rugby Football*, is a thoughtful and detailed treatise on the game. On British rugby in the 1880s, from his observation on the Natives Tour of Australia and the United Kingdom in 1888–89 during which 109 matches were played, he wrote: 'I was not very impressed with the play of the Britishers for, with all the players they had available, I saw no one to compare with Jack Taiaroa . . . I never played against a team which made a radical change in tactics during the course of a game. They all seemed to have tumbled into a grave and stuck there.' Nothing much seems to have changed. This same criticism made by Ellison over 100 years ago can be made of the England rugby sides of the last decade or so.

Jack Taiaroa, a cousin of Ellison's, played in Sydney in 1884. A match report of the game against New South Wales mentions 'Tairaora [sic] by one of his wriggling runs nearly got behind the New South Wales goal-line'; 'Taiaroa ran well after the kickoff'; 'Taiaroa nearly got in, losing the ball just as he crossed the goal-line'; 'Taiaroa ran to the New South Wales twenty-five flag'. It is interesting that all the references to Taiaroa's play were in the context of his running the ball. A five-eight, solidly built, Jack Taiaroa was the prototype of the Maori Player, a line that runs through George Nepia to Waka Nathan and Zinzan Brooke in the modern era. In the 1884 match against New South Wales, Taiaroa was acclaimed as 'the hero of the day. His running, dodging and collaring astonished both players and spectators who duly meted out their applause to this prince of footballers'. On the tour he scored nine tries in the nine matches.

It's worth remembering that the New Zealand Wars, fought during the 1860s over an unscrupulous grab for Maori land by the settlers, were still a strong memory for Pakehas (European New Zealanders)—and for Maoris—when Taiaroa and Ellison were playing. More than a memory, in fact, if the story of the New South Wales player and his pistol is accepted. This fear of the Maori was deeply imbedded in the Australian consciousness well before the 1880s. In a memo written in 1787, a year before he established the first convict settlement at Sydney, Governor Arthur Phillip outlined why transportation to New Zealand was—literally—a fate worse than death by hanging for any unfortunate convict facing the death penalty: 'There are two crimes that would merit death—murder and sodomy: for either of these crimes I should wish to confine the criminal till an opportunity offered of delivering him as a prisoner to the natives of New Zealand, and let them eat him. The dread of this will operate much stronger than the fear of death.' But the inclusive imperative of the New Zealand rugby ethic was so strong, even at its beginning, that there was never any hesitation or question about bringing Maori players into the game and encouraging them to take leading roles on the field as captains and tacticians and off the field as administrators.

The contrast of this inclusiveness—one of the greatest strengths of New Zealand rugby—with the exclusive pattern in Australian rugby that was set in this period is stark. And it worked to the disadvantage of Australian rugby standards and achievements. Jack Pollard in his magisterial book, *Australian Rugby: The Game and the Players*, says in the first entry, 'aboriginals', that 'research suggests that Cecil Ramali and John Howard, who played in the same two international matches against New Zealand in 1938, were the first of their race to play rugby for Australia'. The records confirming this achievement have been lost. The fact that the newspapers of the day didn't comment indicates, perhaps, a certain unwillingness in the rugby world at the time to draw Aboriginal players into the highest reaches of the game. The first (officially recognised) Aboriginal Wallaby in modern times, Lloyd McDermott, a quick and skilful winger, represented Queensland and Australia in two Tests against New Zealand in 1962. In the 1980s, the Ella brothers gave the Wallabies magical ruthlessness that was an important part of the team's ascension as a world rugby power. Later, Australian rugby embraced players with a Pacific Island background such as Willie Ofahengaue (left stranded in Brisbane airport after touring Australia with a New Zealand Schoolboys team, thanks to New Zealand visa problems—has the errant New Zealand official ever been suitably punished?) and Ilie ('O') Tabua.

As Thomas V. Hickie points out in his definitive study of the origins of Australian rugby, *They Ran with the Ball*, the game survived a crisis in Sydney in the 1870s (when proposals to abolish scrums were frequently raised) through the energetic efforts of a 'narrow-based elite' which 'successfully reformed the code and warded off challenges to the code in that period'. This success, Hickie writes, put this elite 'in control of an expanding and successful code in the 1880s and 1890s'. But the victory was at a long-term cost to Australian rugby. The game in Australia, unlike the New Zealand inclusive model, adopted an exclusive ethic. This meant that, until the 1980s when the inclusive principle began—finally—to win through, Australian teams were selected from a narrow (middle and upper class) group of players.

When the Jesuits decided to become a leading teaching organisation in Europe in the 17th century, they embarked on a 30-year study of education to work out the principles they would use in shaping the practice and curriculum of their schooling. One of their principles was this: 'Give me the children until they are seven and anyone may have them afterwards'. This principle of the 'mould' explains, as well, the general superiority of New Zealand rugby over Australian rugby up to the 1980s. From the beginning of New Zealand rugby the dream of being an All Black was a dominating male motif. Middle age for most New Zealand men is the time when they finally reconcile themselves to the fact that they won't ever be All Blacks. Wilson Whinerary, an All Blacks captain in the 1960s, has written about this hunger of the male New Zealander to play rugby for his country:

> I know of one great rugby administrator, coach [and] manager who held every office and enjoyed every honour in New Zealand rugby who, on the occasion of his acceptance of life membership of the NZRU, said that he would have given it all away just to have worn the black jersey once. In my view, there has never been a truly great All Black that hasn't felt a genuine pride in wearing the fern and known some kind of inner stirring every time he pulled the jersey over his head.

By contrast, the passion of Australian players to belong to a national side was generally never as strong as their adherence to their state side. The lack of uniformity and intense national pride in the Australian game, as it was developed at the turn of the century, is identified by this sign: Australian sides often played in the blue of the New South Wales colours, or in maroon and blue stripes which combined the colours of Queensland and New South Wales. The national rugby colours of green and more recently gold were not as quickly established as was the black of the New Zealanders.

Whereas gold, a precious but basically useless mineral, came to stand as a metaphor for Australian rugby, New Zealanders took a barbed wire approach to their game. They played to win. They were ruthless. If inflicting pain was necessary for victory then pain was inflicted. And there was a national passion for the game which embraced all classes and people from every walk of life—unlike the Australian scene. The New Zealand historian Jock Phillips, who has made a speciality of the study of masculinity in the New Zealand culture, quotes the *Grey River Argus*, a radical newspaper serving the coal miners of the West Coast of New Zealand, describing rugby in

1882 as 'the national game'. By the 1880s, only ten years after the first rugby match in New Zealand, there were over 50 000 players and 300 teams affiliated with the new national Rugby Union. Rugby in New Zealand began as 'the pastime of the elite', Phillips notes, but this social barrier was down almost as soon as it was erected: 'An examination of Auckland club teams in 1890 and 1893 suggests that the occupational characteristics of rugby players were similar to the range of men on the electoral role . . . The classlessness of rugby, of course, eventually became central to the game's mythology'.

Aspects of the elite, upper-class attitudes remained, however. Officials at times had difficulties adjusting to the more vulgar behaviour of players and their supporters. The *Bulletin* reported on 3 November 1894 that Auckland Rugby Union officials were 'narked' over an incident on the Onehunga wharf when farewells were being made to a team of Sydney players:

> Several ladies, friends of the executive officers of the [Union], were at the wharf, having gone out specially to say farewell to the gentlemen of the team. But there were also in their four-wheelers a bevy of notorious nymphs de pave, who were more than affectionately farewelled by certain of the departing guests. These women were first cheered as the lines were cast off, and then cheers were given for the Auckland boys, who had no option but to be silent after such an insult to the respectable women present. North Islanders have cried off NSW footballers for some years to come.

This *Bulletin* prediction, fortunately, was not fulfilled.

On the rugby field the New Zealand method was based on skilful, strong forwards who played a vigorous rucking game and backs who endeavoured to break the advantage line on every play. This method predominated from the muddy fields of Dunedin to the rock-hard grounds of Auckland, to the backblock paddocks of Taranaki. There was a fierce national pride, too, in the black jersey and silver fern and a continual and obsessive aspiration of all New Zealand teams to win the accolade of 'The Invincibles'. Results, not glowing plays, were what mattered.

And winning results were quickly achieved. The advantages to All Blacks sides up to the 1980s of this pragmatic barbed wire approach to rugby manifested itself from the outset in the international arena in the first Test between Australia and New Zealand, which was played at the Sydney Cricket Ground on 15 August 1903.

The first Test: New Zealand 22–Australia 3

Tena koe, Kangaroo
Tupoto koe, Kangaroo
Nu tireni tenei haera hei
Au, au, au, a
How do you do, Kangaroo!
You look out, Kangaroo!
New Zealand is invading you!
Woe, woe, woe to you!

After that mocking and prescient haka the New Zealand rugby team took up its position at the Paddington end of the Sydney Cricket Ground. A stiff wind was at its back. The Australian rugby side, in this first battle against the New Zealanders, had made the mistake of giving away the wind, an indication of the haphazard Australian disregard of the fundamental principles of the game. A large crowd of more than 30 000 people waited with trepidation and excitement as at 3.32 pm James ('Bull') Joyce, a second row forward from the Glebe club, kicked off for Australia.

The New Zealand team was to become more familiarly known as the All Blacks two years later on the tour of the United Kingdom. A journalist was struck by the way the forwards ran as backs, so his article referred to a New Zealand team of 'All Backs'. This was transcribed at his newspaper office as 'All Blacks', a reference to their playing kit. The Australian rugby team gave itself the tag 'Wallabies' on the 1908 tour of the United Kingdom. According to Jack Pollard in his *Australian Rugby: The Game and the Players*, the 1908 tourists 'intended the name should only apply to Australian rugby players who had won a tour overseas'. But this restriction, rightly, did not stick. All Australian representatives are now Wallabies.

Few people among the spectators at the first trans-Tasman Test gave the Australian XV much chance of success. The tourists were a formidable combination. They had played eight matches leading up to the Test and had won them all, scoring 242 points and having only 10 points scored against them. There was a hardness about their play and their physiques, too, that made them difficult opponents. Before the Test the *Sydney Mail* carried a photograph entitled 'A typical New Zealand footballer'. It showed a stern-faced Archibald McMinn, 'a broad-shouldered giant', a loose forward about 193 centimetres tall, of rangy build, his hands on his hips, hat on his head, wearing the

Spectators at the first rugby Test between Australia and New Zealand in 1903.

traditional all-black kit with the silver fern on the left breast and large shinpads worn outside his black stockings.

Like many New Zealand forwards of succeeding generations he had a lean and hungry look about him. On the field he fulfilled this look but, like many other New Zealand forwards, he was a skilful runner and passer of the ball. For Manawatu, his New Zealand provincial side, he occasionally played at five-eighth or on the wing. Another photograph in the same newspaper, the week after the Test, shows this same McMinn bursting away from a lineout and setting off upfield during the Test itself. Several other New Zealanders rush forward to support him. The New Zealand captain, James Duncan, in the number 10 jersey, is sprinting up in support, raising his gloved right arm to indicate to McMinn that he is available for a pass. One of the Australians, who is only a matter of metres away, has his hands by his sides as he stops to look—much in the subdued manner of a retired gentleman surveying his garden—at the fleeing New Zealanders, who are racing away like robbers from the scene of the crime. At the end of the lineout, another Australian player has his head down and is strolling across the field as if oblivious to the New Zealand breakout.

It was McMinn who set the New Zealanders strongly on attack by kicking what was described as a 'skyscraper' towards the Austra-

Archibald McMinn who played in the first Test.

lian line. The New Zealanders pressed hard. They forced a penalty and Billy ('Carbine') Wallace, the outstanding fullback, kicked the goal from the sideline. The first of thousands of points to come had been scored by a New Zealand side in an international. Stanley Wickham, the Australian centre, one of the first of the great Australian running backs, soon equalised with a penalty. The score stood at 3–3. The New Zealanders' superior quickwittedness came to the fore during the next important phase of the game. Duncan McGregor, the New Zealand wing, marked the ball near the halfway line. Under the laws of the game at that time he was able to let Wallace attempt the dropkick for goal. The kick, with the wind pushing the ball high in the air, was successful and the New Zealanders were 7–3 in the lead.

Then occurred what the report of the match in the *Sydney Morning Herald* called a 'peculiar incident'. After some play near the sideline the touch judge's flag went up. Players from both sides stopped except the ball-carrier, McGregor, who sprinted on towards the tryline. After investigating the sprig marks the referee, Dr R. Waugh, a Sydney man, decided that the runner had not gone into touch and that the try stood.

This black satin banner was presented to the 1903 All Blacks by the New Zealand residents of Sydney.

From that point in the match onwards, the New Zealanders were dominant. They ended up as easy winners, 22–3. For most of the second half, even though the wind was gusting against them, the New Zealanders played in Australia's half of the field.

One commentator in his analysis after the Test expressed his pessimism about the chances of Australia ever turning the tables against the New Zealanders: 'It seems hopeless to expect to ever score a substantial victory against the Maorilanders . . . though we may never inflict defeat on them as they have on us, we could with, say, annual meetings look forward to considerable improvement in our method of playing Rugby'.

The affirmation by Phil Kearns, the Wallaby captain, just before the 1994 Bledisloe Cup Test, that the Australian players no longer 'feared' the All Blacks—and the result of the Test—finally put to rest that pessimistic but realistic assessment made in 1903.

THE MYTH OF WILLIAM WEBB ELLIS

In his history of the game Jack Pollard, the Herodotus of Australian rugby, notes that the 'first football matches played in Australia were reported on 25 July 1829 in the *Sydney Monitor*'. The first club was formed by the University of Sydney in 1864. This founding set the pattern in Australia (not really broken until the 1970s) of Rugby Union being an upper-class game based in the Greater Public Schools and the universities. The New Zealand pattern, with the town of Nelson pioneering the first rugby match in 1870, was that of a game based in the general community—a game for lower, middle and upper classes and for both Pakeha and Maori. In 1864 Elred Harmer, an MP in the New South Wales Parliament, introduced a Bill to ban rugby. Harmer told the House that rugby matches were 'vicious displays of brutish fist fighting'. Pollard reports that other MPs disagreed, defending what happened on the playing fields as 'youthful exuberance', and Harmer's Bill lapsed for want of a seconder.

Despite Harmer's view of what seemed to be allowable on the rugby field, the teams did play according to rules. Pollard writes that Sydney University 'adhered to its own rules, which were based roughly on what was believed to be the practise in England, where a 16-year-old schoolboy named William Webb Ellis originated rugby in 1823. Ellis became bored during a game of soccer and, with a 'fine disregard for the rules, took the ball in his arms and ran with it, thus originating the distinctive features of rugby'. This 'fine disregard for rules' quotation comes from the wording of a famous inscription placed on the appropriate wall at Rugby School.

To one seeking an understanding of the evolution of rugby and particularly its laws, however, the story of William Webb Ellis picking up the ball and running with it during a football match at Rugby School is of little help. The story is a myth. The event never occurred. If, say, the entry for RUGBY is looked up in the 30-volume *New Encyclopaedia Britannica* the curious fact is revealed that, in five densely written pages about the code and its history, there is no mention of William Webb Ellis. There is only a reference to one of the 'distinctive features' of Rugby Union being that 'players may use their hands and catch, throw or run with the ball (a practice introduced at Rugby School in the 1820s)'. But even the mention of running with the ball in the 1820s at Rugby School is a doubtful claim. In *Blood and Guts: Violence in Sport*, a deeply researched study of how sport legitimises violence, written by Don Ayteo, there is a revealing throwaway footnote: 'Unfortunately, the Ellis saga is a blatant fiction, perpetrated by an overly loyal gathering of Rugby Old Boys more than a century later. As Thomas Hughes, the author of *Tom Brown's School Days* recalled, to run with the ball in the 1820s would have been a short cut to suicide'.

The librarian at Rugby School, Jennifer Macrory, the keeper of the documents, says that Ellis was a day boy and was born in Manchester in 1807. She goes on:

> He probably did run with the ball. The game was very fluid. People expected changes but expected to agree on them. It was not approved of and it was not until the 1830s and 1840s that running—especially for tries—became established . . . it was accepted in 1839 and legalised in 1841 by Tom Hughes, author of *Tom Brown's School Days*. Probably, running was really brought into play by Jem Mackie 15 years after 1823.

This is clearly the statement of someone trying—unsuccessfully—to preserve a myth. An engaging book, published in 1984, entitled *Run with the Ball! A Brisk Dash Through 150 Years of Rugby*, written by Derek Robinson, offers a credible explanation of why and how the hoax of William Webb Ellis was constructed by old boys of Rugby School. Robinson's first point—and it scuttles the Ellis myth at the outset—is that nobody thought Ellis's action was worth recording at the time. 'Indeed it wasn't until 72 years had passed that the Old Rugbeians' Society set up a committee of inquiry into the origins of Rugby football, and by then William Webb Ellis had long since gone to his maker.' According to Robinson, 'a certain Martin Bloxam created the legend of William Webb Ellis 50 years after the alleged event' in an article published in *The Meteor* (the Rugby School magazine) in 1880. Bloxam, a lawyer and an antiquarian, left Rugby School in 1820 so 'he certainly never saw him do the deed in 1823'. Bloxam conceded in his article that he didn't know how Ellis's alleged action was followed up or 'when it became, as it is now, a standing rule'.

In 1895 the rugby code in England was split, with the northern clubs forming the Rugby League. Robinson argues that the 'public school ethos of the game for the game's sake was being challenged by a commercial spirit that treated rugby as a spectator sport'. So it was 'no coincidence' that, in 1895, some Old Rugbeians formed a committee of inquiry into the origins of the game. The committee, coincidentally, revived Bloxam's story which had made no impact in the fifteen years since its publication. The Old Boys inquiry ran into trouble, however, with the revered Thomas Hughes. Hughes told the inquiry: 'I don't think Matt Bloxam a trustworthy authority', and then went on, 'the William Webb Ellis tradition has not survived to my day.' The committee then sought out the Reverend Thomas Harris, the only surviving contemporary at Rugby School of Ellis. To loaded questions from the inquiry as to whether he remembered 'Our Hero doing something unusual', Harris simply repeated that he remembered Ellis only as a cricketer.

The point about the William Webb Ellis myth is that it was concocted by Rugby School old boys to entrench the Rugby School rules as the laws of the game in the 1890s. Subsequently, English rugby officials have used the hegemony established by the William Webb Ellis myth to entrench their control over the code. The All Blacks who toured the United Kingdom in 1905, for instance, had to argue with English referees before most of their matches to get them to accept the New Zealand rucking method as being within the laws of rugby. They still have trouble with the English interpretation of the ruck. Back in 1905, though, many Englishmen regarded rucking as putting the men in front of the rucked ball in an offside position.

In the hundred years since the Rugby League Split, English officials have tended towards a static view of the rugby game, with set pieces being ends in themselves. It is as if they are still bewitched by those huge, seething but generally immobile masses of boys swarming over a ball buried deep in the melee—in their version of football at Rugby School in the 1840s. The English rugby establishment, too, uses the hoax to give itself credibility in its obsession to retain control over the code. These officials, it should never be forgotten, were passionately opposed to the notion of a Rugby World Cup when it was put forward by Australian and New Zealand officials. But, when it became obvious that the first Rugby World Cup in 1987 was going to be an overwhelming success, the English rugby establishment tried to muscle its way into the action. The late John Kendall-Carpenter became the chairman of the Rugby World Cup committee. He proposed that the World Cup trophy be named after William Webb Ellis. He then told the other committee members that he had found a 'marvellous silver cup' that could be purchased for $110 000. This is the trophy that the winning All Blacks captain, David Kirk, held above his head at Eden Park in 1987 and that Nick Farr-Jones, the Wallaby captain, flourished at Twickenham in 1991.

A close look at the trophy reveals, however, that at the top of the cup there is a miniature model of a *soccer* ball, supported by garlands. Can English officials—who willingly perpetuate a hoax of William Webb Ellis and are prepared to have the trophy for the Rugby World Cup commemorate another football code—be allowed to dominate the running of rugby in the face of the success, in every aspect of the code, of rugby in Australia and New Zealand?

What was the form of rugby played by the two fledgling Test sides? Judging from the old film clips of ghostly figures silently rushing down the field, it was rugby that would certainly be recognisable today, with the ball moved from hand to hand, players grassed in tackles, the ball kicked and the enthusiastic chase put on. And judging from photographs of these games at the turn of the century, lineouts were even then a 'dockyard brawl', as they are today, with players pushing into each other and closing the gap so that leaping was virtually impossible. With the absence of the five-metre gap between the thrower and the first man in the lineout that applied at this time, lineouts, even more than in the modern era, were grabbing rather than leaping contests. Most of the Australian commentators noted the 'different game' the New Zealanders played as they bumped opponents aside in their forward rushes and the way they 'walked over them' when running with the ball. Whereas the Australians tended to adopt a 'sportsmanlike' approach, the New Zealanders relied on 'brute strength . . . rather too much' and on 'considerable, if unchecked, illegal interference'.

The *Bulletin*, in a brilliant period in the 1900s when its radicalism and vigorously written articles made it compulsive reading, occasionally referred to rugby as 'the undertaker's friend'. Hacking, the stopping of a player by kicking him in the shins, was abolished in 1877 but rugby remained a game for players with a certain imperviousness to pain. A month after the 1903 one-off Test at the Sydney Cricket Ground the *Bulletin*'s New Zealand rugby expert, 'Offside Mac' (William McKenzie, one of the famous McKenzie family that dominated the administration of New Zealand rugby in the 1920s and 1930s, the inventor of the wing-forward position and such a noted seagull as a player that he was the original 'Offside Mac' in a long line of players given this nickname over the years), wrote this vivid description of the toughness in the New Zealand method of playing rugby:

> Since its inception, Maoriland Rugby has been gory—therein lies the charm. The climate produces a particularly virile race, which must get rid of its surplus energy somehow—football allows the vent. Maorilanders are in their barbaric age. They know little of literature: less of art. Their love of freedom and glory is at present wholly centered in the spectacle provided by 30 men engaged in a manslaughtering struggle for a piece of inflated leather. The element of danger provides the fascination for the crowd, which will always attend to see anybody slugged, especially if the cost is not much . . . Nowadays every Maorilander footballer is insured

against accident, and wears shin guards, ankle and knee protectors, and coverings to save his ears from mutilation. Fractured ribs and wounds requiring five stitches are so common that they are never chronicled by the newspapers. Of course, if a player breaks his neck his name is mentioned.

A book, *Players and Slayers,* written five years after this by the Wellington journalist Leo Fanning, the brother of Bernard Fanning (a burly secondrower who played for the All Blacks in the inaugural 1903 Test at the Sydney Cricket Ground), gives a suggestion of the rugby at the time being more a field of broken bones than of broken dreams. Law 47, apparently, was often disregarded by New Zealand teams: 'Law 47. NO HACKING, or HACKING OVER, or tripping up shall be allowed under any circumstances. No one wearing projecting nails, iron plates, or gutta percha on any part of his boots or shoes shall be allowed to play in a match'.

Grahame Willis, a stalwart of the Norths club in Sydney, and an avid historian of rugby, says that when his club was formed in 1900 it originated from the Pirates club and wore an intimidating black uniform with the skull and crossbone across the breast. One of the original Norths players, Blair Swannell, a player with the reputation as 'the ugliest man who ever played rugby', an Englishman who settled in North Sydney after touring with a British Isles team, was kicked in the face in the second Australia v New Zealand Test played at Dunedin on 2 September 1905. An All Blacks (Third) 15—the best players were in the British Isles on the famous 1905–06 tour—won 14–3. The point of the story is that no Australian player came to Swannell's defence. Yet the great Maori player and administrator, Tom Ellison had described rugby in 1902 as 'the good, manly, soldier-making game'. Poor Swannell, unsupported by his team-mates on the rugby field, put that notion to the real test during the First World War where he was killed leading a charge at Anzac Cove, Gallipoli, on 25 April 1915.

It is unlikely that the New Zealanders would have passively allowed one of their team-mates to be kicked in the face as Swannell was without the opposition 'paying for it'. Jock Phillips, a New Zealand social historian who has a fascination with the impact of the 'manly' rugby culture on New Zealand culture in general, quotes in *A Man's Country* the *Temuka Leader* asking, after the local team had declined in rugby prowess: 'Has all the pluck and muscle of the neighbourhood migrated or degenerated?' Part of the manliness of the New Zealand rugby ethic was to stand up to players who tried to bully their opponents—as well as trying to bully *your* opponents if you could.

New Zealanders accepted that rugby was 'a dangerous pastime' and took the proper precautions on the field. And off the field, with the insurance cover remarked on by 'Offside Mac'. Australians, unfortunately, seemed to tolerate being subjected to physical pressure and, more importantly, failed to establish an insurance policy to cover the problems created by the inevitable crop of injuries suffered by players.

Within four years of the splendidly contested and well-attended first Test, this administrative oversight over insurance cover was instrumental in almost destroying the game of Rugby Union in Australia.

THE BASKERVILLE HOUND

During the 1980s the notion came to several entrepreneurs and a number of players that the 'amateur' principles of Rugby Union exposed the game to a takeover by the best players who, after all, generated millions of dollars in the Tests they competed in. Rumours of circuses abounded but never eventuated. There was, though, a rebel tour of South Africa in 1986 by a team of New Zealanders, the Cavaliers, which was made up of most of the current All Blacks side. This tour gave a clue to the possibility of player power diverting big money from the national rugby unions directly into the pockets of the players. Nothing is new under the sun and it is no surprise that the players of the 1980s were going through the same struggle with administrators for a share of the profits they were creating that their predecessors had gone through at the turn of the century. The unlikely entrepreneur at the turn of the century who had the enterprise to try to make rugby in the southern hemisphere a professional code was a Wellington news clerk, Albert Baskerville.

According to one of his brothers remembering back over a timeframe of 40 years, Baskerville was working in the Wellington Post Office when an employee, 'Old Harry', fell to the floor with a coughing seizure. A newspaper he had been reading fell away from him. Baskerville caught sight of an article in the crumpled news sheets which related that 40 000 people had paid more than a thousand pounds to see a game of Northern Union (Rugby League) at Bradford in Britain. Baskerville immediately set about getting tour guarantees from the Northern Union clubs and began recruiting local players for a privately financed overseas tour.

The difference between the 1990s and the 1900s for entrepreneurs wanting to make money out of rugby is that the balance of power between players and administrators now lies with the administrators. A discipline imposed on the players who toured with the Cavaliers, for instance, was that they were barred from selection for two Tests in 1986. The so-called 'Baby All Blacks' took the field against France and in the first Test of that season's Bledisloe Cup matches. That young team, with emerging stars like David Kirk, John Kirwan, Joe Stanley and Mike Brewer in it, defeated France and played with spirit and resolution in defeat against Alan Jones's Wallabies. It is unlikely, too, that the public would accept a 'professional circus' of players in preference to the traditional Tests, even if the Tests were of a lower standard than the matches played by the breakaway professional players. Rugby people have an instinct for the traditions of the contest. This explains why Tests against a World XV in the NZRU centennial year drew much smaller crowds than did Tests played a few months later against the British Lions.

At the turn of the century, though, the administration of rugby, especially in Australia, was not as competent and resilient as it was near the end of the century. There were precedents, too, that encouraged the push towards player power. Tours were run on the basis of the touring side collecting a share of the gate. But the touring side was firmly under the control of its local rugby union. Entrepreneurs had run tours—a notable example of such a tour was that conducted by a New Zealand Native team that played 108 matches in Australia and the United Kingdom. The promoter of the tour was Thomas Eyton. In Australia, Jack Lawlor, a Victorian Rules coach, was co-opted to arrange football matches (choice of code of rules to be negotiated) in Victoria. According to Eyton, Lawlor cost the promoters of the Native team two hundred pounds. The tour itself was not a financial success. The 1905 All Blacks, too, had played before huge crowds on their tour. Over 45 000 people turned up to watch them play England at Crystal Palace (some estimates placed the number at 70 000). In 1907, at the Sydney Cricket Ground, a crowd of 48 677 saw New Zealand defeat Australia 26–6. The crowd was larger than that for the 1994 Bledisloe Cup Test at the Sydney Football Stadium and only slightly smaller than the crowd for the 1979 one-off Test Australia v New Zealand at the Sydney Cricket Ground, won by the Wallabies 12–6, when Bledisloe Cup mania really began in the modern era. The 1905 All Blacks side, as well, made extra money by advertising products. Newspapers carried advertisements, for instance, with this message:

The NEW ZEALAND TEAM think B.D.V. CIGARETTES are a VERY

EXCELLENT SMOKE, and they have been greatly appreciated by the members.

Manchester Hotel, 3 November, 1905 (Signed) G.H. Dixon, Manager

THE ABOVE TESTIMONIAL WAS SENT TO MESSRS GODFREY PHILLIPS & SONS BY THE MANAGER OF THE NEW ZEALAND TEAM

The money motive, then, was part of the rugby ethic at the turn of the century. The devotion to the amateur principle was, in part, an invention—like the myth of William Webb Ellis running with the ball at Rugby School in 1823—to keep Rugby Union in the control of an upper-class English establishment. Professional sport, too, was flourishing at this period; for example, sculling contests on Parramatta River for large purses were popular sporting events at the time. It was hardly surprising, then, that a number of New Zealand players, with money on their mind, were persuaded in 1907 to join a team to tour England playing northern rules rugby, or Rugby League as it became known, for what could be substantial payment. Although this rebel team outfitted itself in the traditional all black kit, and each player was required to contribute between 50 and 100 pounds for tour expenses (a stiff requirement, with politicians, for instance, being paid about 150 pounds a year at the time), the knowledgeable New Zealand public, without irony, nicknamed the team 'The All Golds'. (They believed the players had sold out for 'gold'.) As the SS *Warrimoo* pulled out of Wellington harbour, bound for Sydney and then England, the cheers of the wellwishers on the docks were overwhelmed by the jeers and insults of a large and what the newspapers called 'an unpleasant' crowd.

When the 1908 All Golds finished their English tour (18 wins, 2 draws, 14 losses), they played a further 10 matches in Australia, including three Tests, in which they emerged as winners on every occasion. But then tragedy struck the team. Baskerville, aged only 25, contracted pneumonia and died in Brisbane. Ian Heads in his marvellous account of the New South Wales Rugby League, *True Blue*, makes the point that Baskerville 'did more than anyone else to get Rugby League going in the Southern Hemisphere.' His death certainly curtailed the later development of the code in New Zealand. Ironically, the first game of Rugby League in New Zealand was a benefit match for Baskerville's mother played at Athletic Park on 13 June 1908 in front of 10 000 spectators.

The Union splits in Australia, too

A week before the All Golds started off on their great adventure, on 8 August 1907, a fateful meeting took place at Bateman's Hotel in George Street, Sydney, a popular drinking spot near the centre of the city. About 50 rugby players, some of them nervously looking around before entering the hotel's door, met to discuss the possibility of starting a professional football league, a rugby league, with some older men of great charisma. The leading light at the meeting was James J. Giltinan, a well-known cricket umpire and a persuasive personality. Backing him were the legendary cricketer Victor Trumper and a local politician Henry Clement Hoyle, who was a strike agitator on the railways in 1890, a Labor MP for the inner-Sydney electorate of Surry Hills and later a State minister. Hoyle established the strong links between the Labor Party and Rugby League ('the working man's game') that persist to this day in Australia. Ian Heads, the historian of the Rugby League code, believes that the 'nonpareil Dally Messenger, 'The Master', was . . . almost certainly present' at the meeting as well.

Two days after the meeting the *Sydney Morning Herald* carried this item: 'At a meeting of players interested in the professional movement it was decided to form the NSWRL'. Further inside the newspaper, the *Herald* reported that all the players at the meeting had signed the following statement: 'I . . . hereby agree, if selected by the controllers, to play Rugby football against the New Zealand professional team at Sydney in any one or all the matches on August 17, 21, 24'.

On the afternoon of the day those reports were published in the *Herald*, Saturday 10 August, Australia and New Zealand played the third Test of the 1907 Rugby Union series. The match ended in a 5–5 draw, the best result the Australians had achieved. (The other Test results in the series were 26–5 and 14–5 to New Zealand.) About 35 000 people watched the draw played out at the Sydney Cricket Ground. Among the Australian backs were the outstanding halfback, Chris McKivat, and Dally Messenger, both of whom had (secretly) signed the declaration of availability to play professional rugby.

Later that month the Rugby League Tests were played to Rugby Union rules and although the play was described as 'disappointing', the gate takings were impressive, with 700 pounds for the New Zealanders and 700 pounds for the new NSWRL. When the SS *Ortona* steamed out of Melbourne for England on 27 August the All Golds had gained some much-needed income and one more player, Dally Messenger, who was deemed to be an honorary New Zealander for the tour, the greatest compliment a New Zealander can pay to an Australian.

The Messenger magic

In the 19 June 1931 issue of the *Sydney Mail* the newspaper's rugby writer, 'Light Blue', a former New South Wales player one imagines from his pen-name, reached back into his memory of over 40 years of watching and playing the game to contemplate the question: Who was the greatest footballer in the history of New South Wales rugby? Like an astute expert turning his port in his glass, watching the play of the light on its tawny levels and turning each sip in his mouth round and round to appreciate the delicacy of the vintage, 'Light Blue' went through some of the 'champions' he had seen: the New Zealanders, Billy Wallace and Bert Cooke, and the Australians, Stan Wickham, Harold Horder and Tom Lawton . . . and then the 'Champion of Champions', Dally Messenger.

> As a contemporary, the writer played against Messenger: at school and in junior football . . . He possessed remarkable stamina, flashing speed, uncanny judgment, amazing intuition, and perfect technique, all the attributes of the champion . . . Football instinct told Messenger what the

> opposition would expect the ordinary man to do: therefore, he did the extraordinary—almost the impossible—thing and, of course, succeeded. Critics have said he was never in position and that he was an individualist, and while at times some of this adverse comment was no doubt warranted, it was only applicable because his comrades could not sustain his excellence. Messenger was so ubiquitous that he was everywhere the ball was, and therefore always in position. He was never cornered, never caught in a jam. He always tested the other chap's nerve and carried the fight everlastingly into the enemy territory. Those who remember his dive over the heads of two opponents to score a try against New Zealand will appreciate those opinions. It was this amazing co-ordination of mind and muscle which stamps him as the greatest footballer that it has ever been my pleasure to see.

When a lover of rugby reads that marvellous tribute to a player who was obviously remarkable in skills and spirit—a turn-of-the-century David Campese, perhaps, for whom 'Light Blue's' loving and detailed description is also extremely apt—an ache comes over one for the lost players who were taken from the game by the Great Split in rugby. And for all those players who were, in turn, brought up in the Rugby League code and who never had the chance to play the beautiful game of Rugby Union. Bobby Fulton played one game of Union when he was given dispensation during his compulsory military service duties in Canberra to play for the ACT against a touring All Blacks side. What a Rugby Union player he would have been! And so too Reg Gasnier, Peter Sterling, Brett Kenny and all the other great Rugby League players over the years.

A number of talented New Zealand and Australian players went across to Rugby League, and the money, almost immediately after the 1907 split: the New Zealanders 'Jum' Turtill, Edgar Wrigley, 'Massa' Johnson, and 'Bolla' Francis; and the Australians 'Dinny' Campbell, the dazzling Chris McKivat and Dally Messenger. A tour made by an Australian Rugby League team to the United Kingdom in 1908 was a financial disaster. The first Test against England was played on a bitterly cold wet day, with wind blasts rushing across the Park Royal, in northwest London, freezing the players and the tiny crowd of 2000 spectators. Enter the entrepreneur James Joyton Smith, who in 1909 promoted a series of matches between the 1908 Wallabies (who had also toured the United Kingdom in 1908, winning the rugby event at that year's Olympic Games) and the Kangaroos, the Rugby League equivalent of the Wallabies. The Kangaroos won the first match against the Wallabies 29–6 and then lost the next two matches in the series 34–21 and 16–15. This act of bodysnatching against the Rugby Union code (which was emulated in cricket years later by Kerry Packer when he formed his World Series Cricket circus) set up Rugby League in Sydney in the decisive years before the First World War.

Without the mass defection of the 1908 Wallabies, Rugby League would never have survived in Sydney. The professional code would have withered away in bankruptcies and writs in much the same way as it did in London at the same time. But the Wallabies gave credibility to professional rugby. In the 1910 season Rugby League started with an overdraft of 200 pounds and ended with a credit of 1410 pounds. The credit in 1911 was 3887 pounds. The Rugby Union code in Australia struggled against this dramatic turn of support against it from players and spectators.

In *Australian Rugby: The Game and the Players* Jack Pollard argues that the Rugby League game itself, its more open play and its scope for more running by forwards and backs, was the great attraction to the players. Money was basically irrelevant, he argued, except for one or two star players. There was, in fact, despite the seemingly big annual profits, no big money in the Rugby League game for the players. Pollard's claim may explain why more Australian Rugby Union players at this time turned to Rugby League than did New Zealand players. A New Zealand Rugby Union supporter even on a rack could not be forced to acclaim Rugby League as a better game to play.

Australian Rugby Union therefore steadily lost a succession of great players over the years: Trevor Allen (described by the BBC after the Wallabies tour of the United Kingdom in 1947–48 as 'one of the three greatest players this century'), Rex Mossop, Phil Hawthorne (a special guest player for the 75th anniversary matches of the South African Rugby Union and a dual rugby international), Russell Fairfax. The 1977–78 Australian Schoolboys team that toured Japan, France, Britain and Holland, scoring 553 points for and only 97 against and winning all sixteen of its matches (arguably the greatest rugby team to leave Australia), had players in it of the quality of Wally Lewis, Michael O'Connor, Tony Melrose, Chris Roche and Tony D'Arcy who turned to the Rugby League code.

Up to the 1980s the drain of talented players from the Australian game meant that the Wallabies were at a disadvantage for nearly 80 years against the All Blacks who generally were able to present the best of New Zealand's rugby talent in the national side. George Nepia and Bert Cooke played Rugby League towards the end of their rugby careers. Aside from them, though, the most notable in the modern era defection was Joe Karam, a chunky, accurate goalkicker, who decided to play club Rugby League in Auckland rather than tour with the All Blacks to South Africa in 1976, where his goal kicking would have

won the series for the New Zealanders. In the years after New Zealand's triumph in the 1987 Rugby World Cup, though, a number of talented players changed codes: John Gallagher, John Schuster, Matthew Ridge and Daryl Halligan. These defections were a savage blow to the strength of the All Blacks. For the first time in the history of New Zealand rugby the All Blacks could not be said to be the best team of rugby players the game had nurtured in the paddocks from Southland to Northland. And the relatively poor results of the All Blacks since this slide of defections to Rugby League started indicate what a loss these players have been to New Zealand rugby.

The author often contemplates what might have been in the battles between the Wallabies and the All Blacks over the years if the Great Split had, somehow, been contained and all the marvellous players 'lost' one way or another from Rugby Union had been available for selection for the code's national teams, and sighs: Oh my Dally Messenger of so long ago.

A WIN FOR AUSTRALIA

Men In Black, an account of each Test played by the All Blacks since 1903, based on original sources and written by R. H. Chester and N. A. C. McMillan, notes that for the second Test of the 1910 series which was played on a Monday, 27 June, at the Sydney Cricket Ground, 'the home team was much better on the day. The Australians were almost incessantly on attack and were seldom called on to defend for more than a few minutes at a time'. Although the first Test had been played on the Saturday, 25 June, with New Zealand winning 6–0, the All Blacks could not complain about the difficulties of having to back up for two hard matches in too short a time. The Australians made only one change to the team that 'missed chances' two days earlier. The New Zealanders had four changes to their side. In theory, at least, the Australians should have been wearier than the New Zealanders.

The key to the Wallabies' victory was possibly, as it has undoubtedly been in a series of Tests played over the years especially at Wellington's windswept Athletic Park, that the Australians played with the wind in the first half. Early in the match, from an attacking position established by the wind advantage, the Australians put on a passing rush and Bert Gilbert, a fine centre who later played Rugby League, went over for the first—and more decisive—of his two tries. This match was only the second time that the All Blacks had failed to score in a Test. There was a 3–0 loss to Wales in 1905, with a controversial and long-running dispute over what was called 'Deans's try'. The second Test of 1910 remains the only occasion, though, on which the Australians have kept the New Zealanders scoreless. By contrast, six New Zealand sides (in 1910, 1914 (twice) 1951, 1955, 1962) have kept Australian teams scoreless.

Several days before this historic Test in 1910 L. G. Abrams gave notice that he would move at the next meeting of the Sydney Metropolitan Rugby Union:

> 1. That employers of the members of the SMRU who may be selected to represent the State or this union, shall be reimbursed the amount of the player's salary or wages should leave of absence be granted him on full pay . . . 3. That a special committee . . . be appointed to witness Northern Union Football games and report at once as to the advisability of the competition matches being played next season under such rules (or improvements) and amateur conditions as laid down by this union.

The motion, which essentially was a call for the Rugby Union code to join the Rugby League, was not endorsed. We may speculate that Australia's victory some days before the motion was discussed may have strengthened the resolve of delegates to confront, rather than submit to, the feeling that Rugby Union was doomed in Australia. And, if this is the case, the winds that swept across the Sydney Cricket Ground on Monday 27 June 1910 should have the same place in the history of Rugby Union in Australia as the 'divine' winds that blew the Armada out of the English Channel in 1588 have in the history of England.

The four spells Test

With winds sweeping Athletic Park with a velocity that seemed to have the force of their journey from the South Pole behind them and with heavy rain pelting down like driving nails into the players and spectators, the first Test of the 1913 series, won by New Zealand 30–5, was played in four 20-minute spells. This was the first—and only—occasion on which a four-quarter system was used in a rugby Test between New Zealand and Australia. The *Dominion*, an outspoken morning newspaper in Wellington, carried a provocative account of the match:

> Outclassed by the All Blacks, the Australian Rugby team cut a rather poor figure at Athletic Park in the gale and rain of Saturday afternoon . . . One-fifth of our enthusiastic 5000 sat in the comfort of the stand: 4000 stood in the clay mud, huddling together for warmth and protection from the elements, a patient and enduring umbrella and over-coat brigade. The dozen pressmen who toiled while everyone else there made holiday burn with gratitude for the thoughtful union who facilitated their work by providing them with accomodation from which they could ascertain with certainty how strong the wind was, how wet the rain was, and what an excellent shower-bath was obtainable by anyone who momentarily took one eye off the overflowing roof-gutter.

That ironic account failed to stir the energies of the officials. But a journalist reading it 80 or so years later identifies with the sentiments of the writer. In the age of high technology there is still a scramble for telephones after a Test to get the story into the newspaper. With night Tests, as with the 1994 Sydney Test, this scramble becomes a matter of survival for the journalists. While the corporate boxes make merry with the gluttony of a Roman feast, most unions in Australia and New Zealand—a pleasant exception is the Queensland Rugby Union at Ballymore—somehow find it difficult to provide a tea urn for the writers, some of whom turn up hours before kickoff to prepare for their match report.

Rugby has made many advances over the decades but the hospitality of officials to journalists, boorish in 1910, still needs much improving. Launching his history of Australian rugby Jack Pollard, whose book literally saved the memory of a great deal of the Australian game after the offices of the ARU were twice flooded, told a gathering that he did not get 'a sausage' of support from the Australian Rugby Union.

THE GREAT WAR NEARLY KILLS RUGBY

On 5 August 1914 the touring All Blacks played New South Wales in a match intended to provide a portion of the funds needed to send Australian athletes to the 1916 Berlin Olympic Games. During the match the news that the British Government had decided to stand by France and that war, accordingly, had been declared on Germany was posted on the big scoreboard of the Sydney Cricket Ground. The first two Tests in the series had been won by the All Blacks 5–0 and 17–0. With the guns of August booming along the European warfront, the rugby tour by the New Zealanders was rushed to conclusion. The final Test on 15 August was played in front of a small crowd of 5000 spectators at 1.30 in the afternoon, the first time such an early kickoff time had been arranged in these matches. The All Blacks won 22–7. But the players on both sides clearly had their minds on other matters. The early start was designed to allow the All Blacks to depart Sydney on a ship leaving the port for New Zealand towards nightfall.

The Australian officials were determined to get behind the war effort. The ideal of Empire loyalty was strong among Rugby Union men. The official view was that the best policy for the game and for the nation was for Rugby Union in Australia to be closed down for the duration of the First World War as an encouragement to young, able-bodied men to enlist for war service. The young men heeded the call. It has been estimated that 5000 Australian rugby players went on active service. This figure represents about 98 per cent of the playing numbers in the game in Australia (outside of the schools) in 1914.

The war fever was such that the *Sydney Mail*, a journal that provided an extensive coverage of Rugby Union matches for its mainly country readership, did not carry any mention of the final Test. The 15 July 1914 issue had been its annual 'Football Number', with a cover featuring a drawing of an Australian player contesting a lineout with an All Black. On the inside of the journal were a number of photographs of the first Test, with the New Zealanders clearly driving into the rucks in the traditional New Zealand manner, with the forwards bound to each other and moving in low and hard. But as soon as war was imminent special War Issues were published, devoted entirely and exhaustively to every aspect of the Great War.

The last rugby comment the journal carried was a note on 15 July on the the match between the New Zealanders and New South Wales, in which the *Mail* editorialised

> Why, we must ask, should New Zealand be content to allow the game to bristle with illegal ruses? . . . New Zealand teams have always shown that they know all the 'tricks' of the game. It must be admitted that they honestly and in the finest sporting tradition play the game as they have been taught it. That sort of teaching, however, belongs to another period, and strict refereeing would raise the game to a standard contemplated by the framers of the rules. The methods of the visitors seemed so unnecessary. If on Saturday they had played under the strictest refereeing they would have won. Criticism from the loser's point of view is perhaps likely to be misinterpreted, but the interests of the sport must be the first consideration. Hence this appeal for strict refereeing.

Every aspect of national life was exploited to create propaganda for the war effort. The *Sydney Mail*, for instance, carried a story in its 22 June 1915 issue which was headed: 'Think I'll Give Up Football'. A long paragraph told of the 'heroic fortitude' of a young Canadian, Captain Francis Whitchurch Townend, who had had his legs shot off at the knees and had horrible wounds to his arms. While his wounds were being dressed he said to the nurse: 'I think I'll give up football next year'. The paragraph ends on this poignant note: 'As he was being carried to the hospital, where he died, he was perfectly collected and laughed quietly, and apologised for all the trouble he caused'.

There is something extraordinary and quite chilling in the way thousands of wonderful, vibrant young men were prepared to treat war as 'the great game'. In a fascinating sociological study, *Sport in Britain: A Social History*, Gareth Williams provides some telling details of the mindset of these rugby players and their attitude to the war effort. The British fondness for football, Williams argues, 'was seen as an element in their superiority over the Germans'. The annual Mobbs Memorial match between the East Midlands and the Barbarians, Williams notes, was inaugurated in 1921 to commemorate Edgar Mobbs of Northampton and England. Mobbs used to lead his men across the barbed wire and mines of No Man's Land by punting a ball towards the enemy lines and following up hard after it.

It was magnificent, perhaps, but it was not war. Mobbs's 'preposterous act of bravado' (Paul Fussell's phrase) led to his being killed at Passchendaele.

Rugby almost suffered the same deadly fate in Australia. Rugby Union went into recess in New South Wales, Queensland and Victoria. The closing down enabled Rugby League to entrench its place in Sydney and Brisbane. As well, the Catholic schools, with the teaching brothers steeped in an Irish, working class and anti-British tradition, generally switched to Rugby League in this period. The notable exceptions in Sydney were the two North Shore schools, St Joseph's and St Ignatius, with the former taking its boarding students mainly from the conservative country districts and the latter from affluent middle-class Catholic families. These schools retained an allegiance to Rugby Union. Especially in the case of St Joseph's, 'Joeys', a factory for Wallabies, it is difficult to see how Australian rugby could have survived as a competitive force against other international sides if this school had become a factory for Kangaroos.

Conscription was introduced in New Zealand in 1916. This decision led to the policy of the New Zealand Rugby Union restricting participation in rugby matches to players under 20 years of age. The eligible age band for conscription was 20 to 45. According to Chester and McMillan in *Men in Black*, this decision meant that 'the public interest in the game also waned, especially at club level'. Rugby League in New Zealand, though, which had been thriving in Auckland, followed the Australian rugby precedent and closed down for the war. This accident of history, based on what we now can see was a mistake of judgment on the part of the two sets of officials concerned, meant that New Zealand rugby was able to re-establish itself quickly, in terms of playing numbers and the quality of the players, after the war. The 1924 All Blacks in the United Kingdom were so dominant that they won all their Tests (unfortunately Scotland refused a match against them, thereby preventing the New Zealanders from achieving a Grand Slam) and gained the title of 'The Invincibles'. The Rugby

League code, on the other hand, struggled to revive itself in New Zealand after the Great War.

But so shattered was the Rugby Union game in Australia by 1919 that it was a decade before the Queensland Union was re-established, in 1929, and Australian rugby could put a national side on the field for a Test against the All Blacks.

1929: An ambush is sprung

The rugby battles between New Zealand and Australia have featured three successful ambushes. In 1979 Australian officials duchessed their New Zealand counterparts into allowing a one-off Bledisloe Cup Test match at the Sydney Cricket Ground—which the Wallabies won 12–6. New Zealand rugby was in a resurgent mood with the All Blacks on their tour of the United Kingdom in 1978 gaining their first—and only—Grand Slam sweep of the Tests against Wales, England, Ireland and Scotland. As the New Zealanders had last lost a Test in Australia in 1934 (at Sydney 25–11), the over-confidence of the New Zealanders is possibly understandable.

Then, in 1993, New Zealand officials were able somehow to convince their Australian counterparts that the one-off Bledisloe Cup Test for that year, which was scheduled for August, should be brought forward in the year. The result was that the Wallabies faced a New Zealand side that had played several hard Tests against the Lions, while the Australian's preparation had consisted of one bad-tempered Test against Tonga. The All Blacks victory (25–10) was virtually inevitable.

The first ambush, though, goes back to 1929. With the re-formation of the Queensland Rugby Union a fully representative Australian side was available to selectors for the first time since the First World War. Queensland rugby was strong, with Queensland winning the 1928 inter-State series with New South Wales. Victorian rugby, too, was strong. The Waratahs, a New South Wales team playing as a national side, had made a brilliant tour of the United Kingdom in 1928, playing an exhilarating brand of running rugby and winning three of its five Tests (Ireland, Wales and France). Alex Ross emerged as one of Australia's greatest fullbacks; Cyril Towers and the Rhodes Scholar Tom Lawton were backs of the highest quality; and Sid Malcolm, the halfback, was rated as the best player in his position in the world.

As they did in 1979 the New Zealand officials took too complacent an approach to the request for an All Blacks tour of Australia in 1929 to mark the re-emergence of the Queensland Rugby Union. The presumption, clearly, was that even a representative Australian side would be no match for the All Blacks, who the year before had squared a series in South Africa for the 'world championship' with the Springboks. Provincial rugby in New Zealand, moreover, was extremely strong with the Ranfurly Shield, a challenge trophy donated in 1901 by the Governor-General of New Zealand, Lord Ranfurly, stimulating many torrid games of Test-match intensity such as the famous 'Battle of Solway' between Wairarapa and Hawkes Bay at the Solway Showgrounds in Masterton on 9 July 1927.

The New Zealand side for the first Test against Australia on 6 July 1929 contained no fewer than fourteen changes from the side that had defeated the Springboks 13–5 on 1 September 1928. The only player to make both sides was Ruben George McWilliams, a tall rangy loose forward from the Waikato province. With players like Jack Manson Tuck, a halfback also from Waikato, Eric Snow from Nelson, a loose forward who was at the end of a long career, Alfred Clarence Waterman, and Wiremu Rika Heke, a 37-year-old 'colossal chap who plays aggressively' in the forwards, the 1929 tour had elements of a 'consolation prize' in it for some of the players. The fullback, though, was the famous and fearless Maori, George Nepia, who was not selected for the tour to South Africa because of the colour bar imperative. The team also had a young centre, Charlie Oliver, a New Zealand representative at cricket and rugby, who was being groomed to succeed the incumbent centres: Bert Cooke, a wiry genius with the quickness and deadliness on the break of a frog's tongue, and Mark Nicholls, the mastermind behind the famous victory in the rain in the final Test against South Africa at Newlands in 1928.

Professor Garnet Vere Portus, a Rhodes Scholar, who played twice for England in 1908 and became an Australian selector in the 1920s provided, as the rugby correspondent for the *Sydney Mail*, a colourful account, with its intimation that something special was on for the Australians, of the first of the Ambush Tests:

> A thin trickle of people which began to cross Moore Park at 11 a.m. had swelled to a steady stream at 12.30 p.m. and by half past one was a rushing torrent . . . An hour later the incoming tide had covered all the green spaces on the hill—convincing evidence enough (if any were needed) that the old code had definitely come back to favour. Nearly 40 000 watched the match. One lady left her home in a distant suburb at 10.30 a.m. She was determined to see this game. And who shall blame her? It was Mrs Ford. Has any Sydney mother ever before had two sons playing in an Australian Fifteen?
>
> . . . At 3 minutes to 3 came Lawton, stepping delicately at the head

"THE NEW CHAMPION"

of his men. For the first time an Australian Rugby Union XV appeared in green jerseys . . . The crowd roared its welcome to its stalwarts, and just as heartily cheered the All Blacks—a sombre and businesslike procession led by Lillburne.

With Australia leading 9–8, and time running out, the description of play in the last minutes of the Test that Portus provided could have been used 65 years later for those dramatic, thrilling minutes of the 1994 Bledisloe Cup Test:

> New Zealand made desperate attempts to snatch back victory. Twice Ross saved us, once off McWilliams's very boots. But the Black stormed back. Riki was nearly over in the corner. Then a jumble of black jerseys bumped over the left corner flag. Then the Green vanguard cleared, with Palfreyman in the lead. But New Zealand came back. Their tide was at the flood. A thrust to the right was checked by a homeric tackle from Hamalainen. Still the pressure continued. Would that confounded bell never ring? People were either very silent or very vociferous, and everyone was getting a headache. Slowly the Green men pushed the game back to their twenty-five, then on to the halfway. A free to New Zealand! What for? What matter? The bell rang and we had won.

The first Test 9–8 to the Australians; 17–9 in the second Test at Brisbane; and 15–13 in the third Test at the Sydney Cricket Ground.

For the first time in their history of playing rugby Tests the New Zealanders had lost a series—and by a clean sweep. Portus concluded that a change in strategy towards an appreciation that rugby Tests are won upfront in the forwards contributed significantly to Australia's series triumph:

> We won the rubber from New Zealand in 1929 very largely because we held them in the van. And, despite all that has been said about the scintillating play of the Waratah backs, it was on our forwards that we relied when the pinch came this year . . . A good vanguard can, at a pinch, carry medium backs; but the best backs in the world are lost behind indifferent forwards.

This fundamental principle of rugby, so apparent to New Zealanders who are used to playing under a greater variety of field conditions and weather than Australians are, was lost to Australian rugby almost as soon as it was learnt. The resurgence of Queensland rugby in the 1970s, which was in part due to a deliberate policy of playing against New Zealand provincial sides and learning the secrets of their craft, brought back—finally—the understanding that rugby power comes from the barrel of the forwards.

A NOTE ON TEST LISTS

In *Australian Rugby: The Games and the Players* Jack Pollard has a listing of Australia's international record, as accepted by the Australian Rugby Union. He records Australia's first Test in 1899 against the British Lions (Australia 13–3). And he lists fifteen Tests against New Zealand and the New Zealand Maoris between 1924 and 1928.

R. H. Chester and N. A. C. McMillan in *Men In Black* date New Zealand's first Test at 15 August 1903, against Australia at the Sydney Cricket Ground. They then list the Tests discussed so far in this book but do not list the matches played in the 1920s that are accepted by the ARU. In their preface Chester and McMillan make the point that 'there has been some conjecture as to the definition of an "International Match". In 1967 the New Zealand Rugby Football Union published the history of their first seventy-five years. Compiled by historian Arthur Swan, this official publication listed those matches classed by the NZRFU as "International". We have followed this official classification . . .'

And so have I in this book. My opinion is that the NZRFU list is more rigorous—and truer to the Test ideal of *matches between countries*—than the ARU list is. The ARU list, for instance, accepts a match played between the touring Australian side and a New Zealand Maori side at Wellington in 1928 (Maoris 9–8) as a Test. The ARU list, in fact, admits sixteen matches against the New Zealand Maoris as Tests. This can't be right. It carries the inclusiveness of rugby too far and diminishes the integrity of Test rugby. If the New Zealand Maoris warrant Test or international status, why not the New Zealand universities side? Or an Australian universities side? Or a Black South African side? Or other matches played by the New Zealand Maoris in the Pacific Islands?

This argument, however, as to what constitutes a Test match becomes an academic dispute after 1929. With the introduction of fully representative Australian sides for the first time since the First World War, the lists of the ARU and NZRFU for rugby Tests between New Zealand and Australian teams coincide. The beginning of the Bledisloe Cup era marks this development.

THE PRESENCE OF LADIES

According to Sean O'Hagan in his excellent history of the Otago Rugby Union, *The Pride of Southern Rebels*, 'the presence of ladies' at rugby matches in New Zealand was encouraged up to the end of the 1920s by allowing them in free. The policy behind this move—which might be considered by modern administrators for matches which are not expected to draw crowds of more than about 10 000 people to grounds holding up to 40 000 people—was that players might be less thuggish with a large number of women watching and that male spectators might behave themselves with ladies around them. O'Hagan quotes the exposition given on this matter in the New Zealand context in the finest book ever written about rugby, *The Complete Rugby Footballer* by David Gallaher and Billy Stead, published in 1906:

> Everywhere ladies were admitted free to both grounds and stands, and, while this is a nice compliment to pay to the sex, it is, from the business point of view of the Union, very much more than a compliment. It is one of those seemingly trifling details that are really important factors in establishing the success of the football of a country . . . It may not be always realised how powerful is the influence of womankind in a game like this.

O'Hagan also quotes an article in a Dunedin newspaper of 1890 on the 'presence of ladies' at rugby matches which has a very 1990s twist to it:

> There is the matter of the objectionable manner in which a number of men persist in smoking to the great discomfort of lady visitors . . . I regret to notice that the practice is still being continued, and I would urge the necessity of stringent steps being taken to enforce its discontinuance, if for no other reason than it is a desirable thing to encourage the presence of ladies at football matches as having a tendency to check rough play.

Lord Bledisloe and the Cup

There is no evidence that Lord Bledisloe, the Governor-General of New Zealand between 1929 and 1935 and the alleged donor of the Bledisloe Cup, knew one end of a rugby ball from the other. The remarkable files of the *Sydney Morning Herald*'s library hold a typewritten biography of Lord Bledisloe, 'The English Statesman', that was sent out to newspaper offices throughout the British Empire by a Whitehall press office in October 1929 to mark his New Zealand appointment:

> Charles Bathurst, barrister, politician, agriculturalist and First Baron BLEDISLOE, was born in Sept. 1867, and educated at Sherborne, Eton and University College, Oxford. After leaving Oxford he was called to the bar in 1894 and practised as a Chancery barrister and conveyancer for 16 years. In 1910 he was elected Conservative MP for S. Wilts and made a member of the Council of the Duchy of Lancaster . . .

This biography was updated by Whitehall in March 1934 when Lord Bledisloe was coming to the end of his term as Governor-General.

> In November 1929, Lord Bledisloe was appointed Governor-General of New Zealand . . . His knowledge of and interest in agriculture made him the most popular Governor of the Dominion in many years. He did everything in his power to strengthen the Empire bond in New Zealand. The fact that every article he wore was made there from Dominion materials gave great satisfaction . . . In May, 1932, he and Lady Bledisloe presented to the people of New Zealand one of the country's most historic relics. This is a house built by James Busby, a British resident, in 1834 at the Bay of Islands, outside which the Treaty of Waitangi, which put an end to disputes between the Maoris and the British, was signed in 1840 . . . The Governor's munificent gifts won him and his wife a lasting place in the affections of the people of the Dominion.

Even in the oily world of public relations these accounts of the life and career of Lord Bledisloe are unduly obsequious. Bruce Hewitt, a distinguished New Zealand journalist, the head of the New Zealand Press Association for many years, started his career as a reporter in the early 1930s. An article he wrote for the *Sun-Herald* in 1988 gave an entirely different perspective on the so-called 'most popular Governor'. Hewitt remembers Lord Bledisloe as a man 'who had little interest in football, and his outdoor activities were limited to farming and long-winded speech-making at country shows'.

Lord Bledisloe was once photographed at the Canterbury Show at Christchurch, according to a story Hewitt tells. The next day the photograph of a beaming Lord Bledisloe was run in the *Christchurch Times*—with a caption describing the show's beribboned champion ram. This incident triggered off Lord Bledisloe's 'long-running differences with the New Zealand press . . . To a generation of reporters he became 'Chattering Charlie,' and there were harsher names when his complaints led inevitably to sackings in those bleak, jobless, and depression days'.

An official of Lord Bledisloe's stature who is offside with the press is in clear need of a public relations gesture, or gestures, to persuade the public that he is a man of compassion and devotion to the New Zealand people. The gift of Waitangi House fits this need. And so, too, does giving his name to a Test match competition between the rugby teams of New Zealand and Australia.

An observant reader will notice that the inference in the last sentence is that Lord Bledisloe did not actually donate the Bledisloe Cup, as popular memory and the naming of the trophy indicate. A curious fact about the official biography issued to the media at the end of Lord Bledisloe's term in office is that there is no mention of the Bledisloe Cup in it. Years later, too, when Lord Bledisloe, now in his anecdotage and sounding even more like P. G. Wodehouse's Lord Emsworth and his passion for pigs, toured Australia and New Zealand in the 1950s there was not one mention in the numerous press articles of the time, now residing in the *Herald*'s files, of the Bledisloe Cup and the lord's connection with it. Clearly, Lord Bledisloe, perhaps through his secretary, formally agreed to stand with his predecessor Lord Ranfurly as a patron of Rugby Union in the colonies and then promptly turned his chattering and his attention to farm matters. This view, though, is at variance with the official version which is set out in Keith Quinn's *The Encyclopedia of World Rugby*:

> The Bledisloe Cup was presented in 1931 by Lord Bledisloe, then Governor-General of New Zealand, as a trophy to be played between the

Test teams of Australia and New Zealand . . . The first game for the trophy was played at Eden Park in Auckland in 1931, New Zealand winning by 20–13. The game, played in front of Lord Bledisloe, was notable for the small crowd that turned out (only 15 000) and for the scoring of 14 points by the New Zealand fullback, Ron Bush, of Otago. It was then the New Zealand record for the greatest number of points scored in a Test match, let alone a debut, though Bush did not get to play for his country again.

But *did* Lord Bledisloe watch the match at Eden Park? Gordon Slater, a noted New Zealand author and journalist, is adamant that he was not even in Auckland when the Test was being played. 'Neither Lord Bledisloe nor his cup was at the Test match', Slater writes in his monumental *On the Ball: The Centennial Book of New Zealand Rugby*. 'He was in Wellington to attend the commercial travellers' smoke concert, at which he told them that the world was topsy-turvy, particularly in the sphere of industry and commerce.'

The 1931 Test at Eden Park involved the first Australian side in eighteen years to play a Test in New Zealand. Public interest in the match, however, was lukewarm. This was hardly surprising as the Australians were one of the least successful sides to have ever toured New Zealand. The Australians had drawn with Otago (3–3), defeated the New Zealand Maoris (14–3) in a match that is designated by the Australian Rugby Union as a Test match, lost to Southland (12–8) and Canterbury (16–13), defeated Hawkes Bay and Waikato (27–11, 30–10) and lost to a Combined Nelson side and to Bay-Buller (11–10, 14–5) in the leadup to the Test.

We go back now to Gordon Slater:

On the day before the game, it was announced from Wellington that the Governor-General had presented a cup for competition between New Zealand and Australian Rugby teams and that the first match for the trophy would be the Test at Auckland the following day. Mr S. S. M. Dean, president of the New Zealand Rugby Union, and Mr T. C. Davis, manager of the Australian team, expressed their appreciation of the offer. The design of the cup was to be decided upon later, but it would be symbolic of both countries.

This story of Lord Bledisloe earbashing the commercial travellers with an eternity of platitudes at their smoke concert in Wellington fits Bruce Hewitt's description of him as 'Chattering Charlie' far better than the official version of the leader in love with his people and eager to demonstrate his passion for the national game of rugby.

The most likely explanation for the creation of the Bledisloe Cup is that New Zealand officials were perturbed at the lack of pulling power of the Australians—and, possibly, at the low standard of play of the tourists. They were no doubt mindful that now that Test matches against Australia had been revived a large number of the Tests the All Blacks would play in the future would involve Australia. Before the First World War, from 1903 to 1914, the All Blacks played 24 Tests, 14 of them against the Wallabies. But only three of these 14 Tests against Australia were played in New Zealand. This ratio of away Tests against the Australians clearly had to be balanced out. This meant more Tests in New Zealand against the Australians—more than the previous average of one every four years. But how could the officials get around the fact that the New Zealand public was uninterested in the outcome of these New Zealand and Australian Tests compared, say, with Tests against the British Lions and the South Africans? The four Tests played in 1930 against the Lions (a series won by the All Blacks 3 Tests to 1) drew crowds of 27 000 at Carisbrook, 30 000 at Lancaster Park, 40 000 at Eden Park and 40 000 at Athletic Park. These crowds meant a windfall for the NZRU but the problem was that the Lions and the Springboks toured New Zealand only once every decade or so.

But here were the Australians, who were destined to be regular tourists, only two years after defeating the All Blacks in a three-Test series (New Zealand's first losing series ever) unable to draw even reasonable crowds to their games. Not even a cartoon from an Australian newspaper after the third Test in 1929, depicting a kangaroo throttling a kiwi and a kookaburra on a scoreboard showing the results of the Tests chortling 'Ha! Ha! Who would have thought it' and with the provocative caption 'The New Champion', seemed to arouse the nationalistic fury of New Zealanders.

For the New Zealand officials the response to this problem was obvious. Why not set up a trophy along the lines of the successful Ranfurly Shield competition? The *Encyclopedia of World Rugby* has this entry under 'Ranfurly Shield':

> The Ranfurly Shield is a challenge trophy, decided on only one match between New Zealand unions and with the odds stacked heavily in favour of the holders, who have the home ground advantage . . . Yet, for all its seeming inequalities, the Ranfurly Shield has evolved an aura, mystique and passion which, to an outsider, may seem slightly unreal. In 1901, the Governor of New Zealand, Lord Ranfurly, offered a trophy to the New Zealand Rugby Union. The offer was accepted and the trophy commissioned from England. It arrived as a shield—complete with a centrepiece depicting soccer goalposts and a round ball!

An equivalent of a Ranfurly Shield for New Zealand–Australian rugby competition—that was the way, the officials must have thought, to revive interest in the rugby rivalry. Get old 'Chattering Charlie' to agree to the idea, to continue the Governor-General link. No problem that he was totally ignorant about rugby and had no interest in it. He needn't come up to Auckland even, as there was no cup to present right now. But the words 'Bledisloe Cup' had a fine ring to them and might just lift the New Zealand–Australia Tests into crowd-drawing matches in the way the Ranfurly Shield had enthused the New Zealand public for local provincial rugby.

SHEEP AND GOALPOSTS

Touring New Zealand is a rugby purgatory for visiting sides. But there is one heavenly light amid the gloom—the All Blacks invariably play a poor first Test. In many cases, some of the provincial matches are much harder to win than the Tests are. The 1986 Wallabies, for instance, were thrashed by Canterbury 30–10 but won the Test series two-one,—and could have had a clean sweep except for a refereeing error. Because New Zealand sides generally feature players from a number of provinces the new combinations usually haven't had time to settle in before the first Test. This problem is exacerbated for New Zealand teams by the ridiculous International Rugby Board ruling that a Test side not be allowed to come together before the Wednesday of a Saturday Test. The 1931 All Blacks for the first Bledisloe Cup Test, for instance, had players from Otago, Canterbury, Wellington, South Canterbury, Auckland, Southland, Hawkes Bay and Nelson in the starting fifteen.

'"Take off thy shoes for the place whereon thou standest is holy ground" may well be the injunction to any visiting football team on arrival in New Zealand', a *Sydney Mail* journalist covering the 1931 tour wrote. He went on:

> One of the wags of the New South Wales team of 1921, when asked the question: 'What are the staple products of New Zealand?' significantly replied, 'Sheep and goalposts.' Yea, verily, football is a serious business—a national affair—in New Zealand, and the All Blacks jersey is a sacred vestment for the demigods chosen to wear it and its badge of honour, the silver fern.

The journalist was struck by the 'chubbiness of the schoolboys and their lustiness and beefiness'. He saw a connection between 'the big hefty chaps' working out in the open and 'the virility always associ-

ated with New Zealand football'. The softer grounds too, he argued, provide 'varied experiences' for the players who had to learn how to cope with slippery grounds, wind and wet balls, thereby gaining 'a more liberal football education than in Australia'.

Phil Wilkins interviewed a couple of the 1931 tourists for the *Australian* some 50 years after the tour. Their memories were still vivid. Harold Tolhurst, described by Wilkins as a 'rock of a man' after five heart attacks, square-shouldered and strong of opinion, remembered Invercargill, the last New Zealand town before the South Pole:

> The night before the game, they took us over on a boat to Stewart Island off the bottom of the South Island and filled us with Bluff oysters and whisky. The oysters were the local delicacy there but they set like leather in our bellies. I wasn't a drinker, but we couldn't walk for a day after those oysters.

Tolhurst, a winger as a player and a referee who later refereed two Tests between New Zealand and Australia in 1951, actually scored a try against Southland but had no memory of how he did this.

The second old timer, Bryan Palmer, told Wilkins:

> Southland beat us alright. It would have taken a hippo to digest those Bluff oysters. You needed a hacksaw to cut them. It was a heartbreak of a tour, the first by the Wallabies after the World War, the most stupid in history. There were no planes in those days. We had a three-day boat trip to Auckland, caught the midnight horror train to Wellington, got a ferry to Lyttelton and then on by train to Dunedin. We didn't have a coach, we were leg-weary from travelling, we hadn't had a decent training

session and ran straight on against Otago, the Ranfurly Shield holders. We started in snow and the weather turned to wind, sleet and ice. God knows how we held them to a 3–3 draw.

Harold Tolhurst's last memory offered to Phil Wilkins came back to the rugby and the men he'd played against: 'Rucks were just as willing in New Zealand then as now. They kicked the hell out of me in the Test. But they were nice blokes'.

The Curse of the First Test struck the All Blacks as they struggled to defeat a side no one, either in the Australian camp or in the New Zealand camp, considered had the remotest chance of winning. As well as the curse working for them, the Australians finally had ground conditions that were similar to those they were used to back home and which suited their speedy backs. Eden Park at Auckland was built on volcanic rocks. The field was so hard for the Test that a 'distinct vibration' was heard as the players charged around the ground. A 'hollow ring' was heard when the goalkicker made his mark in the ground with his heel in placing the ball.

The *Sydney Morning Herald*'s account of the 1931 Test was headlined:

TEST MATCH

All Blacks Win

SERIES OF PENALTIES

Australia was defeated yesterday by 20 points to 13 in the only international match of the season against New Zealand. Twelve of the winners' points came from penalty kicks. The Australians gave a brilliant display in the first half. At the interval they led by 13 points to 11, but they could not score in the second half . . . New Zealand winning the toss, opened the play with the benefit of a slight wind. Within five minutes of the start Hart scored for New Zealand, Bush converting. The visitors secured the ball from successive scrums and lineouts and Malcolm gave a good display of passing. Steggall, after a dashing run, transferred to Cowper, who raced across and scored near the posts. Ross converted, thus evening the score. A penalty kick, the first of several, was kicked by Bush a minute later, and then the Australians scored their second try. Towers, sent away by Malcolm from his own 25, got beyond two defenders, and reaching Bush kicked over the latter's head. Judd picked up, transferred to Towers again, who scored. Ross converted thus putting the visitors ahead. Steggall distinguished himself again by taking a well-timed pass from Malcolm, and dashing through the defence scored just when being tackled. The visitors were now leading 13–8. The margin was soon reduced by Bush with a penalty goal . . .

The second spell was characterised by sterling play. At times, the visitors assumed a dangerous offensive, but the All Blacks were more than their match. A further penalty goal by Bush placed New Zealand a

A. W. Ross, Australian fullback for the first Bledisloe Cup game.

> point ahead. The All Blacks were now showing their traditional form, and after varying play, Bush from a penalty goal kicked his fifth goal making the scores 17 to 13 in favour of New Zealand. The Australians were awarded a penalty near the touch-line. Ross made a splendid attempt, but the ball hit the post. Australia launched further swift attacks but the opposition was sound in defence. Within two minutes of time, Bush registered New Zealand's second try after securing the ball from Solomon just as the latter was to be tackled by Ross. Bush failed with the kick, the game ending New Zealand 20: Australia 13.

There is no mention in this report of a Bledisloe Cup at stake in the Test. At this point the Bledisloe Cup was a concept that existed essentially in press releases.

So there was no presentation of the trophy after the match to the New Zealanders. As a gimmick to create interest in a Test that few New Zealanders had been interested in, the Bledisloe Cup concept—initially at least—must be deemed a failure. Certainly, it did not capture the imagination of New Zealanders as the Ranfurly Shield did from its outset. The New Zealand captain, the five-eighth Archie Strang, for instance, was confronted by the manager of the stock agency at which he worked, the day after the Test. The manager brandished the morning newspaper and exclaimed: 'I see you are still playing football, Strang. Well, I just want you to know that if you break an arm or a leg you won't have a job here'. 1931 was a Depression year. Strang, with a captaincy record for the All Blacks of one Test and one victory, at the age of 25 retired from rugby.

The Australian captain, the mercurial Syd Malcolm, a tiny but brilliant player with a face like Punch, dealt with the Depression and rugby-playing in a more novel manner. According to Bruce Hewitt, he put an order book in with his rugby gear and sent back a full quota of New Zealand sales of the new novelty sweets appropriately called—if the later history of the Bledisloe Cup is acknowledged—Lifesavers.

ASHES REGAINED.

WIN FOR ALL BLACKS.

WALLABIES SUFFER DEFEAT.

VISITORS' GOOD REARGUARD.

BUSH KICKS FIVE GOALS.

The only Rugby test between the All Blacks and the Wallabies was played at Eden Park on Saturday, and resulted in a win for the All Blacks by 20 points to 13. The All Blacks' score was made by two tries, one of which was converted by Bush, who also kicked four penalty goals. Bush kicked magnificently and as a result 14 of New Zealand's points were registered by him. The Wallabies scored three tries, two of which were converted by Ross.

By their success the All Blacks have regained the ashes lost to Australia two seasons ago. In the first spell the Wallabies had all the better of the play and scored three really brilliant tries. The All Blacks settled down better in the second half, during which the visitors failed to score.

The match was really a duel between the All Black forwards and the Wallabies' backs. The visiting rearguard gave a fine exhibition of polished passing, which was in strong contrast to that of the All Black backs. Its speed and accurate handling, with penetration by the inside men, always made it a dangerous attacking force.

The All Black inside backs were extremely disappointing, Strang and Lilburne repeatedly taking their passes standing and their tackling being weak at times. Corner was not in the same form as that which gained him All Black honours last season, and at times sent out some impossible passes. Page, who replaced Oliver, in spite of the fact that the inside men were at fault, was disappointing except for good defence.

Threequarters Starved.

It was a great pity to see Hart, and Ball having to make their own opportunities. Hart, especially, played a very good all-round game. Credit for the All Blacks' rather lucky win must, therefore, to a great extent be handed to the fine goal-kicking of Bush and the work of the pack, especially in the second spell.

The match was played under splendid weather conditions, the ground being in good order. There was an attendance of about 15,000 spectators.

The teams were as follows:

ALL BLACKS.

Fullback.—R. G. Bush.

Threequarters.—N. Ball, R. Page, G. F. Hart.

Five-eighths.—H. Lilburne, W. A. Strang.

Halfback.—M. Corner.
Wing-forward.—F. Solomon.
Hookers.—A. I. Cottrell, E. Jessup.
Lock.—E. R. G. Steere.
Supports.—G. Purdue, D. Max.
Back Row.—W. Batty, T. Metcalfe.

WALLABIES.

Fullback.—A. W. Ross.
Threequarters.—W. Hemingway, C. H. Towers, D. L. Cowper, H. Tolhurst.
Five-eighths.—J. Steggall.
Halfback—S. J. Malcolm.
Front Row.—M. R. Blair, E. Bonis, W. H. Cerrutti.
Middle Row.—M. White, B. Judd.
Back Row.—J. Clark, T. Perrin, L. J. Palfreyman.
Strang captained the All Blacks and Malcolm led the Wallabies.

The All Blacks won the toss and played with the sun and slight wind. Immediately following the kick-off a scrum was formed, the All Blacks hooking the ball, but Corner was caught in possession. Steggall intercepted a pass from Corner brilliantly and started a passing movement which gained considerable ground and earned the applause of the spectators. The All Blacks retaliated, and Strang made a fine cross-kick, which had Ross in trouble. Hart dashed up while the visiting fullback was waiting for the bounce, kicked on and gathered possession well, to score well out unopposed. Bush landed a fine goal.

All Blacks	..	..	..	5
Wallabies	..	..	..	0

Malcolm Shines.

The All Black forwards were being penalised for offside and play was being confined to the home team's quarters until Ball fielded a cross-kick and found the line well in the Wallabies' territory with a great kick. The visiting backs were throwing the ball about from all positions, and Malcolm shone out in clever play behind the scrum. The All Blacks were in a good attacking position in the visitors' twenty-five but the advantage was lost when Lilburne dropped his pass in a back attack.

Good play by Steggall saw the Wallabies in a likely position, a touch-in-goal resulting. Twice Lilburne was conspicuous for heady play, and twice all advantage was lost through Page failing to gather his pass cleanly. The Wallabies were gaining a little more of the ball from the scrums, but the backs made little headway. The first time the whole All Black back line handled the ball correctly Hart beat Tolhurst, who, however, chased and lowered the All Black threequarter.

It was then the Wallabies' turn. Malcolm started a movement cleverly and Steggall made a splendid opening before drawing Bush. Steggall transferred to Cowper, who outpaced the opposition and scored behind the posts. Ross easily added the goal points.

All Blacks	..	..	..	5
Wallabies	..	..	..	5

A few minutes later Bush landed a magnificent goal from a penalty about five yards inside halfway.

All Blacks	..	..	..	8
Wallabies	..	..	..	5

Better passing by the Wallabies and superior speed gave the visitors the advantage, the All Blacks being kept on defence. Towers then made a lovely opening and with no support when reaching Bush kicked. Judd gathered possession and Towers came up last on the outside to accept a pass and score near the posts. Ross converted.

Wallabies	..	..	..	10
All Blacks	..	..	..	8

Second Try for Towers.

The Wallabies were now throwing the ball about in fine style and gained applause for several spectacular movements. Steggall made a splendid opening by beating the All Black five-eighths, and in a flash Towers was up alongside him to accept his pass and score a fine try near the posts. From a free charge Ross missed the goal points.

Wallabies 13
All Blacks 8

The All Blacks made a brief attack and Bush just missed at goal from a penalty near halfway. A few minutes later the fullback was successful with another magnificent kick.

Wallabies 13
All Blacks 11

In the few minutes remaining before the spell the Wallabies had all the better of the exchanges, but there was no further scoring.

The All Black forwards commenced the second spell with more dash, but a penalty and a magnificent kick by Ross drove them back. The All Blacks maintained the attack, but the passing of the backs was too slow and deliberate. Short kicks by the visiting backs had the home team troubled. The two fullbacks came into prominence for good kicking, and then clever play by Malcolm placed the Wallabies on attack, a force down eventually resulting.

Batty broke clean away from the loose but kicked and Ross saved nicely. Then Bush landed his third penalty goal with another great kick from well out. A little earlier the fullback had narrowly missed with another free kick.

All Blacks 14
Wallabies 13

The All Blacks were now continually on the attack and Steggall stood out for some fine defensive work. A bad offside by a visiting forward outside his twenty-five gave Bush another opportunity and the fullback again raised the flags.

All Blacks 17
Wallabies 13

The Wallabies took a brief turn on attack during which Ross was unlucky when his penalty kick hit the upright. Clever passing by Page, Strang and Hart drove the attack back past halfway. The All Black backs were given several chances, but generally a bad pass spoiled the opportunity. The All Blacks had the better of the remaining exchanges, and just on time Corner made a clever opening on the blind side. Solomon further improved the position and drew Ross before sending on to Ball. The All Black wing took advantage of his only real opportunity during the match by scoring wide out. Bush failed to convert and the game ended with the score—

All Blacks 20
Wallabies 13

Mr. S. Hollander, Christchurch, was referee.

1934: Australia wins the Bledisloe Cup

Why was Australian rugby so strong coming into the 1930s and so weak—compared with New Zealand rugby—throughout the 1940s, 1950s, 1960s and 1970s? In 1929 the Australians inflicted the first series whitewash the All Blacks had to endure. Then, two years later, an Australian team that lost most of its tour matches was defeated in the Test, although as a newspaper account noted 'the honours were with Australia, who scored three tries to two by the victor'. A year later, scoring four tries to three, the Wallabies defeated the All Blacks at the Sydney Cricket Ground, 22–17. Two weeks later, the All Blacks exacted their revenge at the Exhibition Ground at Brisbane, 21 (four tries) to 3 (one try). The series wound up at the Sydney Cricket Ground with another All Blacks victory, 21–13. Two years later, the Wallabies again won the Bledisloe Cup with a stupendous victory, scoring 25 points (four tries) to 11 (three tries). This was the heaviest defeat inflicted on New Zealand by Australia. And it took another 30 years for the Wallabies to better the winning margin of 14 points, a result achieved with a 20–5 victory against the All Blacks in 1964. The first Test win in 1934 was turned into Australia's first Bledisloe Cup triumph with a 3–3 draw at the Sydney Cricket Ground in the second Test of a two-match series.

This admittedly small run of Australian wins (five victories, a draw and three losses in nine Tests) represents one of the best sequences the Wallabies have constructed against the All Blacks. Part of the reason for this outcome was the outstanding talent of backs like Syd Malcolm, an inventive halfback who has been rated as an 'extraordinarily astute tactical thinker', Cyril Towers, a masterly centre, and Dr Alexander Ross, a shrewd captain and one of the finest fullbacks Australia has produced. The packs during this successful sequence of Tests included players like Edward 'Weary' Dunlop, a tall and fiery lineout forward from Victoria, and Aubrey Hodgson, a 1930s version of Ray Price, a snarler of a loose forward who terrorised opposition backs and sometimes his own with the fury and aggression of his play.

Terry McLean, the doyen of New Zealand rugby writers, a journalist who has seen and reported All Black sides since the 1930s, reckoned in 1979 that 'the greatest display by a forward that I ever saw was given by an Australian named Aubrey Hodgson in 1936'. According to McLean, Hodgson was 'stupendous' when he played for the Wallabies against Wairarapa in the small town of Carterton:

> Wherever he moved in the lineout, the ball came to him. Wherever he ran in the open, ball in hand, there were great spaces—kamikaze kids had not been chosen for Wairarapa. It was an extraordinary display, and though I have seen a bundle of great forwards all over the world in the past 43 years—God bless me, is it so long?—none in the space of a match played as Aub did that day.

Hodgson turned on a similar display of ferocious and effective rugby in the second half of the first Test in Sydney in 1934. His fierce tackling upset the New Zealand backs and his long runs with the ball contributed to the most dominant half of rugby a Wallaby side has ever played against the All Blacks, with the home side scoring 19 points and the New Zealanders failing to score a point.

Remarkably, at halftime the All Blacks led 11–6. What caused the

historic turnaround in the second half. 'Light Blue' in the *Sydney Mail* gave a masterly analysis. He noted that in the first half the Wallaby inside backs were not moving up on defence. This left gaps for the New Zealand captain, James 'Rusty' Page, to exploit. The Wallaby forwards, too, were allowing the All Blacks to pour through the lineouts and rucks. These mistakes were put right at halftime:

> First, Mackney and Bridle co-operated, one taking the half, Corner, and the other the five-eighth, Page, as occasion demanded. Then Ross adopted a stratagem which probably won the game. He asked for scrums, instead of lineouts, and hooker Bonis—the hero of many encounters with international opponents of world repute—nobly assisted the players by winning most of the scrums. Previously a menace in the lineouts, the All Blacks were thus thwarted and placed on the defensive. The result was that Australia got 'on top,' and excellent leadership of the pack by Jessep—an Australian-born but New Zealand-taught footballer—kept them on top.

Evan Morgan Jessep had a foot in both camps in the rugby wars between New Zealand and Australia. He went to New Zealand from Australia as a child of four. A rugged man, a big player for his time, he played hooker for the All Blacks on their tour of Australia in 1932. He then stayed on in Australia, settling in Melbourne, and as part of a strong Victorian state side forced his way into the Wallabies for the

Tests of 1934. He was the first New Zealand representative to play for and against the All Blacks in Tests.

He was also the first All Blacks hooker to pack down in a three-man front row in a Test. For during the 1932 series the All Blacks finally gave away the 2–3–2 diamond scrum. The decline in back play that marked New Zealand rugby for decades can be attributed to this—necessary but unfortunate—decision. The 2–3–2 scrum was a backs' delight. The ball came out of the diamond scrum quickly, giving backs a great deal of room to set up their plays and engage in man-on-man contests. In this environment New Zealand produced many backline wizards from Billy Wallace to Bert Cooke. Sometime in the future the 2–3–2 scrum will be brought back to rugby, with the forwards reduced to a pack of seven men.

The 1920s and 1930s, however, were decades when there was a great deal of experimentation with scrum formations. The practice in Britain for a long time was typically informal and unthoughtful. The first three forwards to the mark formed a front row, the next two a second row and the last three a back row. The Australian practice was to use the eight-man British scrum formation but with players trained to play a specific position, as the New Zealanders did. For some years the South Africans experimented with a four-man front row before devising the 3–4–1 formation.

The effectiveness of the South African scrum formation was—literally—rammed into the Wallabies during their tour of South Africa in 1933. The vice-captain of that team, Syd Malcolm, discussed the merits of the South African formation and scrumming philosophy in a fascinating article published in the *Sydney Mail* of 31 March 1934. 'Hard, solid pushing', Malcolm wrote, 'has always been regarded as the first article of South African football faith, and the 3–4–1 formation is suitable for a pack composed of big men imbued with this idea.' Malcolm ended his article on this ominous (for the All Blacks) note: 'I still consider the 3–2–3 a superior scrum for general purposes; but I would, nevertheless, employ the 3–4–1 at which we became so expert, in the forthcoming contest against the All Blacks'.

For its part, New Zealand rugby seemed to have forgotten any lessons about scrum formations and techniques that were picked up on the 1928 tour of South Africa. New Zealand teams reverted to the 2–3–2 scrum during the tour of Australia in 1929. And even though the 3–4–1 scrum had been used by the All Blacks, finally, in 1932, it is clear that there was no enthusiasm, or belief, in its advantages. In New Zealand provincial rugby the scrum was neglected as a way of exerting pressure on the opposition. Many teams failed to develop specialised forwards in the front row. This neglect, which was based

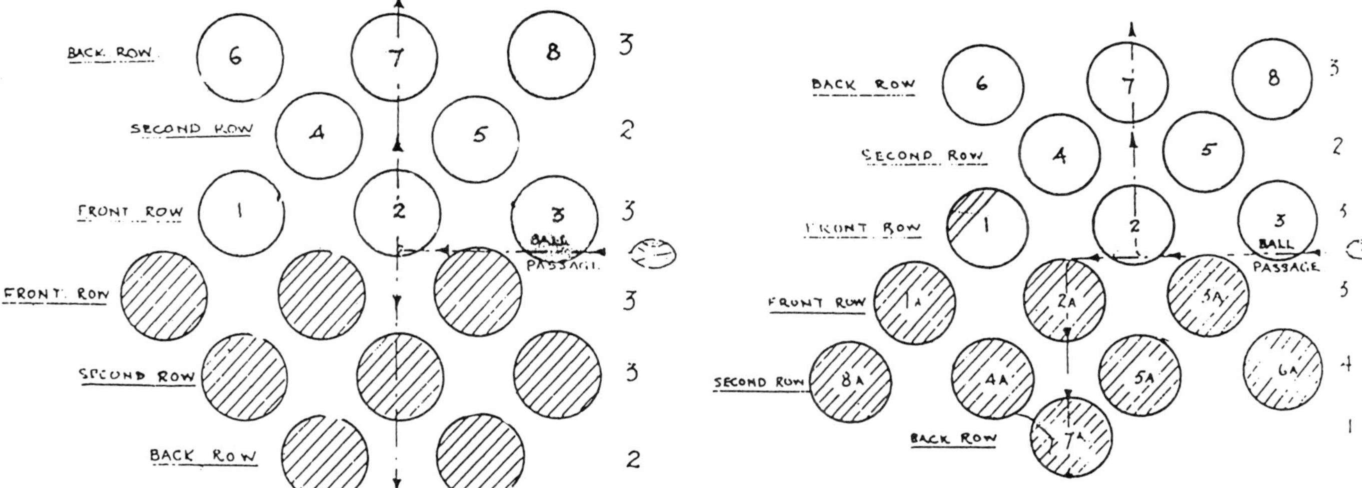

Diagrams of the Scrum Formations During the Wallabies' Tour of South Africa

Figure 1 (left): Orthodox British scrum formation 3.2.3 versus an African formation 3.3.2. Figure 2 (right): Orthodox British scrum formation 3.2.3 (as used by Australia before South African tour) versus typical South African 3.4.1. formation. Note the wider scrum base and better passage for ball on the ideology that the scrum was merely a device to get the ball to backs, had its revenge. During the final Test against the Springboks at Eden Park in 1937, when the series was in the balance, the South African captain, Philip Nel, who captained against the Wallabies in 1933 also, uttered the fateful words when the first New Zealand kick went into touch: 'We'll scrum it, ref.' New Zealand, in a replay of the devastating second half of the Test against the Wallabies in 1934, were starved of the ball. The result on both occasions was a compelling defeat for the All Blacks.

Australian rugby was to forget this lesson of scrum dominance over the years. The All Blacks, defeated four Tests to none in South Africa in 1949 at least came back from that tour with the principles of the scrum—explained to them by former Springboks halfback and then selector, Danie Craven—deeply embedded in their psyche. Although the scrum option instead of lineouts was abolished after the war, the harsh lesson that at scrum-time might is right was accepted by New Zealand teams and duress was, accordingly, inflicted on Australian sides at scrum-time up to the late 1970s.

One other critical aspect that governed the sequence of Wallaby victories in the early 1930s was also lost—the effectiveness of a truly representative team. The 1934 Wallaby pack that scrummed the All Blacks out of the first Test had two Queenslanders in it, three Victorians and only two players from New South Wales. The backs had four New South Wales players and three Queenslanders. Australian rugby had to wait until the late 1970s (the era when the Wallabies became successful again) for a similar representation of Queensland players in a Wallaby Test team. Queensland officials still smart from the treatment meted out to their players during the 1950s and 1960s. New South Wales officials often told them that the Wallabies were weakened by the inclusion of the Queensland players. Since the resurgence of Queensland rugby in the 1970s the exact opposite has been the case.

We have a good idea about the way the Wallabies played in this golden era and the strategy behind their methods. Cyril Towers, the outstanding centre, a 'player without a weakness, with a rare blend of fierce aggression and bravado', according to the rugby historian Jack Pollard, passed his ideas on through the famous Randwick club to Bob Dwyer who used them to build his reputation as a coach at Randwick and then for the Wallabies. The way Randwick has played right up to the present day, as the 'Galloping Greens', was the way Wallaby sides in the early 1930s played. In his book, *The Winning Way,* Dwyer talks about the Randwick method of the flat backline and the club's abhorrence of the kicking game:

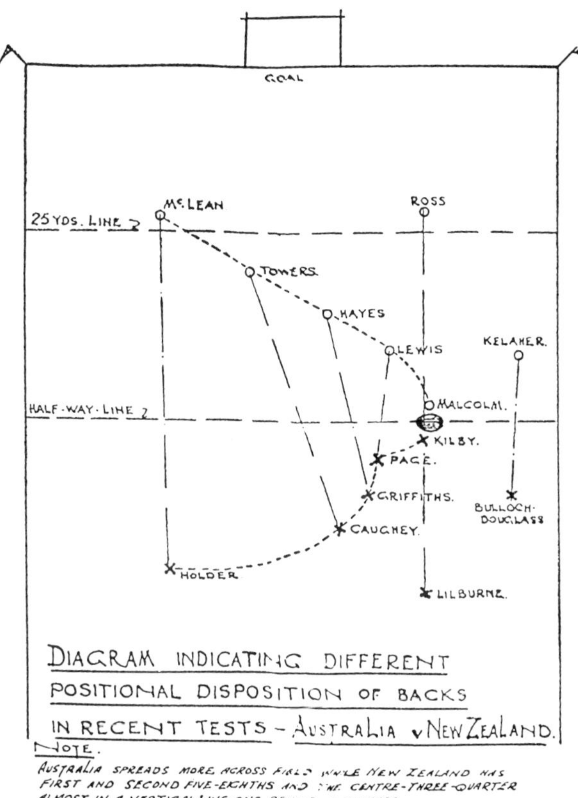

The person who introduced me to the concept was a great player of the past named Cyril Towers, who had played centre for Randwick and for Australia in the 1930s when both teams were using this type of backline play. In his later years Towers often came down to the Randwick club to do a bit of coaching or simply yarn with the players about Rugby and how he thought the game should be played. No matter how many points we won by, Cyril would always tell us we were no good. As a Randwick player in the 1960s I often found myself talking to him about technique and tactics, and it was during these conversations that he started telling me about the backline game he had played thirty or more years before . . . The logic of what he was saying must have gradually seeped into my thinking, however, because one day, probably about 1975, I realised I had grasped it. Suddenly, it was obvious to me that Cyril's concept of backline play was right, and as soon as I accepted that fact it opened up a different world of analysis for me. At once there was new scope for moving and manipulating opposition defences. The challenge was to get the opposition to react in the way you wanted them to react, as if they were puppets on a string. The extra dimension which this adds to the game gives enormous satisfaction to the players, because they feel they are doing something above the ordinary, so they have an incentive to try and play harder and better.

1936: THE ALL BLACKS GET THEIR REVENGE

Predictions in rugby sometimes work in inverse proportion to what they assert. The 1936 Wallabies were rated by Australian officials and sportwriters as 'the best Wallaby team to leave Australia'. This 'best' team lost the Bledisloe Cup and endured the second largest losing margin in Bledisloe Cup history when it was defeated at Dunedin by a revengeful All Blacks side, 38–13. The 38 points conceded in this Test stand as the most points conceded in a Bledisloe Cup Test. Thirty-six years later, the 'Woeful Wallabies' of 1972—surely the year marking the lowest point in Australian rugby?—were defeated 29–6, 30–17 and 38–3, the worst sequence of defeats suffered by either side in the Bledisloe Cup series. Until 1972, though, the 1936 'best ever' Wallabies rate, as far as results are concerned, as the most unsuccessful Wallabies.

Where did the over-confidence come from? There were, of course, the results of 1929 and 1934 to indicate how competitive the Wallabies had become. As well, the thinking in Australian rugby circles before the tour to New Zealand began was that the All Blacks had a serious and possibly chronic weakness in the alignment of their backs. As usual, 'Light Blue' in the *Sydney Mail* was at his best explaining why the New Zealand method was wrong and why the Australian method of back alignment was the correct one. The Wallabies adopted the Welsh system of one five-eighth and two centres who lined wider and straighter (following the Cyril Towers doctrine) than the New Zealand formation did. The New Zealanders stood their two five-eighths and the one centre close together, almost in Indian file behind one another. Cyril Towers, 'an authority of team tactics and fieldcraft', was quoted as saying that the All Blacks were an easy team 'to hold defensively'. Because they were lined up so deep the New Zealand backs could be pushed across the field when they tried to run with the ball.

Against this, though, the 'I' formation, which was used very effectively by the Canberra Rugby League side in the 1994 grand final, provided 'greater mobility' according to 'Light Blue'. This became particularly apparent 'if a change from open to blindside movements is contemplated'. A great strength of New Zealand rugby has been its willingness to, in effect, widen the field by playing the blindside and then switching play to the more open spaces away from the sideline.

T. P. McLean, who was still writing about rugby in the 1990s and who remains a figure of reverence for New Zealand journalists when he makes his dignified entrance into the press box at Eden Park on Test days, analysed the 1936 tour, in one of his earliest excursions into writing about the sport, for the *Sydney Mail*. He wrestled with the Australian team's record and the high hopes held for it before it left Sydney. In the first Test, won by the All Blacks 11–6, the team was 'beaten by five points when, with any luck, it should have won by fifteen'.

The second Test thrashing McLean attributed to an incident that occurred shortly after halftime, with the Wallabies leading 13–11:

> K. Storey, the Australian fullback, standing fairly deep, ran up to take a high kick, saw he could not get to it, and waiting for the bounce, made a wild kick at it. He missed, and George Hart, New Zealand's flying winger, picked up the ball and ran over to score. The try was converted, and New Zealand's easy five points seemed to take the steam out of the Wallabies.

A similar incident, this time working in favour of the Wallabies, with Rob Egerton running on to the ball from a fortuitous bounce, turned the first Bledisloe Cup Test in 1991 decisively in Australia's favour. But the All Blacks, to their credit, continued to try to win the Test. The 1936 Wallabies, though, were made of insubstantial stuff. McLean reported that, after Storey missed with his speculator, a stupid play anyway given the fact that he had plenty of time to gather in the ball and send it spiralling down the field, the Wallabies collapsed: 'I have never seen an international team wilt so completely as the Wallabies. It was inexplicable that a side should go from good to very bad so completely'.

The last Test before the real war

New Zealand rugby was humiliated in 1937 when the touring South African Springboks ('the best team to leave New Zealand') won the series against the All Blacks, the first time a series between New Zealand and South Africa had been won and not squared (1921 and 1928). As the next team to face the All Blacks, the Wallabies, although

having the advantage of playing at home, suffered three defeats inflicted on them by a side that wanted to exact revenge. On the tour, in nine matches, the New Zealanders scored 279 points to 73. And in the Tests the All Blacks scored 58 points (including ten tries) to 29 for the Wallabies (including five tries). There was a ferocity in the play of the All Blacks that left shattered Australian players after all the matches. Four frontline Wallabies, 'four of the best', Ron Rankin (fullback), Max Carpenter (wing), 'Rus' Kelly and Bill Monti (forwards), were unavailable—injured—for the third Test won 14–6 by the All Blacks.

During the third Test, the last for the Bledisloe Cup before the Second World War, Cecil Ramalli, a halfback who burst spectacularly into Test rugby like George Gregan in 1994, was carried off the field on a stretcher suffering from concussion and a broken nose. Ramalli, an Aboriginal teenager, was playing his first season of representative rugby and was brought into the Wallabies in the second Test at the insistence of the critics who rated him the 'greatest halfback' since Syd Malcolm. There is some doubt about Ramalli's background. When I mentioned in the *Sydney Morning Herald* that Jack Pollard in his history of the game had cautiously suggested that Ramalli was 'one of the first Aboriginals to play for Australia', I received a letter from a reader:

> Cecil Ramalli was born to parents of Indian descent who migrated to Australia from India; for many years his parents had a store in Mungindi New South Wales as well as a property named 'Bombay' on the other side of the border. He was a member of the Australian touring side to play in 1939, but on arrival in England War was declared and the tour cancelled. I lived most of my life in the Mungindi district, born there in 1932. My family and the Ramalli family were great friends. He may well have been the first of his race to play Rugby for Australia.

I passed this letter on to Jack Pollard. He sent the reader the following reply, with a copy to me:

> The information about Cec Ramalli, which you conveyed in your letter to Spiro Zavos, confirms the facts on which I based my entry on Aboriginal rugby players in *Australian Rugby: The Game and the Players*. This material came from Professor Colin Tatz of Macquarie University, author of the booklet *Aborigines In Sport*. Tatz told me that in researching Aboriginal rugby players for a new edition of his book he had examined Cec Ramalli's birth certificate. This shows that Ramalli was the son of an Indian father who settled in Mungindi and married an Aborigine.
>
> I knew Cec well when he was an administrator of junior development for the Northern Suburbs Rugby Club and I was one of the coaches. He told me how he had burst on to the international scene with some striking performances just before World War II, but then underwent some horrific years in prison camps and mines which snuffed out his career. I recall Cec standing up at the bar at Norths claiming he had missed out on the job of National Coaching Director because of prejudice against Aborigines. The job went to a white Queenslander named Dick Marks. When Cec left and found I was working on my rugby book, he volunteered the information that he was an Aborigine and had been christened Ali Ram,

which his family revised to Ramalli when he went to Hurlstone Agricultural High School.

Whatever his origins, there can be no doubts about his ability as a rugby player. A photograph of the 1938 Test shows Ramalli, a player of frail build, clutching the ball tentatively and steadying his body for the impact of Albert Bowman, the New Zealand expert at bursting through the lineouts, who has his arms around Ramalli's shoulders ready to smash him to the ground. Bowman is clearly going to run over the top of little halfback as he tumbles to the ground. Is this the occasion of Ramalli's broken nose and concussion? The ruthless physicality of New Zealand rugby—and its effectiveness—is epitomised in this photograph.

The determination to inflict defeat on the Wallabies was driven more by the traditional All Blacks passion to win than by any feeling that Australia was a rugby enemy that needed to be put in its place. The fact was, though, that at this time Australian rugby played the same—small—part in the rugby imagination of New Zealanders as, say, Western Samoan, Tongan or Fijian rugby plays in the imagination of Australians in the 1990s.

An indication of the New Zealand priorities in rugby competition comes from a poem entitled 'September 25, 1937' (the date of the decisive fourth Test between the All Blacks and the Springboks), which was written at the time by a young lawyer, John Carrad, who later in life became an enthusiastic administrator in university rugby in New Zealand.

A ruddy staunch pig-islander
Stood up against the bar:
His ruddy eyes were sombre
And his thoughts were soaring far
Away from ruddy Auckland,
From that gory Eden Park,
And as he drank his beer in silence
While his brow was grim and dark,
And he thought of other, golden days
When the All Blacks were the tops,
When England, France and Ireland
Took the ruddy nasty knocks,
When Wales was skittled
Nineteen to flaming nil
And Cooke and Morrie Brownlie
Scored tries at ruddy will . . .
He thought of how in 1905
The All Blacks beat the best;

Of glorious 1930,
When the All Blacks won the Test . . .

Nowhere in the poem is there a reference to the Wallabies, although the All Blacks had lost two series to them in the previous eight years. There is a sign in this of the New Zealand disregard, at that time, for Australian rugby. Admittedly, a cartoon depicting the third Test in 1938 showed a smug kiwi sitting on top of the Bledisloe Cup as if a meaningful triumph had been achieved. The reality, however, was that for New Zealanders, even those as devoted to their rugby as John Carrad, a victory over Australia was as insignificant as a defeat of the All Blacks by the Wallabies.

It was to take 40 more years before this attitude was changed. Because a 40–year era of All Blacks dominance over the Wallabies, accepted as the natural order of things as day following night, was under way.

THE SECRET OF THE ALL BLACKS

P. G. Wodehouse, who was tall enough to play in the second row but too gentle a man to be a hard player, once described the game of rugby in these words:

> The main scheme is to work the ball down the field somehow and deposit it over the line at the other end, and in order to squelch this program each side is allowed to put in a certain amount of assault and battery and do things to its fellow man which, if done elsewhere, would result in fourteen days without option, coupled with some strong remarks from the bench.

Most New Zealanders would accept that ironic summary as a reasonable description of the way in which All Black teams have played rugby over the decades. The basic secret of the All Blacks is that—except on a few mad occasions such as the third Test against the Wallabies in 1986—they have always accepted that rugby is a body contact sport in which the courage to dominate the opposition physically is a first principle of playing the game successfully.

Sometimes this imperative to dominate spills over into untoward foul play. Richard Loe's elbow into the nose of the Wallaby winger, Paul Carozza, in 1992 at Ballymore, was against the spirit of the game and not in the interests of New Zealand rugby. Two years later, at the Sydney Football Stadium, Loe found himself being penalised for rough play almost on suspicion by the referee. These infringements meant that the All Blacks were starved of possession in the first half and lost the Test because of this. This tough-bodied approach to rugby, though, has seldom been carried to the level produced by Richard Loe. This is not to suggest that fists were never thrown. They were. But generally there was a reason. And the reason often involved imposing some sort of law and order on a lawless opposition.

This Wild West approach was exemplified by a famous story concerning the 'Iron Man' New Zealand prop, Johnny Simpson, and Phil Hardcastle, the wily, tenacious Australian secondrower. During the 1946 Test series in New Zealand (won by New Zealand 31–6, 14–10) Hardcastle had created havoc in the New Zealand lineout, especially in the second Test. The scrum problem of the 1930s was fixed with an overwhelming 23 to 6 scrum count for the All Blacks in the first Test at Dunedin. So when Hardcastle started his tricks again in the first Test at the Sydney Cricket Ground in 1947 Simpson was prepared to take action. 'Hardcastle', he shouted out, 'if you do that again I'll clock you.' Whatever it was, it was done again. Some lineouts later, Hardcastle caught the ball, held it through his legs so that his head was sticking out of the maul. Simpson wound up for the punch. Charlie Willocks, the New Zealand secondrower, an inquisitive man, sensed that something was about to happen. He stuck his head up out of the maul at the precise moment that Simpson's fist was flying through the air. Seven stitches—for Willocks, and no more matches on the tour for him . . .

The second secret of the All Blacks over the years is the team's pragmatic inventiveness to the problems rugby poses as a game. The elements of the New Zealand system were developed in the 19th century when most New Zealanders lived on the land and were used to being inventive with the equipment they had at hand. New Zealand farmers to this day can do just about anything with fencing wire, except perhaps make babies with it. So the pragmatic, inventive farmers played a pragmatic, inventive game of rugby. The pattern was summed up by Charlie Saxton, the outstanding All Blacks halfback of 1938 and later a superb administrator, as the Three Ps: Possession, Position, Pace. The New Zealanders, for instance, developed the ruck in the 1880s, rolling the ball back with the foot, to ensure that a team could retain possession of the ball instead of having to 'hack' it through to the opposition's pack. As late as 1905, some experts on the laws of Rugby Union in the United Kingdom insisted that such rucking put the rest of the pack offside. Rucking, though, liberated the game from developing into an endless moving maul much like the Eton wall game, where tries were rare, to a game where the backs—and forwards—can be brought into play to run with the ball as fast as they can.

Finally, the dynamic inside the culture of New Zealand rugby and, perhaps, the real secret behind the success of the All Blacks was (and is) an obsession with playing to win. New Zealanders feel enhanced when the All Blacks win and diminished on those occasions when they lose. The cultural and sociological significance of this visceral identification with the All Blacks on both a national and an individual level was memorably described by the writer John Mulgan in his book, *Report on Experience*, which was written during the Second World War:

> Our main pursuits were only cultural in the broadest sense. They were horse-racing, playing Rugby football, and beer-drinking—especially playing football . . . Rugby football was the best of all our pleasures: it was religion and desire and fulfilment all in one. Most New Zealanders can look back on some game which they played to win and whose issues seemed to them then a good deal more important than a lot that has happened since. This phenomenon is greatly deprecated by a lot of thinkers who feel that an exaggerated attention to games gives the young a wrong sense of values. This may well be true, and if it is true, the majority of New Zealanders have a wrong sense of values for the whole of their lives. But to be frank, and since we live in a hard world, and one that has certainly not in my time got any softer, I found in war-time that there was considerable virtue in men who played games like professionals to win, and not, like public-school boys and amateurs, for exercise . . . Englishmen spent some time and casualties in finding war ungentlemanly before they tossed the rules overboard and moved in on the same basis as the New Zealanders. I don't know that the cunning and professionalism of my fellow countrymen is to be commended on abstract grounds, but these are comfortable qualities to have around in war-time. Oddly enough, I don't think these things affected their natural kindliness, nor the kind of ethics that they expect from people in private life. It was only that they looked on war as a game and a game to New Zealanders is something they play to win, against the other side and the referee. Personally, I still prefer games that way and find them more interesting.

With a style of play built around these secrets the All Blacks created a record that made them one of the greatest teams in the history of international sport. By 1947 a remarkable record had been put together. From the first New Zealand team in Australia in 1884 up to the beginning of the 1947 tour of Australia by the All Blacks, New Zealand national teams had played 267 matches against Australian opponents for 229 victories, only 28 losses and 10 draws. Points for were 5827 and against 1621.

A major law change of the postwar era was the abolition of the right to call for a scrum in place of a lineout. The lineout became the focus of attention from the pragmatic New Zealand selectors. This was an era, too, before the maul. Rugby was a setpiece, run, tackle, ruck, kick game. Continuity of play was extremely difficult to develop, so much so that the staple of training in New Zealand was the exercise that put the ball through the backs, the last handler falling to the ground on the blast of a whistle for the forwards to rush across and ruck the ball back for another back movement and so on, and so on. The blast of the whistle seemingly went on forever.

The calculation was made in 1947 by the New Zealand selectors that the All Blacks could expect about 60 lineouts in each Test. Throughout the 1946 Test series the Wallabies had actually outjumped the All Blacks and had shown, especially with the highstepping Charlie Eastes on the wing, much more pace out wide. The 1947 All Blacks, as a matter of selection policy, were the tallest side ever sent out of New Zealand. Of the thirteen forwards sent to Australia in 1938 only five were over six feet tall: eight of the twelve forwards in 1947 were six-footers. They were extremely fit, too, as most of them had served in the armed forces only a few years previously.

A win by New South Wales in the opening match of the tour raised (false) hopes among Australian officials and journalists of a Bledisloe Cup series win by the Wallabies. The victory, however, flattered only to deceive when the crunch came in the first Test. The opening paragraph of a Brisbane newspaper's match report told the story:

> They say that earthquakes have come to Queensland! We'll let the secret out. It's these black shirts from the Shaky Isles. They gave the Aussies a touch of the tremors in the first Rugby Union Test at the 'Ekka' yesterday! The Kiwis polished off the Wallabies 13 points to five before 25 000 Union football–hungry souls in a match where the perfect combinative qualities of the Enzedders triumphed over the jittery and disjointed Aussie inside backs.

Although the margin of victory was not large, the superiority of

the All Blacks was obvious. The Australian selectors embarked on an exercise of 'wholesale changes'. The 35-year-old Graham Cooke, a noted lineout jumper who had played against the All Blacks back in 1932, was recalled. The first-Test captain, Phil Hardcastle, so lucky to escape having his head blasted off by Johnny Simpson, was metaphorically decapitated by the Australian selectors, being dropped right out of the team. Eight changes in all were made. The pack was told it had to play much tougher than it did in the first Test. The Wallaby wingers were instructed to use a 'torpedo' throw into the lineout, to nullify the superior jumping and blocking by the All Blacks. This is the first reference to such a throw I've been able to come across. The usual lineout throw in those days was the overarm bowling motion which had the great disadvantage that it was hard to vary the speed and the loft of the throw. The lineout count with the Australian wingers using the torpedo throw came out at 27 all. And, although the score of 27–14 against the Wallabies was larger than in the first Test, the result was seen as an endorsement of the decision to play a tighter game with less emphasis on running the ball on every play.

'Ditch the Waratah tactics and Australia will develop footballers capable of beating any nation in the world', the All Blacks manager,

Harold Strang, told journalists before the Test. After the match, a relieved Strang commented: 'I thought I had given you the good oil too soon'. The series victory relieved Strang of another problem. The Bledisloe Cup, a huge and weighty object, had not been brought with the team because—and this was the official reason—'their air luggage was limited'. Might there not be, though, another reason? Confidence in an inevitable New Zealand victory, what is sometimes called 'arrogance', is also part of the All Blacks secret. Why bring the Bledisloe Cup across to Australia when the All Blacks would have to lug it all the way back to New Zealand again after the series was over?

The Blackest Year for the All Blacks

Headlines in the sports section of the New Zealand *Free Lance* of 7 September 1949 summed up the anguish and shock of New Zealanders:

> AN ALL BLACK DAY IN RUGBY: TWO TEST DEFEATS
> Penalties Give Springboks Win For Second Time, Australia Too Good For Uninspired Home Side

On the same day, separated by thousands of miles and a few hours in time, the All Blacks lost two Tests. Bad (and in New Zealand eyes biased) refereeing was behind the loss to South Africa 9–3 (three penalty goals to one try). Incompetent administration was to blame for the defeat by the Wallabies. With 30 of the best players touring South Africa, the New Zealand Rugby Union was careless about the prestige of the All Blacks—and condescending to Australian rugby—by agreeing to a two-match Test series for the Bledisloe Cup.

To make the task of the third-string All Blacks harder, the team for the first Test at Athletic Park was selected only a day before it ran on to the field. No coach was provided, either. Presumably the thought was that, with players arriving in Wellington from the various provinces up to Friday evening, a coach wouldn't actually have a team to put through its paces before kickoff time.

It was perhaps no coincidence that the Wallabies outthought the All Blacks with their game plan. The Wallaby five-eighths continued with the rejection of Waratah rugby based on the running game and kicked for position on most occasions. New Zealand possession was spoilt, particularly from the lineout, by the use of the 'impetuous'

Wallaby flanker, David Brockhoff, adopting Hennie Muller tactics of attacking the five-eighth, Ben Couch, virtually when the halfback was set to deliver his pass to him. In South Africa and in New Zealand the All Blacks had no answer to this marauding style of play. Norman McKenzie, one of the best thinkers in New Zealand rugby and the analyst for the *Free Lance* said of Brockhoff's play: 'He is big and fast, and when New Zealand gained possession he headed straight for Ben Couch at first five-eighth. It was perfectly legitimate play and on many occasions he compelled Ben to act contrary to prior intentions'.

New Zealand rugby had ideological and practical difficulties coping with this Brockhoff/Muller tactic of the flanker taking off to tackle the five-eighth like a bullet from a gun. Throughout the 1930s, New Zealand wing forwards, who adopted a similar tactic from the scrums, were accused of being 'cheats'. With the advent of the 3–4–1 scrum, the 'seagull' forward had become unfashionable in New Zealand rugby. Vic Cavanagh Jnr, the formidable coach of the dominant Otago side of the 1940s and 1950s, developed the quick-ruck game with the second five-eighth (in New Zealand terminology) running at his man or the Brockhoff/Muller loose forward. But Cavanagh's expertise and profound insight into the strategies of rugby were not sought for the South African tour (the coach was Alex McDonald, an All Black in 1905) nor for the home series against the Wallabies. Cavanagh stayed in Dunedin and coached what was basically an Otago second

XV (eleven of the All Blacks touring South Africa were from Otago) to retain the Ranfurly Shield, ending the season with a 16–5 victory over a star-studded Auckland side. The great tragedy for New Zealand rugby was that Cavanagh was never given an All Blacks side to coach. A similar tragedy seems to be playing itself out in the case of the gifted Aucklander, John Hart.

Ironically, Brockhoff, a man with a passion for rugby, had a number of conversations with Cavanagh when the Wallabies were in the South Island. He brought the Cavanagh concept that hard-rucking forwards win matches back to Australian rugby when he coached the Wallabies in 1979. A practical problem for the New Zealanders in 1949, though, was that the 'stand-up ruck' or what we now call the maul was not allowed. Referees were instructed to call out 'Put the ball down!' when a stand-up ruck was formed. If this didn't happen the side with the ball, generally the All Blacks, was automatically penalised. The point about this is that there was no option after winning a lineout but to get it back to the halfback to pass on to a five-eighth—who was in the sights of the Brockhoff/Muller marauder. The more ball that was won, when a Brockhoff or a Muller was playing, the more of a liability possession tended to become.

Rex Mossop has given an engaging account of this 1949 tour, one of only two in which the Wallabies have so far won the Bledisloe Cup in New Zealand (the second occasion was Alan Jones's 1986 Wallabies), in his rugbiography *The Moose that Roared*. On being selected Mossop was forced to 'chug-a-lug' a large jug of beer and then sing a song. He chose 'I Want to Take You on a Slow Boat to China'. On tour he learnt the remedy to stop his cauliflower ears aching from the giant New Zealand secondrower, Tiny White—bathe the ears in hot milk several times a day. The mind boggles at the possibility of his adding some flour to the milk: the Mossop ears might have been subjected to a cauliflower sauce remedy. An elated Mossop gave some indication of the uninhibited broadcaster he was to become when he was asked to send a cheerio call back to Australia after the second Test (Australia 16, New Zealand 9) at Eden Park. Without any hesitation he grabbed the microphone and yelled out: 'Hi Dad, hi Mum, hi Kirk! We've beaten the bastards! You beauty!'.

On a serious note in his book Mossop makes the claim that the New Zealand team that lost the Bledisloe Cup could not be regarded as a third XV because the 'predominantly Maori side they put in against us was one to be reckoned with and would have been the nucleus of the team to South Africa had the colour bar not been in force'. This is half right. Aside from Bob Stuart on the flank, who captained the 1953 All Blacks to the United Kingdom, and Tiny

White, the finest lineout jumper in New Zealand rugby up to Andy Haden, the New Zealand pack in the first Test in the 1949 Bledisloe Cup series, for example, was made up of good but not outstanding provincial players. Both Stuart and White were at the beginnings of their careers as All Blacks. Alan Blake, one of the flankers, was a Maori. He was 27 and the Wellington Test was his only match for the All Blacks. Ron Bryers, a secondrower, the other Maori in the pack, was 30 and played his only Test at Wellington. As far as the forwards were concerned, then, the All Blacks pack was very much a third-string combination. The backs, though, were up to the best All Blacks standard: Jack Kelly was a brilliant running fullback who could also play on the wing; Roy Roper had an outstanding series in the centres the next year against the Lions and Jack McLean was a noted tryscorer from Auckland and a controversial omission from the South African touring party; Johnny Smith, a Maori, was rated by Mark Nicholls as 'the greatest player for his wingers the rugby world has ever seen'; Ray O'Callaghan was a skilful second five-eighth with a huge, thumping left-foot punt; Ben Couch, a Maori, was a mercurial five-eighth; and Vince Bevan, who was not a Maori but was assumed to be so because of his looks, was out on his own as the best New Zealand halfback of the era.

The magnitude of the All Blacks fall from power in 1949, 'The Year of the Six Test Losses', can be marked by these incredible statistics: from 1903 up to 1949 the All Blacks played 64 Tests, won 44 of them, drew 4 and lost only 16. At the *end* of the 1949 season, 70 Tests had been played but there now were 22 losses, a not quite so incredible record.

The Era of the Unsmiling Giants

The dark night of the soul that the All Blacks went through in 1949 took the joy out of New Zealand rugby. An even more obsessive win-at-all-costs mentality than had previously existed infected the New Zealand approach. The kicking game was adopted as the only way to defeat the Brockhoff/Muller marauders. Talented backs, instead of being looked upon as the glory of the game as they were when Mark Nicholls, George Nepia and Bert Cooke flourished in the 1920s and 1930s or when Bob Scott, James Sherratt and Fred Allen starred with the legendary Kiwi Army Team of 1946, were now overlooked in favour of players with a boring steadiness to their play. If a back had prodigious running skills, as in the case of Ron Jarden (who was rated by Aub Hodgson in 1951 as 'the best winger I've ever seen'), every effort was made to starve him of the ball. Efficiency of execution rather than flair became the standard. Black, a colour that is really an absence of colour, became the literally true sign of the New Zealand game. The game was played ruthlessly. The means always justified the ends for the All Blacks.

The demeanour of the players, too, became as grim as the pattern of play imposed upon them. Some great sides were thrown up (the 1957, 1987 and 1988 All Blacks in Australia, and the 1967 and 1972 All Blacks in New Zealand and the United Kingdom)—but this was despite, rather than because of, the black pattern. The great sides emerged because there is a genius among New Zealanders for playing rugby. As the All Blacks won Test series after Test series—after 1949 the Wallabies were not to win the Bledisloe Cup until 1979—they created the image for themselves of the Unsmiling Giants, robot players of stoicism and efficiency who were prepared to endure anything and do anything—as long as they won. The Darth Vader era ended, as it had to, in 1991 when the methods of intimidation and pressure on the field and surliness off it saw the All Blacks lose the public relations battle to the Wallabies, in Ireland before the World

The Union men could have been sheep

By ARTHUR MAILEY

Writing about footballers on a wet day at the Sydney Cricket Ground is about as satisfactory as reading in a blackout.

The boys go out on the field all spick and span, prancing about, and smelling of glycerine oil and resin.

You are able to identify everyone by their numbers, the shape of their chassis, or cauliflower ears.

Ten minutes later the numbers are completely obliterated, and lumps of Bulli soil are bulging from their ears and nostrils.

Their snow-white pants are black, and I defy anybody, including the umpire, to say who's who.

The chap who broadcast the match fairly staggered away from the mike after the game, and for him I had a somewhat brotherly sympathy.

After all, he had to mention a name occasionally, whereas I had a chance of getting away with shapes.

I really went to the wrong ground at first.

I thought the All Blacks v. Australia match was being played at the "Agra."

I watched the ewes and rams for a while, and, while I do not claim to know which was which, I think I would have made a better fist of the Sheep Show than the affair next door on the "black soil plains."

I would suggest that in future, when the Sheep Show clashes with an international Rugger match, the rams and ewes should parade on the S.C.G. and the footballers do their stuff on the "Agra."

Had that happened yesterday I'm sure that many members in the long room wouldn't have noticed the difference.

Anyhow, since the sheep clip was responsible for something over six million pounds I suppose sheep should have the choice of grounds.

While this is not a hint, I feel that if New Zealand could send across a few boxes of the promised butter it will be a step in the right direction regarding the choice of non-Bulli grounds.

Cup semi-final. The public relations defeat foreshadowed a loss on the field to the Wallabies.

The Unsmiling Giants era—which, admittedly, was a period of remarkable success in terms of Test wins—began with the 1951 tour of Australia. The All Blacks arrived in Sydney with a single ambition—they had to win back the Bledisloe Cup. Not even Arthur Mailey, the old leg-spinner and humourist, was amused by the first—mudbath—

Test at the Sydney Cricket Ground (New Zealand 8 – Australia 0). 'Writing about footballers on a wet day at the Sydney Cricket Ground', he noted, 'is about as satisfactory as reading in a blackout.' Ron Jarden, the wonder winger, a player who could have been a 1950s early edition of David Campese and who earlier in the tour had set a record for the highest individual total scored by an All Black in one game when he scored six tries and converted ten against New South Wales Central West, was starved of the ball. 'Neither of the wings, Jarden or Erceg', wrote the NZ Press Association correspondent, Bruce Hewitt, 'had many chances. Both of them were on their toes ready to make play'. They had to be alert because they would have frozen out on the wings otherwise. As so often happened in his Test career the brilliant Jarden, a matchwinner if the ball was played to his wing, had to create his own magical plays. In the first half he grubber-kicked to within metres of the Australian goal line where the ball was run into touch by a Wallaby. Jarden quickly retrieved the ball and threw it to the prop Kevin Skinner to score the only try of the Test.

A dry field for the second Test (New Zealand 17 – Australia 11) was no encouragement for open play. The All Blacks won back the Bledisloe Cup by kicking the leather off the ball and relying on Ron Jarden to score tries, Campese-like, from opportunities lesser players could never have converted. Thirty seconds from the kickoff, for instance, the ball rolled clear from a ruck, Jarden picked it up, fended off the burly Eddie Stapleton and ran around the fullback Peter Rothwell for the quickest Bledisloe Cup try up to Jason Little's 16-seconds-from-the-start-of-play effort in 1994. Minutes from fulltime, with New Zealand leading 14–11, the All Blacks backline—finally—put on a passing movement. The fullback Maurice Cockerill came into the line as an extra man and Jarden was given some room to run in. He easily ran around Stapleton and Stockwell to score in the corner. Between those flashes of genius from Jarden the All Blacks pursued an attrition game. Phil Tresidder reported that 'the crowd showed disapproval of the monotonous line-kicking, in which both sides tried to exploit the obsolete "kicking out on the full" rule. The All Blacks were much more skilful and accurate with their plugging of the touchline than the Australians, but neither side gained much praise from the crowd'.

For the first time since 1903 the All Blacks failed to pull in the crowds. The two Tests attracted crowds of about 17 000 on each occasion, about half the usual number of spectators for a Bledisloe Cup Test. The Australia v England Soccer Test at the same venue, the Sydney Cricket Ground, a week later, drew 46 000 spectators. And the Rugby League Test against France drew 60 000, with a gate of 11 200 pounds (compared with the Rugby Union Test gate of 2220 pounds). The newspaper, the Australian *Truth* saw the end of Rugby Union in these figures: 'A great game is dying and its death is being hastened by a host of armchair generals who apparently think it can and will survive because everything is lovely'.

But the report of Rugby Union's death, like that of Mark Twain's, was exaggerated. The next season the crowd-pleasing Fijians drew a huge crowd of over 40 000 spectators to their inaugural Test against the Wallabies. The Australian crowds wanted to watch Rugby Union, but they also wanted to be entertained and not bored while doing so.

Life for the touring All Blacks, though, was as grim off the field as on it. Looking back on the 1951 tour, his first for the All Blacks, the marvellous secondrower Tiny White found that his trick of passing at the top of his jump (a skill only John Eales has performed better than White) was not wanted by the dour Otago-based captain, Peter Johnstone. He was told he had to put the ball on the ground for the forwards to drive on—always. The result was that the ball was never released quickly to the backs. 'To me', White recalled decades later, 'our rugby was dour and uninteresting, and in the finish the spectators were staying away. It was the most forgettable rugby experience of my life.'

But the Bledisloe Cup was regained. The end justified the means.

The missing Bledisloe Cup

And up to the 1980s the policy of the end justifying the means, the application of the 'might is right' dogma, provided handsome results for the All Blacks against the Wallabies. It was not until 1979, for instance, that the Wallabies won their first Test match at home against the All Blacks since 1934. Several generations of Australian rugby followers had never seen the Wallabies defeat the All Blacks. Those 40 000 spectators at the Sydney Cricket Ground on 11 August 1932 who saw the Wallabies inflict their heaviest defeat on the All Blacks, 25–11, were surely a dwindling community by the time the next victory was achieved 45 years later. And in New Zealand Australian supporters had to wait until 1986—when New Zealand rugby was ripped apart by the controversy over the South African tour of the Cavaliers (almost an All Blacks side in coloured jerseys) and by the horrendous civil disturbances provoked by the tour of New Zealand in 1981 of the South African Springboks team—for an authentic Bledisloe Cup series win in New Zealand.

For New Zealanders, during this long period, Australian rugby did not count. The only things that mattered in a rugby context were the Test series against South Africa, in New Zealand (1956, 1965 and 1981) and in South Africa (1960, 1970, 1976). The home side won its series on every occasion. The holy grail of New Zealand rugby became—and remains to a certain extent—for the All Blacks to win a Test series against the Springboks in South Africa. The intensity of the pursuit of this ideal was heightened by the perception, which grew stronger after each tour of South Africa, that unsatisfactory refereeing lay at the heart of the All Blacks' problems. There may be something in the complaint. Since the introduction of neutral referees in South Africa-New Zealand Tests, with Clive Norling blowing the whistle as the pioneer neutral referee during the 1981 series, the All Blacks have won five Tests against the Springboks, lost one and drawn one. This record has only served to fan the flames of longstanding New Zealand paranoia about the integrity of South African referees.

Throughout the period up to the 1980s, therefore, there was a lack of intensity in New Zealand over Wallabies–All Blacks encounters. There were few references to the Bledisloe Cup in the New Zealand press during these decades. The All Blacks tradition, for instance, of filling the Bledisloe Cup to the brim with 26 jugs of beer and drowning the lot after a winning series was forgotten. The Cup itself disappeared for a number of years. Bruce Hewitt, the NZPA journalist in Australia, claims that 'it turned up eventually unharmed under a great deal of dusty cardboard Maori huts and Mount Cooks in the back storerooms of the old New Zealand Government Tourist Bureau in Temple Court, Melbourne, where it had evidently been taken for display purposes and forgotten'.

THE 1957 ALL BLACKS: THE GREATEST?

The All Blacks who defeated New South Wales 36–10 at Auckland on 19 September 1925 are regarded as the finest New Zealand side between the two world wars. Thirteen of the team that swept aside New South Wales were members of The Invincibles, the undefeated All Blacks who toured the United Kingdom, France and Canada in 1924. T. P. McLean in his enthralling book *Great Days in New Zealand Rugby* has this to say about the 1925 All Blacks: 'Experience, vigour, enterprise, imagination, power and sublime confidence were to be seen in everything they did. How difficult it is to deny that this was the finest of New Zealand teams!'. The first side to lay claim to 'the greatest' after the Second World War was the 1957 All Blacks. This splendid side demolished the Wallabies in the two Tests in the series (25–11 and 22–9) and amassed 463 points in 13 games on its tour of Australia.

At Grenfell, against a country side, the prodigious kicker, the All Blacks fullback Don Clarke, booted 32 points. For the tour, he finished with three tries, 44 conversions, 20 penalty goals, one dropkick and one dropkick from a mark. The ratio between conversions and penalties is interesting. That would be reversed in the modern game, and the mind boggles at just how many penalties Clarke, whose range was from his own 10-metre mark, might have kicked in the modern, penalty-obsessed era. Two young forwards destined for greatness played their first matches for the All Blacks on this tour: Wilson Whinerary, who didn't miss another Test until 1964; and Colin 'Pinetree' Meads, acknowledged as the finest All Black since the Second World War, who was still the heart and muscle of the New Zealand pack in 1971. Ross Brown (the talented son of a former All Black), who conceded at the end of his career that his main rugby ambition was to play against the Springboks (a goal he achieved—with success—in 1956) rated the 1957 All Blacks as 'one of the greatest All Black sides ever'.

The All Blacks came into the first 1957 Test at the Sydney Cricket Ground after an indifferent performance against New South Wales and a loss (8–3) in their last Test against the Wallabies in 1955 at Eden Park. In the latter match the Dreaded Curse of the Third Test after winning the first two Tests had struck the New Zealanders—as it did again at Eden Park in 1978 and at Wellington in 1990. In these matches the New Zealanders had their minds on other things: in 1990 there was the next year's Rugby World Cup, in 1978 there was the coming tour of the United Kingdom (which resulted in the first and only Grand Slam by the All Blacks) and in 1955 there was the expectation of the long-awaited tour of New Zealand by the Springboks the next year, their first tour since 1937 and one which resulted in the All Blacks' first series win against their toughest opponents.

The opening half of the first Test in 1957 (which was being televised live on Channel 7, the first time in Australia on a commercial television channel) suggested that the New Zealanders were still luxuriating in that 1956 series victory over the Springboks. An exciting first half, in which the Wallabies created most of the thrills, ended with the scores tied at 11–11. Stan Baxter, in the Sydney *Herald-Sun*, reported:

> At half time, yesterday, Australia had to be given a chance—and then came a dramatic change in the game . . . In 12 minutes, the Australian team was transformed from a reasonably optimistic combination to a bunch of near tyros. The blame can be laid at many doors—poor refereeing, the Australian forwards' collapse, and the fumbling efforts of Brian Cox at halfback. The Australian forwards allowed the New Zealand forwards to take over and dictate play in the second half . . . The lineouts went to New Zealand 16–9 and the rucks also went to New Zealand, as expected, 16–9 . . .

Journalists like Baxter had to telephone their story of the Test through to their newspaper's office as soon as the game was over. With television coverage now the norm, though, readers the next day could compare the newspaper account with their own better view of the match, even though it was in fuzzy black and white, to see how accurate the journalist was in his summary of what happened. The time was coming, therefore, when detailed play-by-play match reports were dropped from the newspaper columns. New Zealand print journalists, (who did not have to contend with television until the 1970s), especially those from Wellington (with the six o'clock Saturday night edition of the *Sports Post*) and Auckland (the Saturday night *Eight O'Clock*), had even tighter match report deadlines than their Australian counterparts had. Match reports were generally telephoned through to the newspaper office while the match was in progress. There was an almost insatiable appetite for these reports. Huge crowds of men gathered outside the gates of the *Evening Post* building around six o'clock on a Saturday night waiting for the boys to dash out carrying bundles of *Sports Posts* under their arms. Before the movie started in cinemas, an hour or so later, a sound like the rippling of wind through a forest could be heard as most of the young men ignored their girlfriends and turned over the pages of their *Sports Post* or *Eight O'Clock* to catch up with all the rugby matches played around New Zealand that Saturday.

A feature of the *Sports Post* was the full-page, front page cartoon drawn by Neville Lodge. Lodge would draw two cartoons if a rugby Test was his subject and the editors used the appropriate drawing depending on the outcome of the Test. For the second Test in 1957, in which the All Blacks forwards were so dominant they reduced the Wallabies to a walk, Lodge's cartoon showed a smug, head-geared kiwi in All Blacks colours strutting across the Tasman Sea with the Bledisloe Cup clutched in its wing. A dazed Wallaby, still seeing stars, is pictured on the ground with the thought of a tank in his mind. Many a true insight is conveyed in jest. Lodge correctly identified the storming power of the New Zealand forwards as the decisive factor in the All Blacks victory.

This notion of the primacy of forward power, that if the pack is on top everything else falls into place, was quite obvious to a cartoonist in New Zealand. The concept, though, was still beyond the comprehension of most serious rugby thinkers in Australia.

AN INCREDIBLE UPSET

The superiority of the All Blacks over the Wallabies in this period was never more marked than in the first Test of the 1958 Bledisloe Cup series played in the wind at Wellington's Athletic Park. The Wallabies made their first mistake by giving the wind away to the All Blacks. W. G. Grace once commented that a cricket captain should contemplate putting the other side into bat when he wins the toss—'but he should never do so'. The same principle applies to taking the advantage of the wind. With the wind at their backs, therefore, the New Zealanders quickly established a strong field position and after a series of backline movements the athletic prop Wilson Whinerary went across for a try. This was Whineary's first Test of thirty as captain. He was 23 at the time but already had a presence and an intelligence about him that indicated the makings of one of the finest captains in the history of Test rugby. That first try came after fifteen minutes of play. Ten minutes later Whineary, who was skilful enough as a ball handler and a runner to play number eight on many occasions, scored again. Although the score stood at only 9–0 to the All Blacks and the Wallabies started the second half strongly, it was clear that the result of the Test was not in doubt. R. H. Chester and N. A. C. McMillan in *Men In Black* claim that 'New Zealand was so clearly superior it was only relatively poor kicking that prevented them from winning by over forty points'.

And so, on to Christchurch for the second Test with the Wallabies defeating Otago and South Canterbury and losing to Southland (26–8) in the runup to the contest. 'It was generally felt', Chester and McMillan note, 'that the New Zealand team would repeat their first Test victory without too much trouble'. There is a Roman saying about papal elections: 'Go in Pope, come out cardinal; go in cardinal, go out Pope'. The saying is applicable to rugby as well. Teams—like the All Blacks at Christchurch in 1958 (and in Wellington in 1990)—which go out on to the field expecting that merely turning up will be enough to achieve a victory have already set themselves up for a loss. Things started to go wrong for the All Blacks from the beginning. A penalty shot at goal four minutes into the match was missed. The master goalkicker, Don Clarke, had been injured and his place was taken by a journeyman player from Southland, David Ashby. In his first—and last—Test, the nervous Ashby muffed his kick. Towards halftime Terry Curley—just 20 years of age and already an outstanding fullback, a strong runner, wide-hipped with a massive kick and crashing tackle—stroked across a penalty for the Wallabies. After halftime, taking sustenance from their oranges, the All Blacks put together a fine backline raid on the blindside with Ross Brown exchanging passes with Russell Watt before scoring in the corner. Ashby failed to convert. A brilliant individual try to Alan Morton, in which in a 30-metre dash he beat man after man along the sideline with nifty footwork and subtle swerves, pulled the Wallabies into the lead which they clung to in the last twenty minutes when the All Blacks, finally aroused, threw attacks from all over the field at them.

The underdog showed its teeth 'in what must rate', Jack Pollard asserts in his account of Australian rugby, 'as one of the biggest upsets in our history'. The courage and resilience of a team that knows it has to play above itself in order not to be swept away provides another reason for the incredible victory. The penalty count also helped, with Australia being awarded 19 penalties to 6 by C. R. Gillies, a referee from the Waikato province. If Don Clarke had been playing he might have turned the few shots the All Blacks had at goal into points. There was the brilliance of Alan Morton's try, 'one of the triumphs of his career' according to Pollard: 'Morton took the ball about 30 metres out and somehow made the line, bumping or fending off tacklers to score a remarkable, match-winning try'. At fullback the Wallabies had a wonderful boy, Terry Curly—in Pollard's assessment 'one of the finest fullbacks Australia has produced'. And the Christchurch Test was Curly's masterpiece in his eleven-Test career. 'It was Curly', Chester and McMillan write, 'playing an outstanding game who turned back many of the New Zealand attacks in the last twenty minutes of the game.' Pollard writes that Curly was such a perfectionist with his massive linekicking that 'when he missed the line three times in about 50 kicks in an important game for Australia, the misses had him almost in tears after the game. Three mistakes meant an almost disgraceful game for a player of his skill'. There were no tears at Christchurch, though.

The deciding Test at Auckland, at the Epsom Showgrounds, saw Don Clarke back in the New Zealand side and the familiar pattern

restored. Terry Curly kicked a penalty and the conversion of John Carroll's try for the Wallabies. But Don Clarke kicked a conversion of Colin Meads's try from wide out—and four penalties.

When the Wallabies arrived back in Australia Terry Curly announced his retirement from Test rugby in order to enter the Marist Brothers. The decision, writes Pollard, 'did not surprise his tour colleagues'. The loss of the young fullback, however, was regarded by sound judges as a bigger blow to the Wallabies than was the loss to Rugby League of any of his contemporaries the Thornett brothers, Mike Cleary, Kevin Ryan and Jim Lisle. Ten years later Curly played in a Barbarians match on the eve of a Bledisloe Cup Test at Ballymore. The Australian selectors sauntered along 'just to have a look'. They were so impressed with Brother Terence's play that they asked him if he might consider a 'comeback'. The Wallaby fullback at the time was Arthur McGill, with 88 points in 21 Tests the third most successful Test goalkicker for Australia after Paul McLean and Michael Lynagh. 'I'm too slow', Curly told the selectors, 'whenever I come into the backline these days, I stop almost to a walk.' This response, which the selectors found disappointing given their hope of returning him immediately to the Wallaby colours, was in character. For it reflected the dedication to the highest standards of play that gave him the mental and physical resources to play such a masterly game at Christchurch in 1958.

KEN CATCHPOLE, 'THE GENIUS'

In 1978 I published a book of essays on rugby called *After the Final Whistle*. One of the essays compared the styles of the two outstanding halfbacks (in my opinion) of their generation, Sid Going and Chris Laidlaw: Going, a Maori Mormon, introverted off the field and a dynamic running halfback on the field; and ambidextrous Laidlaw, a Rhodes Scholar, the first exponent of the long spin pass which he threw out sometimes halfway across the field with the backs streaming on to the ball. Several years later I had become an editorial writer at the *Sydney Morning Herald*. I was eager to break the anonymity of my job, so I started to look around for a rugby subject to write about. The Sydney team, at the time, was playing forceful and inventive rugby under their charismatic coach, the former Wallaby secondrower and later president of the New South Wales Rugby Union, Peter Crittle. An interview with Crittle was in order, I thought. I rang him up. I could have the interview, he told me, provided that I gave him a copy of my book on rugby. This was duly done and the interview conducted and reported. Some weeks later Crittle rang me up. 'You're wrong about Going and Laidlaw', he said. 'The greatest halfback of them all was Ken Catchpole. There is no argument about this.' Then, at a rugby dinner in 1994, I heard Crittle go even further than this and describe Catchpole as the 'greatest player ever to represent Australia at Rugby Union.'

Extravagant praise? Perhaps not. T. P. McLean has seen virtually all the great players in a long and distinguished career of writing about rugby (Chris Laidlaw called him the finest rugby writer in the game's history and the finest writer on rugby.) This is what McLean wrote in 1979 about Ken Catchpole:

> Catchpole I rate for many reasons which start with courage and end with loyalty to the game. The fine point was his pass. Years ago, I talked with the great Welshman, Haydn Tanner, who would be a candidate for the greatest scrumhalf of all time—I only saw him play once, indifferently-well, at five-eighth in a British Army side in Italy in 1945. We talked passing. 'There are,' said he, 'three elements to the halfback's pass. They are length versus speed versus accuracy. The greatest of these is speed.' Enter Kenny Catchpole. His was not so much a pass as an

> instantaneous flip. His partner was given a yard, even two yards, before opponents grouped and rushed. At various times in various sorts of company, with players and alickadoos and pressmen, I have discussed the great players we have seen and our candidates for the greatest in various positions. At the most conservative estimate, Catchpole has been the first choice of 80 per cent of us.
>
> The president of the English Rugby Union endorsed this view at a dinner for the 1966–67 Wallabies, after Australia had defeated England 23–11, with this unequivocal statement: 'Ken Catchpole is the greatest halfback rugby has known'.

For those of us who didn't see him play, our only glimpse of his genius comes from some television footage that is played from time to time. When his five-eighth partner, Phil Hawthorne, died in September 1994 some of the television channels showed footage from their archives of the pair in action. One of the clips reveals a darting Catchpole running flat from a scrum before putting a perfect scissors pass into the hands of Hawthorne who virtually strolls through a bemused Welsh defence for a try. Randwick Rugby Club, too, have a video of the great tries scored by the Galloping Greens over the years. One of these tries is the miracle try scored by Catchpole in a club grand final against Norths. Once again Catchpole is caught by the camera running across field from a scrum, along the same tight line that David Campese ran to score his try against the All Blacks at Dublin in the 1991 World Cup semi-final. But Catchpole is about 40 metres out, not 15 metres or so. Suddenly he breaks around the opposing inside centre and bolts on an angle to the corner flag. The fullback comes across and Catchpole jinks and shakes his hips, all at high speed, slips inside the cover defence and scores under the posts. It was a remarkable try from a remarkably gifted player.

Ken Catchpole's first Test against the All Blacks was in 1962, the year of the first home and away series between Australia and New Zealand. The Wallabies wore their gold jerseys for the first time in this series as a sign, perhaps, of the halfback with the golden touch who was captaining the side. Aged 23, Catchpole had already been captain-coach of the 1961 Wallabies to South Africa. His opposite number for the All Blacks in the 1962 Bledisloe Cup series was another Australian, Des Connor. Connor had everything as a player: a strong and accurate pass, a thumping kick, toughness of body and mind, a galloping break, an unquenchable will to win, and vision. His first touch of the ball for the All Blacks in 1961 saw Connor scooting around the blindside and sucking in the French back row before passing to Neil Wolfe, the new five-eighth, who passed on to Don McKay (a new winger) to score the try.

Catchpole was dropped for the third Test in 1962 (the first of the series in New Zealand). Even great players can lose form. This comment in relation to Catchpole's play does not really tell the tale, however. It was not so much a lack of form that worried the Australian selectors as the fact that his brilliance was in attack. With the All Blacks forwards rolling over the Wallaby pack like a division of tanks, there was little scope for Catchpole's genius. The nuggety Ken McMullen had the game and the build to absorb the beatings a Wallaby halfback could expect at this time. The Wallabies produced their best result in this Test, a 9–9 draw, with Don Clarke grimly kicking a penalty right on time to even up the score. So the selectors could justify what they had done.

Catchpole was returned for the next Test at Dunedin and began his famous partnership with Phil Hawthorne. The New Zealand selectors had taken the axe to their pack as a reaction to the drawn Test, dropping Kel Tremain, Ian Clarke and Dennis Young (the blindside flanker and noted tryscorer, a prop and a hooker). The new pack struggled to hold the Wallabies and a try set up by Catchpole for the winger Jim Boyce was disallowed. The Wallaby hooker Peter Johnson, in his account of his rugby career, insisted that the All Blacks were given a helping hand from the referee: 'The first Test decision that allowed Clarke to construct a draw was odious, but the penalising of Catchpole for passing off the ground to send Jim Boyce in under the posts in the second Test was absolutely ludicrous'. Clarke kicked another penalty to win the Dunedin Test 3–0 for the All Blacks. Catchpole was out injured for the last and fifth Bledisloe Cup Test of the season (replaced again by Ken McMullen). By this time the two sides must have been sick and tired of playing each other. The Wallabies lost 16–8, with a new New Zealand five-eighth, Mac Herewini, one of the most gifted inside backs New Zealand has produced in the modern era, having a sensational match, scoring a try and dropping a goal.

In all, Catchpole played eight Tests against the All Blacks for seven losses and only one win. If ever proof is needed that a good rugby team will beat a poor rugby team even with a rugby genius in its ranks, the career of Ken Catchpole against the All Blacks provides the evidence. The one Test victory that Ken Catchpole enjoyed over the All Blacks was at Wellington (20–5) in 1964, a Dreaded Third Test for the All Blacks, after they had won the first two Tests (14–9, 18–3). Catchpole and his five-eighth partner Phil Hawthorne were brilliant that day as they masterminded the biggest win ever (up to that time) by Australia in a Test against New Zealand. The victory also broke the All Blacks' then-record run of sixteen Test wins and one draw since 1959.

A photograph of the Test gives an indication of how even the genius of Catchpole was frustrated by the All Blacks, except on this one occasion. Ken Gray, the strong mobile New Zealand prop forward, is bursting through a lineout on to Catchpole who is in the motion of passing back to Phil Hawthorne. Peter Johnson is trying to pull Gray back by the jersey from pouncing on Catchpole. It is clear, though, that Gray is going to smash Catchpole to the ground, a fraction of a second after he delivers his pass. Although the Wallaby front five are trying to protect Catchpole, there is no protection from the New Zealand back row which is in a position to charge on Catchpole if he fumbles or if he tries to run his way out of trouble.

It was Catchpole's unfortunate fate to play out his Test career when Australian forwards were significantly inferior in size and ability to their New Zealand counterparts. The iron law of rugby is that great backs—even those as supremely gifted as Ken Catchpole—rarely defeat great packs.

THE 1967 SEVENTY-FIFTH ANNIVERSARY TEST

The New Zealand Rugby Union celebrated its 75th anniversary with a Test against Australia, their oldest rivals, at Wellington on 19 August 1967. Two survivors of the original New Zealand team were present: Billy Wallace, the first scorer with a penalty in the New Zealand–Australia series; and George Nicholson, 'Long Nick', a prototype of the New Zealand loose forward, tall and rangy, later a referee (the third Test between New Zealand and Australia in 1913) and an All Blacks selector (1920, 1921, 1929, 1930, 1936, 1937). The old-timers and the crowd of over 42 000 spectators, most of them New Zealanders, were rewarded with a fine display by the All Blacks who were acknowledged later in the year, during their unbeaten tour of the United Kingdom, as one of the great teams in the history of rugby.

Nonetheless, Gordon Slater, in *The Centennial Book of New Zealand Rugby*, claims that the 29–9 victory to the All Blacks did not do justice to the Wallabies:

> If they had had some games together as a touring side they would have been a different proposition. Furthermore the three-quarter Phillip Smith dislocated his collarbone and was off the field for 18 minutes in the first half. He came back and played on with his arm strapped to his side,

earning the admiration of the crowd for his courage and providing further evidence for the need to amend the no-replacement rules.

The 1968 series, in fact, saw replacements being allowed.

The All Blacks finally solved the problem of the Muller/Brockhoff marauder (in this Test the former New Zealander Greg Davis) by running the pacy and big inside centre Ian MacRae to set up a 'crash ball' ruck for the ball to be moved to the side of the field where the opposition's numbers were short. Some harsh words were spoken at halftime (New Zealand 9–Australia 3) to the All Blacks by their captain Brian Lochore, Slater reports.

> In the next period of play the New Zealanders took control and in 12 minutes scored 15 points. Tony Steel, the second cousin of Jack Steel, swung past the Australian full-back and showed the speed that made him a New Zealand sprint champion, too. He scored under the posts after a dash of 50 yards. In one movement Michael Williment fielded the ball near his own posts and opened up play to such an extent that Brian Lochore scored under the Australian posts but the referee recalled him for a forward pass.

A winger, Tony Steel scored two tries for the Jubilee All Blacks; the new centre, Bill Davis, a try; Kel Tremain, the breakaway, an (inevitable) try—one of nine in Tests, a record at the time for an All Blacks forward. Mick Williment converted all four tries and kicked two penalties. And the inventive and skilful five-eighth Mac Herewini dropkicked a goal, one of ten in Tests for New Zealand. The All Blacks marked the celebrations, therefore, with a typically comprehensive and efficient Test performance. The rugby, except for Steel's thrilling run, appealed more to the head than to the emotions. This was textbook rugby, nevertheless, so characteristic of the All Blacks and which made them admired rather than loved (even by their supporters) over the decades. The former Labor federal minister John Button, now a witty and perceptive essayist, analysed the West Coast Eagles and Geelong before the 1994 Australian Football Grand Final in this way: 'There is nothing predictable about Geelong. They are favourites to come second. Following any football team with passion involves tribal loyalties of an exemplary kind; following Geelong is character-building. It heightens the capacity for suffering'. He saw the West Coast Eagles as a team that played 'a disciplined game of tough, skilled, precision football. They remind me of the medieval Italian painter Andrea Del Sarto. He was known as "the faultless painter". Highly skilled, and predictably clever, he became a bore'. Over the decades the All Blacks have been, in Australian Rules parlance, the West Coast Eagles of rugby and the Wallabies—until the 1980s—the Geelong. In

1994, as former Australian cabinet minister John Button suspected, the ruthless West Coast Eagles destroyed the lovable Geelong side—just as the All Blacks, the faultless team, tended to destroy their Wallaby opponents in this era.

THE ALL BLACKS *ARE* NEW ZEALAND

Comparing the All Blacks and the Wallabies with Australian Football teams has a certain historical resonance because Rugby Union in Australia and New Zealand developed its dynamic as a code in opposition to Australian Football.

A form of rugby had been played in Sydney since 1829 (only six years after the alleged William Webb Ellis ball-running incident at Rugby School). The first game played in New Zealand under the new 'Rugby Rules' took place on 14 May 1870. The match was organised by the Nelson club, which in the first two years of its establishment in 1868 played Association and 'Victorian Rules' football. Once the 'Rugby Rules' were brought to Nelson by Charles Munro, who was educated at an English public school, and propagated around New Zealand, the other two forms of football were overwhelmed. As late as 1893, however, former Victorians who had fled the great depression of the 1890s in their State to try to find gold in New Zealand had formed 44 Victorian Rules clubs in New Zealand.

Australian rugby faced a similar challenge from Australian Football. In 1880 the first 'Australasian Rules' match was played in New South Wales between St Ignatius and St Joseph's (both schools now entrenched as rugby schools) to mark the inauguration of the New South Wales Football Association, 'an organisation designed to promote Victorian Rules of Football'. The push was on for the Australian game because on the same day as the schoolboys match, 12 July 1880, a New Zealand 'Victorian Rules' Association was formed.

Goaded by this obvious threat from the 'Victorian science', in 1881 the Southern Rugby Union (SRU), which became the New South Wales Rugby Union in 1892, invited a New Zealand 'Rugby Rules' side to tour Australia the next year. Perhaps the SRU had in its mind the famous 'propaganda' tour of both islands of New Zealand by an Auckland side in 1871, which was credited at the time with hastening the expansion of the 'Rugby Rules' code in New Zealand. Financial and organisational complications forced the offer to be reversed, however, and New South Wales arrived in Auckland in September 1882 to play the first match of a tour of New Zealand. The impetus provided by this tour saw New South Wales play its first-ever rugby match against Queensland in Sydney on 12 August 1882. A Queensland Rugby Union had to be formed to select and outfit the Queensland side. Two years later, the pattern of trans-Tasman rugby tours was stitched into permanence when a 'New Zealand' team toured New South Wales and Queensland. An editorial in the *New Zealand Mail* pointed out that 'in Victoria, where football is enthusiastically played, a fresh set of rules have been devised, which is unfortunate and unwise, because it prevents intercolonial matches'. The editorial concluded with this telling observation: 'Football is our national game'.

No football code in Australia has been able to establish a hegemony, with Australian Football dominating in Victoria, Tasmania, South Australia, Western Australia and the Northern Territory, and Rugby League and Rugby Union (in that order of popularity) being the dominant football codes in New South Wales and Queensland. Rugby Union dominates New Zealand social and cultural life, although now Rugby League has a strong following on television. Crowds of over 40 000 (a quarter of the city's population) will gather to watch Tests at Dunedin in the south and at Eden Park in the north of New Zealand. The result in New Zealand is that rugby permeates every aspect of national life. The Auckland deputy coroner, Mate Frankovich, underlined this assertion when commenting in March 1990 on the deaths of three young men who took their lives after a breakdown of their relationships with women. He said:

> When young people live together they form a strong attachment and it's not as though it is a permanent commitment. One doesn't take it seriously and the other one is left. Many of these young men are just taking their lives. It is a tragedy of our modern society. The great sexual revolution has taken place to solve everything, but it has been quite the reverse. Young chaps who have been living with their girlfriends have nothing to look forward to. Things should be kept low-key. They should be out playing rugby.

The heading to the article carrying the coroner's message was: THERE IS NOTHING LIKE A GOOD RUCK . . .

'You could always get a team together and all you needed was a paddock and a ball', Paul Holmes, New Zealand's main national television current affairs host, told an interviewer not long after he had devoted the entire half-hour show in July 1990 to a spate of defections of All Blacks to Rugby League and the implications for Rugby Union. 'There is some deep appeal of rugby in all of us who had to play the damn game and who got up at two in the morning to hear the latest Test in England . . . If there is an exclusive club to which all New Zealand boys aspire in their lifestyle, it is that exclusive club called the All Blacks.'

In a way that no Wallaby could hope to be, the All Blacks *are* New Zealand. A perceptive essay by Chris Laidlaw (*Pakeha: The Quest for Identity in New Zealand*, edited by Michael King), written in the 1990s when he was the Race Relations Commissioner, poignantly reveals the burden on the psyche that this intense relationship has placed on the nation and the players:

> I had a rather curious introduction to foreign travel. It was with All Blacks teams, whose sense of identity was built around one of our most determinedly national qualities: an ability to play rugby better than anyone else around. And yet beneath the veneer of sporting stardom that accompanies the All Blacks wherever they go, and which opens social and ethnic doors beyond the reach of the average Kiwi traveller, were invariably a collection of uncertain and unassertive beings in personal terms until we hit the field of play. Our nationalism was one provoked by the immediate circumstances, by the pride in consistently winning . . . To be distinctive we had to keep winning. Perhaps that same neurosis keeps us winning even today. I somehow suspect that it might.

For most New Zealanders rugby is not just the national game: it is part of the national character. As the former New Zealand prime minister, David Lange says, rugby games are 'part of the blooding of New Zealand youth', and that youth takes on the characteristics the game brings out in its players—'the camaraderie, that rather flamboyant mateship of rugby that excuses a multitude of sins'. The poet M. K. Joseph satirised (somewhat unfairly) the stereotype of the 'rugby, racing and beer' New Zealand man in 'Secular Litany', his poem of the 1950s:

> That we may avoid distinction and exception
> Worship the mean, cultivate the mediocre
> Live in a State house, raise forcibly-educated children
> Receive family benefits, and standard wages and a pension
> And rest in peace in a State crematorium
> St Allblack
> Saint Monday Raceday
> Saint Stabilisation
> Pray for us

As the brilliant, quicksilver, darting, intelligent Ken Catchpole was the epitome of the Australian rugby player, Colin 'Pinetree' Meads was the personification of New Zealand rugby, in all its ruthfulness, its power, its shrewdness, its energy, its toughness, its high skills exhibited under intense pressure, its stoicism and its absolute dedication to the challenge of winning. Meads, who is regarded without challenge as the finest All Black of the modern era, played 133 matches for New Zealand, 55 of them Tests. Fergi McCormick, a resilient All Blacks fullback, in his rugbiography describes Meads as 'a terrible man with the silver fern on. He regarded the All Black jersey as pure gold. He could do so many things so much better than anyone else in a match that he stood alone as the greatest player I have ever known'.

The first Test Meads played against the Wallabies was in 1957, his last was in 1968. In all, Meads played 15 Tests against the Wallabies of which the All Blacks won 12, lost two and drew one. The closing moments of the Wallaby draw (for anything but a defeat was a victory for the Wallabies in this era) in the Test at Wellington in 1962 was captured in memorable prose by Peter Crittle in the opening paragraphs of his obituary for Phil Hawthorne who died in 1994, aged 50:

> It is August 25, 1962, at Athletic Park in Wellington. The Australian Wallabies and the New Zealand All Blacks are locked in battle at nine points all with the final minutes of an epic Test match ticking away.
>
> The All Blacks win a deeply thrown lineout near the Australian tryline: around the back comes Pinetree Meads, the totemic symbol of New Zealand forward power. One prehensile hand clutches the ball like an orange while the other ranges wide and free, ready to smash anything out of the way that his massive frame might have missed. Huge strides take him straight towards the diminutive figure of the Australian five-eighth, by then the sole guardian of the Australian tryline. But even as Meads prepares to drop his shoulder for the final tank-like charge, Phillip Francis Hawthorne has his measure. He moves gracefully to the right of the charging giant and then comes straight back into his knees with his right shoulder. He drives him sideways with all the power of his well-muscled frame. The Pinetree comes crashing down, the ball is spilled forward, the referee whistles and the match is saved. Phil Hawthorne has just played his first Test match for Australia. He is 18 years old . . .

Colin Meads was not tall (190cm) by 1994 standards for secondrowers (203 cm is what is required in the 1990s) but he was immensely powerful and skilful. During the second Test against the

Wallabies in 1957 (and Meads' second Test), the All Blacks winger Frank McMullen was injured and dropped back to reserve fullback. Meads was put on the wing to fill his position. *Rugby Greats* by Bob Howitt has Meads relating this new experience: 'Pat Walsh who had moved into centre told me to make Alan Morton, whom I was marking, go outside me every time. "I'll get him then", said Pat. I didn't let him inside me, but boy he went outside me a few times. Pat had told me when I got the ball to run straight at him. I did, and it earned me my first Test try'.

In *Mud In Your Eye*, a coruscating insight into the world of rugby, Chris Laidlaw has a chapter on greatness in a player. Meads, a man whose conservative views on life, politics—and rugby—the intellectual and radical Laidlaw is opposed to, is singled out in this chapter for the wonderful way he played for over a decade. 'He never played a bad game', Laidlaw writes. And the elements of his greatness? He was incredibly tough. He played Tests with a split head, with a fractured toe and another time with a huge, gaping gash in his leg. He was unusually fast for a big man, leading the All Blacks selectors to play him (foolishly) at number eight in 1964 when the Wallabies thrashed the All Blacks at Wellington 20–5. He brought to his rugby an extremely cunning mind. In the 1962 Test series against the Wallabies, Meads, with his brother Stan as his companion secondrower, nullified Rob Heming ('one of the greatest lineout specialists I ever marked') by developing a method whereby Stan, a strong leaper, knocked the ball back to Colin to snaffle in his iron grip. There was, too, his tremendous team spirit. During the 'Battle of the Boots' in 1968 against France, Meads shoved one of the New Zealand backs out of a ruck with one hand and with the other grabbed the boot of one of the more indiscriminate Frenchmen—for later retribution.

Towards the later years of his Test career Meads overplayed this desire to be sheriff during the wild west brawls of the rucks and mauls. On 2 December 1967 he was sent from the field in the Test against Scotland, for wildly kicking at a ball that was bouncing near the head of the five-eighth D. Chisholm. He joined Cyril Brownlie, another forthright New Zealand forward, as being the only All Blacks sent from the field during a Test.

The All Blacks' next Test after this sending-off incident, against the Wallabies at the Sydney Cricket Ground on 15 June 1968 (New Zealand 27 – Australia 11), saw Meads disgrace himself—in the minds of Australian supporters—by dragging Ken Catchpole from a ruck so roughly that his groin was so severely injured he had to leave the field on a stretcher. Catchpole never played Test rugby again. John Hipwell was the replacement and the golden line of Wallaby halfbacks—Syd

Malcolm, Cyril Burke, Des Connor, Ken Catchpole, John Hipwell, Nick Farr-Jones and George Gregan (sometime in the future?)—continued with all the certainty of a papal succession. But Catchpole should never have had his Test career snapped like a wanton boy breaking a wishbone.

This fatal impact between the two greatest players of their generation, Ken Catchpole 'The Genius' and the 'Mighty' Meads, may be read as a sign of the Australian and the New Zealand approaches to rugby—the Australian approach concerned (perhaps too concerned?) about style and the New Zealand approach concerned (perhaps too concerned?) about winning.

WAS MEADS GUILTY?

Like beauty, truth lies in the eye of the beholder. Many Australians are convinced that Colin Meads deliberately maimed Ken Catchpole. New Zealanders argue that Colin Meads wouldn't have held off during a number of Bledisloe Cup series before trying to damage the brilliant halfback if that was what he had wanted to do. Anyway, foul play of this nature was foreign to Meads's game. He was a hard player but never a dirty player. And, while the incident remains a cause célèbre among Australians, few New Zealanders are even aware of it. Gordon Slater in *The Centennial Book of New Zealand Rugby* notes that several players were injured during the course of 'this hard match' at the Sydney Cricket Ground: Brian Lochore, the All Blacks captain, injured his left hamstring and muscle; John Brass dislocated his left shoulder; 'Catchpole pulled a groin muscle'.

That laconic summary is the New Zealand version. The Australian version, which also exonerates Meads, is given in Jack Pollard's *Australian Rugby: The Game and the Players*:

> Catchpole was grassed after receiving an awkward ball, and fell in a split position with the All Black and Australian packs falling over him. Colin Meads, the All Black forward, grabbed one of Catchpole's legs while he was pinned under players: 'I could feel the muscles stretch like rubber bands reaching the end of their elasticity and snapping,' Catchpole said . . . He discounts reports that his injuries were deliberately inflicted. 'It was more of a silly accident. How could anyone be that vicious?'

T. P. McLean wrote a book about the 1968 tour, *All Black Power*. A writer who has never been afraid to criticise New Zealand rugby and the All Blacks when he felt this was necessary (he was once barred from Eden Park for his outspoken comments), McLean was concerned at this time about the way 'Australian rugby hates New Zealand'. He quoted the Queensland flanker Jules Guerassimoff ('a loose forward who frightened blazes out of a number of opponents') as saying: 'The All Blacks are the dirtiest bastards going. And the Springboks are the cleanest'.

McLean noted that Queensland was a team that didn't forgo rough play. He then made these telling observations based on his long experience of watching Test rugby:

> New Zealanders punch; Frenchmen kick and punch; Welshmen kick and punch; Englishmen punch; Irishmen kick and punch; Scotsmen punch and sometimes kick; Springboks punch and sometimes kick; and Australians punch and sometimes kick. In other words, unbridled temper is a human misfortune which at times afflicts rugby—too many times in recent years, I regret to say. The substance of Guerassimoff's accusation was not—in my opinion—a fair comment. Rather it is an expression of the latent hostility in Australian Rugby to New Zealand.

McLean's catalogue basically holds up in 1994, with several exceptions and inclusions. The Wallabies rarely punch or kick, one of many reasons why they have been successful in the 1990s as the referees see them as 'the good guys'. The Springboks punch, often kick and occasionally bite. Welsh players have added 'bagsnatching', the grabbing of an opponent's genitals, to their kicking and punching. And the All Blacks, or their abrasive prop Richard Loe, have added stomping and in Loe's case eye-gouging to their repertoire of bad deeds. The stupidity in the Loe approach is that he gave away so many penalties in the first half of the 1994 Test (with the referee concentrating on him because of his reputation for foul play) that the All Blacks were denied any possession and, as a consequence, gave up 17 points to a confident Wallaby team.

RAH RAH RUGBY

In May 1986 the *Sydney Morning Herald* published a provocative article called 'A Matter of Class' which was written by Jason Dasey. The point of the article was established in its first sentence: 'It is probably not a coincidence that Sydney's Rugby Union heartland happens also to be one of its most conservative and affluent areas—the North Shore'.

Only two of the then eleven metropolitan Rugby League teams came from north of the Harbour Bridge, Dasey pointed out, but four of the then ten Rugby Union first grade sides were based on the northside. The North Shore, he argued, was the one part of Sydney where there were as many Rugby Union supporters as Rugby League supporters.

What were the social implications of all this?: 'It has been said that Union is a ruffians' game played by gentlemen, that soccer is a gentleman's game played by ruffians, and that League is a ruffians' game played by ruffians. Is Union's strength on the North Shore, therefore, primarily a matter of class? Is Union the game they play in heaven on earth?'.

Alex Buzo, a well-known author and a famous supporter of the North Sydney Bears, was cited as turning up on a Sunday afternoon to watch his Rugby League team go around at North Sydney Oval having himself played a game of Rugby Union earlier in the day. 'It was considered that Union was a better game to play, while League was a better game to watch', Buzo explained.

Dasey's article provoked a number of letters, including one from Ian McAlpin of Ryde: 'Have you ever known what it is to be a 'Leaguie' on the northside? As a GPS old boy and a member of staff at a Rugby-playing school, the flak and knocking I receive as a League watcher is amazing'.

The point about all this is that in the 1960s and 1970s when the claim could be made that 'New Zealand is rugby', no such claim could be made for Australian rugby. The class lines confirmed in 1907 with the Great Split, when Rugby League established itself as 'the people's game' and Rugby Union entrenched itself as the game of the middle and upper classes, remained in place, as if set in concrete, throughout the system. The implication for Australian rugby is that the pool of talented players available for selection to the Wallabies is limited by the number of rugby players who never play the Rugby Union game. Supporters, too, are limited along the class lines of the game.

In the 1980s and especially in the 1990s (fuelled in New Zealand by a third television channel and pay TV showing a number of Australian Rugby League competition matches every week), Rugby Union in New Zealand was under some pressure from League. This pressure was not expressed so much in terms of a falling away of players or crowds. But with the television interest in Rugby League and the advent of the Auckland Warriors in the ARL competition the notion of Rugby Union being the great national binding force in New Zealand was breaking up. The mystique of the All Blacks remains. But the spell they cast over New Zealand may not be as dominating as it was in the first three decades after the Second World War.

In Australia, the movement was slightly in the other direction. The first three decades after the Second World War were decades of domination, both in the media and in terms of supporters, by Rugby League. But, as the Wallabies became more successful in the 1980s and especially after the 1991 Rugby World Cup victory (when the number of junior players increased by a third throughout Australia), Rugby Union began to infiltrate into the areas where only League had been played and followed. Rugby remains predominantly a Rah Rah game in Australia. Waratah Oval at Concord, in Sydney's inner west, does not seem to be able to attract large crowds—perhaps, as I have told officials almost in jest, because 'the BMWs can't turn west when they cross the Harbour Bridge'. And a bomb let off at a rugby dinner in a Sydney hotel would destroy most of the movers and shakers in the Central Business District. But, while the domination of the middle and upper classes in Rugby Union remains and gives the game a unique tradition, the code is spreading like a slowly moving flood into (for it) less traditional parts of Sydney and Brisbane—and back into Victoria, a State which was strong enough to defeat New South Wales in the 1930s.

'We wuz robbed'

During the 1958 tour of New Zealand by the Wallabies, Des Connor, the gifted Australian halfback, was approached by Tom Morrison, a member of the New Zealand Rugby Union council. 'Would you be interested in playing rugby in New Zealand?', Morrison asked. New Zealand administrators had had their eye on Connor for over a year. Dick Everest, the coach of the 1957 All Blacks, was extremely impressed with Connor's play for Queensland against his team. He told the Australian selectors: 'You're mad if you don't take this kid to Britain'. Connor told Morrison that he was interested in the New Zealand option. The *NZ Education Gazette* was sent to him (oh, the innocent days of true amateurism in rugby!) and Connor was appointed to a teaching post at Takapuna, Auckland. By 1961 he had become an All Black and the brains behind the powerful Auckland side, coached by Fred Allen, that held the Ranfurly Shield for a record number of defences. He returned to Brisbane in 1966 and in 1968 was appointed the Australian coach. His mission impossible was to devise a way of defeating one of the great All Blacks teams which was coached by Allen, one of New Zealand's most successful coaches. Connor had the advantage, therefore, of at least knowing the All Blacks system and the peculiarities of Allen's methods.

With his inside knowledge of New Zealand rugby and an insider's understanding of Allen's determination to play expansive rugby with the All Blacks, Connor worked out a 'hit and run' strategy for the Wallabies for the second Test in the series at Brisbane. The Wallabies had been outplayed at Sydney when trying to play patterned rugby. They were not able to take the New Zealand forwards on in set pieces. So, for the second Test, Connor decided to present a fractured rather than a patterned game to the All Blacks to oppose. The Wallabies were instructed to play short lineouts. If the ball went loose the forwards were to dive on it and prevent the All Blacks from playing their traditional rucking game. The backs were to stand flat and harry their opponents by getting into the New Zealand line when the ball was being moved along the backline. Talking to Bob Howitt many years later for the book *Rugby Greats*, Connor acknowledged: 'I concede the Test was an awful spectacle but we almost succeeded in lowering the mighty All Blacks'.

Connor was surprised that the All Blacks did not counter his guerilla tactics by kicking more and driving the ball more through the forwards. But this was a misreading of the rugby philosophy of his former coach, Fred Allen. A talented five-eighth with a mesmerising sidestep, Allen had captained the famous New Zealand Army side, the Kiwis, on their tour of the United Kingdom and New Zealand after the war. The Kiwis were remarkably fit, and released from the threat of being killed in the war, had played their rugby with the freedom and joy that comes from being young, talented and hard of body and from the sentiment of having a new lease on life. On their New Zealand tour the Kiwis, now tired from playing too many matches in too many countries, lost to Wellington. A Saturday before that match, as a small boy, I had been at Athletic Park when the man on the scoreboard put up the score of the Kiwis playing Canterbury: Canterbury 6 – Kiwis 3. A buzz went around the ground. A minute or so later, the scoreboard man laconically put an extra number after the Kiwi's 3. But there was no escape for the Kiwis against Wellington. The local side played dour, attrition rugby and defeated a lacklustre Kiwi side. This result, according to the knowledgeable rugby broadcaster and writer, Winston McCarthy, convinced many highplaced administrators and coaches in New Zealand rugby that 10-man rugby in the Wellington style was the best format to guarantee wins. Fred Allen made a pact with himself that he would reverse that Wellington–Kiwis outcome and its ramifications throughout New Zealand by bringing back the Kiwi style of expansive running rugby to the New Zealand game when he had the opportunity.

As the Auckland and then New Zealand coach this is just what he did. When his All Blacks side, therefore, was confronted with the negative play of Des Connor's Wallabies it was for Allen the second round of the Kiwis against Wellington. Rather than bow to the negativism by resorting to a kicking game, Allen encouraged the All Blacks—foolishly as it happened—to continue to play the running game. But the more the ball was run the more successful the spoiling tactics of the Wallabies became. The Wallabies were like shooters on a pheasant hunt gunning down the New Zealand backs as they fluttered through their backline attacks.

Into the last minutes of the Test the Wallabies, with a try to John Hipwell and five penalties kicked by Arthur McGill, were leading 18–14. Desperate and panicky, the All Blacks tried one more running attack. Chris Laidlaw, captain of the All Blacks for the first and last time, made a break from a lineout.

Bill Davis, the New Zealand centre, raced through a gap and started to set up his winger Grahame Thorne for the run to the tryline. But Thorne was jostled by Alan Cardy and pushed out of play. Davis, with no passing option left, kicked towards the tryline and fractionally after the kick was brought down in a flying tackle by Barry Honan, the Wallaby centre. Gasps of relief from the spectators greeted the tackle. The ball dribbled into the in-goal area and was touched down: the end of the Test and victory at last for the Wallabies against the All Blacks in Australia.

But what is this? Oh no! The referee, Kevin Crowe, watches the touchdown and now he raises his arm for a New Zealand try and runs towards the goalposts. The Wallabies watch him with bewildered, shattered looks on their faces. Fergi McCormick kicks the conversion and the All Blacks are—suddenly—the winners 19–18.

Was the referee justified? Or were the cries of 'we wuz robbed' from Australian players, officials and supporters justified? T. P. McLean, an eyewitness, believed that Cardy's interference on Thorne was 'so deliberate as to warrant an extreme penalty'. But he, along with all the other journalists, reported that Cardy's offence was not the action that provoked the awarding of the penalty try. 'I awarded the try', Crowe said after the Test, 'because in my view Davis, had he not been tackled, would probably have scored'. This can be said, of course, for many tackles in a rugby match. The implication in Crowe's statement was that the tackle was made after the ball had been kicked and was, therefore, illegal. Chester and McMillan in *Men in Black* confirm the view that 'Mr Crowe subsequently made it clear that the late tackle by Honan was the infringement for which the penalty decision was made'.

The trouble with this view is that the tackle on Davis was not illegally made. Barry Honan has a series of photographs of his tackle which were published in T. P. McLean's book on the tour. The first frame shows the ball released from Davis's hands ready to be kicked and Honan moving in for the tackle; the second frame shows the ball on the boot of Davis with Honan, diving forward both feet off the ground, clutching the waist of the New Zealander; the third and fourth frames show the ball clear of the boot and the tackle being completed. On this evidence, scrutinised in tranquillity admittedly, there can be no doubt that the tackle on Davis was a legal one.

Twenty years after his controversial decision Crowe gave a final interview to the Australian journalist Dick Tucker. 'I never said it was for Honan's late tackle', he insisted. 'I awarded it for Cardy's deliberate interference on Thorne just outside the quarter line. The All Blacks had an overlap and Cardy took Thorne out of play.' An official, he claimed, told journalists—without checking with him—that the Honan late tackle was the cause of the penalty try decision. Why, though, did Crowe leave it so long to clear the air? The point is that, while the late tackle reason was doubtful, there was little doubt that Cardy's interference on Thorne justified a penalty try award.

The penalty try was justified in another sense, too. If Cardy had not pushed Thorne out of the play the worst that would have happened for the Wallabies would have been a try in the corner. That try would not have been converted. The Wallabies would have won the Test by a point, instead of losing it by a point. And why wouldn't the try have been converted? When Thorne did score a try some time before the penalty try incident, taking the All Blacks to one point away from the Wallabies, in the words of McLean 'McCormick made a quite shocking attempt to place a goal'. Under even greater pressure, and from the sideline, the odds on McCormick kicking the All Blacks to a victory in the last minutes of the Test were about as good as someone winning Lotto. An irony in the selection of McCormick in the All Blacks ahead of his rival Mick Williment lies in the fact that Williment was such a good goalkicker that Allen preferred not to have him in his side. The logic used by the New Zealand coach and chairman of selectors was that when a side had a dominating goalkicker it tended to play for penalties. Having McCormick at fullback, the All Blacks were forced to play for tries and forced to use McCormick's hard-shouldered running.

A further irony is this: Crowe did Australian rugby a favour in presenting the All Blacks with a win. If the Wallabies had won the Ballymore Test using the negative spoiling tactics devised by Des Connor this style of play may have become the standard for Australian rugby. The expansive tradition of the Waratahs, which has been the basis of the successes of the 1980s and 1990s, would have been jettisoned for an Australian version of the—unsuccessful—Scotland and Ireland style of trying to win by making a nuisance rather than by making tries.

Scrap the Bledisloe Cup

After a Sydney Bledisloe Cup Test in 1951 Col Windon, the Wallaby captain, invited the All Blacks to his house for his engagement party. There was no likelihood of anything like this comradeship between the players being demonstrated after the 1968 Tests. The two Tests were spiteful, bad-tempered matches with players from both sides at each other like unleashed doberman dogs. At Brisbane Cardy and McCormick, for instance, engaged in a running battle. After one imagined provocation McCormick threw the ball down and angrily kicked Cardy. The Wallaby winger retaliated with a sharp punch to McCormick's chin.

T. P. McLean summed up the mood of many people—New Zealanders in the main but some Australians also—when he wrote:

> I cannot help feeling that a great kindness would be done to all hands if the two Rugby Unions between them agreed to encase the Bledisloe Cup in concrete before consigning it, with due ceremony, to the stormy waters midway between Australia and New Zealand. With all due respect to the shade of the noble Lord Bledisloe, it's meaningless. Worse, it's mischievous . . . There's a tendency for Rugger types on both sides of the Tasman to use wounding words like 'mug' and 'no-hoper' when discussing the Wallabies vis-a-vis the All Blacks. Justifiably, one might suppose.

THE WOEFUL WALLABIES

Further indignities were in store for the Wallabies and their supporters. The 1972 side that toured New Zealand attracted to themselves the shameful title of 'Woeful Wallabies'.

The first match of the tour, against Otago, was lost 26–0. The tour should never have begun with such a hard match. Once again, Australian administrators had accepted an itinerary that put the Wallabies on the back foot from the opening of the tour. Otago had a strong side and the rucking game that has become synonymous with the province's style was given a boost by one of the wettest winters that province had experienced. The Wallabies, brought up on hard ground, stepped out in a gingerly manner on to a Carisbrook mudfield. 'Is this where they grow oysters?' one of the Wallabies remarked when he saw the waterlogged ground. After the match, in which the Otago forwards were overpowering, the Australian manager Joe French remarked: 'These Otago forwards are like one of our native fishes—they only come up for air every half hour'. The Wallabies had a win, (36–7) against Nelson Bay and another loss (15–10) to Buller-West Coast, one of the weakest provincial sides in New Zealand, before going down to the All Blacks in the first Test 29–6. After five minutes of play, the All Blacks halfback Sid Going burst around the blindside of a five-yard scrum to put the new five-eighth, John Dougan, in for the first 4-point try in international rugby. The All Blacks won the second Test 30–17 and the third Test by the biggest winning score and margin against a Wallaby side: 38–3. The headlines in the Sydney *Sun-Herald* told the story of the woes of the Wallabies:

KIWIS SLAUGHTER WALLABIES
AUS FARE BETTER BUT LOSE AGAIN
ALL BLACKS MASSACRE WALLABIES

In the three Tests the All Blacks scored 97 points to the Wallabies' 26. The pathetic performance of the Wallabies, with their best player being the former New Zealander, the 33-year-old Greg Davis ('Davis was all over the place, tackling anything that moved but he lacked support', a match report of the third Test noted), convinced administrators in Australia that something urgent needed to be done to lift Australian rugby and the Wallabies out of their rut. In October 1972 a special committee was established to investigate the declining standards of Australian rugby. The committee examined how administrators managed rugby in South Africa and New Zealand. Their report, published after six months of investigation, recommended competitions and tours for schoolboys to keep them interested in the game; the introduction of a national coaching scheme; mini rugby for schoolboys; the establishment of an Australian Schools Rugby Championship; and the appointment of team managers and coaches for Wallaby sides several months before an overseas tour. A planned Wallaby tour of Canada and Argentina was cancelled to save money. The Adidas company was approached, successfully, to sponsor the Wallabies' tour of France.

The emphasis of the report was on the need to develop and keep the talented youngsters who played rugby but then gave it away for other sports when they left school. At the senior level, the report laid down guidelines for the Wallabies and their management to follow in order to become as well-organised and competitive as their New Zealand and South African opponents.

The report of the investigation (which involved 42 meetings and inquiries all over Australia and New Zealand) is worth consulting as it gives a detailed (and bleak) view of where Australian rugby was positioned at that critical period in 1972. Extracts from the report are given in Appendix 2 on page 188.

Since the report, with its 30 or so recommendations most of which were accepted, there have been no more 'Woeful Wallabies'. The three men who wrote the report deserve to be named for their crucial role, off the field, in ensuring that the Wallabies became successful on the field: John Howard, Bob Templeton and Bill McLaughlin.

THE BEST NEW ZEALAND EXPORT SINCE THE TOHEROA

On holiday in Sydney in 1960, I read in a newspaper that a New Zealand side, Tauranga, was to play a New South Wales XV. After so many years it is hard to remember where the match was played—somewhere in the Eastern Suburbs of Sydney, I would guess. My vague memory, too, is that Rod Phelps, a versatile back much like Darren Junee in the 1990s, played strongly for New South Wales and may have pulled the match out of the fire for the local side. The crowd was sparse and, being able to stand right on the touchline to watch the play, I was able to see at close quarters just how much power top grade players put into their running and tackling. What does remain in my memory, though, clear and shining as if it were yesterday, was the remarkable performance of one of the flankers on the Tauranga side. He was smallish for a forward, a wiry man, with thinning blond hair, a long face with a beaky nose, inexhaustible energy, ferocious in the tackle, with elbows and knees flying on the run with the ball in his hands. He was everywhere across the field. It seemed as if he had been instantly cloned during a play as, almost freakishly, he would make a tackle in one part of the field, then pop up on the other side to make another tackle, then another tackle and then a charge with the ball tucked in his arm after it had been wrenched loose from the opposition.

The flanker's name, I found out, was Greg Davis. Back in New Zealand I wrote an article for a sporting magazine, *Sports Digest*, proclaiming the advent of a tremendous new forward star and a future All Black. But it was not to be. Davis was an All Black triallist when playing for Auckland in 1961. But the competition for a position on the side of the scrum for All Blacks at the time was intense, with players like Peter Jones, John Graham, Waka Nathan, Kel Tremain, Tom Lister and Ian Kirkpatrick available to the New Zealand selectors. Davis came to Sydney in 1963 as 'the best New Zealand export since the toheroa', according to the journalist Dick Tucker.

At the end of the 1963 season he was selected for the Australian touring party to South Africa. He ended his international rugby career in 1972, as one of the valiant but ineffective triers in the 'Woeful Wallaby' side in New Zealand. By then he was—unfortunately—well past his sublime best. The New Zealand journalist Lindsay Knight argued that when Davis retired early in the second half of the second Test of that year's Bledisloe Cup series and was replaced by Reg Smith 'the Wallaby pack went much better and for the first time was able to contain the All Black forwards'.

On this tour, though slowed down by innumerable injuries to his knees, Davis achieved his greatest ambition—to captain the Wallabies against his former country. As captain in all three Tests Davis took his number of caps as Wallaby captain to 16, equalling the then record of John Thornett and ahead of Ken Catchpole (13) and Trevor Allen (10). Ever optimistic, he expressed the confidence before the series that his sole aim was 'to knock off' the All Blacks: 'I reckon we can do it'. But there was to be no repeat of 1964's stunning 20–5 win by the Wallabies over the All Blacks, a victory that Davis inspired with his fiery play around the field. It was not long after that Test, in fact, that Aub Hodgson (named by T. P. McLean as having played the greatest loose forward game he'd ever seen) nominated Davis as 'the greatest breakaway Australia has ever had—he's fantastic. Davis is superior to me or Wyllie Breckenridge in what he can do'. Phil Wilkins, in a fine tribute to Davis in *The Australian*, quoted the view of Bill McLaughlin, the president of the Australian Rugby Union, that Davis was one of the world's finest breakaways: 'Greg was the greatest leather hunter I have ever seen. He'd be tackling a man and he'd leave him in mid-air if he saw the ball was loose. Jules Guerassimoff was a cruel tackler, harder than Greg. He'd knock them back to the goalposts. Between them they made a devastating pair'. As an example of Davis's commitment and disregard of pain—necessary attributes for a dominating loose forward—Wilkins told the story of how, when the Wallabies were playing in Ireland in 1968, Davis had his nose splattered across his face. A doctor told him he needed to have an operation on it, 'whereupon the breakway retired to a nearby room and knocked his nose into reasonable shape with a soft-drink bottle'.

When the Wallabies were in New Zealand in 1978, Greg Davis, wearing a cap to hide a huge scar across his head from an operation to remove a tumour, looking thin and wearing thick bifocal glasses, turned up to watch the team train at Rotorua. 'I'd been counting the days until you got here', Davis told the Wallabies. He made it clear where his rugby loyalties remained: 'I'll be in even brighter spirits if they beat the All Blacks in the last Test on Saturday'. The Wallabies achieved this wish. A year later, though, before the historic one-off 1979 Bledisloe Cup Test at Sydney, there was a minute's silence for Greg Davis whose funeral was taking place in New Zealand at about the same time as the Test was due to start.

Davis was once asked whether he regretted never being an All Black. 'It is sometimes just as hard to hit the top in Australian rugby as in New Zealand', he replied. The *Encyclopedia of New Zealand Rugby* compiled by R. H. Chester, N. A. C. McMillan and R. A. Palenski (1987 edition) lists 41 New Zealanders (including Davis) 'who have been capped for overseas countries'. The book also lists 136 players 'unlucky not to represent New Zealand'. This relates to another telling point that Davis made when asked about his aspirations to be an All Black: 'After all, there have been quite a few top New Zealand players who have never made the grade there'. This comment has a double sadness in it. Greg Davis had to leave New Zealand to get the recognition in rugby that his great talents and passion for the game deserved. But what of all the players like him who had the passion and the desire and the ability but were never given the chance to demonstrate this at the highest levels where their class would shine through? The what-ifs and the might-have-beens in rugby are, as they are in life, always poignant. Contemplation of the glorious career of Greg Davis and his short life takes me back to my convent school days, when the nuns were insistent that we understood that life was imbued by what the Roman poet Virgil called *lacrimae rerum*, the tears of things.

A NOTE ON WIND

On 25 May 1974 Andy Leslie, the new All Blacks captain who was selected more for his qualities as a leader than as a player, faced a crucial decision: should he play with or against the gale at the Sydney Cricket Ground in the first Test of the series? The wind was so fierce that parts of Sydney were blacked out for hours. In the outer suburb of Mulgoa a young man was swept to his death by a racing torrent of stormwater as he tried to cross a flooded bridge. Houses had their roofs lifted. It was the coldest day of the year. Alan Clarkson, the *Sun-Herald*'s Rugby League writer, began his report of the South Sydney v Newtown match with the assertion that the match should 'never have been played'. At the Sydney Cricket Ground, the goalposts whipped backwards and forwards as if they were being shaken by an angry invisible giant. The pelting, driving rain and the raging, tousling wind whacked the faces of spectators and players like a thousand cracking whips.

Some years ago I interviewed Fred Allen and Brian Lochore, both former All Blacks captains and coaches, on what a captain should do if he wins the toss on a windy day.

Fred Allen stated the FOR argument this way:

I personally always believed in taking the wind. It often turns out, especially if it is a strong wind, that when you are playing against the wind and it comes your turn to play with it, you have exhausted yourselves so much defending that you can't take full advantage of it. As far as I am concerned, I believe in taking all advantages if you get the opportunity.

Brian Lochore's AGAINST argument ran this way:

I usually gave the wind away when I won the toss. Of course, there are always exceptions. If I was playing in a team of underdogs that lacked confidence in their ability, I would take the wind in the hope of getting points up. My reasons for playing against the wind are: firstly, that most points in any game are scored towards the end of it, when the defence is not as well organised and the players are a little tired. If you have the advantage of the wind during this period, it makes it easier to get on attack and use your scoring moves. Secondly, the first 20 minutes of most games are spent sizing up each other. This means that you only have 20 minutes to play with the wind anyway. Also, playing in a strong pack means that you do a lot to subdue the opposition by driving from the lineouts and generally controlling things up front. It is ideal to play into the wind under these circumstances because you are using your attack in the forwards as a means of defence. Finally, every team's defence I think is much tighter in the first half, which makes it harder to take full advantage of the wind.

These conflicting arguments were obviously mulled over by Andy Leslie. As a Wellingtonian he was used to playing in the wind virtually every Saturday of the season. This experience lead him to the right decision. 'We'll play with the wind', he told John Hipwell, the Wallaby captain.

The match (won by New Zealand 11–6) started off disastrously for the All Blacks. The Wallabies won a penalty near the New Zealand posts after only eight minutes of play. Paul McLean's kick at goal hit one of the shaking posts and rebounded across the in-goal area where Ray Price, the fiery breakaway playing his first Test for Australia, slithered across the pools of water to touch down in the Hill corner. Price looked up and saw his family and friends all standing up cheering for him. A big banner was raised in the raging wind: THE RAY PRICE STAND. Smacking the ball into the surging gale, Paul McLean converted the try.

Jim Webster in his report of the Test in the *Sun-Herald*, with the headline BLACKOUT FOR BOLD AUSTRALIA, gives a vivid picture of what was a memorable comeback by the All Blacks:

In the first half, New Zealand won five fewer lineouts than the Wallabies, but after the break they crushed Australia 28–8. It was a similar story in

> the rucks and mauls and Australia was so starved of possession, their eclipse was inevitable . . . The sight of the All Blacks captain Andy Leslie down on his haunches sweeping water away with his arm for fullback Joe Karam to kick his first goal to take the score at halftime to 6–3 vividly sums up the conditions . . . Ian Kirkpatrick, the All Blacks 16-stone breakaway with immense power, became particularly prominent in the second half brushing close to the rucks and mauls, the ball tucked to his side, splintering the defence as he went. Trying to stop his charges must be similar to trying to hold back a falling oak tree. He scored the last try of the day, a deserving reward.

This match provides the proof of the Fred Allen approach to taking the wind, as have a number of other Bledisloe Cup battles. The 9–9 draw at Wellington in 1962 between New Zealand and Australia, a Test the All Blacks were expected to win comfortably, had a halftime score of 3–0 to New Zealand after playing into the wind. With the wind behind them, the All Blacks scored another six points but the Wallabies, with seven new caps (is this a record?), managed to score nine points into the wind (three penalties) when they could score none with it to snatch an unlikely draw. At Wellington again in 1990 the Wallabies won the Test after playing into the wind. But towards the end of the Test the New Zealand captain, Gary Whetton, gave away an easy kick at goal to level the scores in favour of trying to score a try. All Blacks regard draws as losses and as New Zealand had already won the series this may explain Whetton's curious decision. The decisive vindication of the 'playing with the wind' theory came in the 1982 Test series in which every match was played in high winds. Playing with the wind at Christchurch, the All Blacks won the first Test 23–16; playing with the wind at Wellington, the Wallabies won the second Test 19–16; playing with the wind at Auckland—and enduring a converted Wallaby try in the opening minutes of the match—the All Blacks won the third Test 33–18.

A rugby captain should take the W. G. Grace approach to the wind mentioned earlier: think about giving it away occasionally—but never do so. This sentiment is supported by the best of all possible precedents. At the beginning of the famous football match at Rugby School in *Tom Brown's School Days*, Old Brooke won the toss and took the advantage of the wind for the Schoolhouse.

Cornelsen's Match

There have been two original strategems introduced into rugby in the modern era. One was the 15-man maul developed by North Harbour in the 1980s, with Wayne Shelford as the impact point of the battering ram. The other was the up-the-jumper trick devised by the New South Wales Country coach, Daryl Harberecht.

In the 1975 match between New South Wales Country and Sydney, Country scored a last-minute try using the up-the-jumper ploy to snatch the match, 22–20. Was the ploy legal? Harberecht was asked after the match: 'There is nothing in the laws to say we could not do it . . . To be quite frank, the idea has appealed to me as a form of deception since a discussion a couple of years ago about the laws of the game. Somebody said that there was nothing to stop a player from shoving the ball up his jumper'. The player Harberecht selected to run with the ball up his jumper, as his team-mates scattered across the field, some with their arms folded over their stomachs, was a rangy breakaway, Greg Cornelsen. 'Cornelsen was chosen', Harberecht explained to journalists, 'because he is the fastest of the forwards and is a strong runner.'

We now fast-forward to 9 September 1978 for the third Bledisloe Cup Test between New Zealand and Australia at Eden Park, Auckland. The tour had been a dismal one for the Wallabies. The first two Tests were lost—at Wellington by one point (13–12) after Ken Wright missed a penalty shot, on full time from an acute angle after the All Blacks had interfered with a quick throw-in, and at Christchurch (22–6) with the All Blacks scoring three tries to nil. Talking about that second Test, Greg Cornelsen said that in the first ruck the All Blacks drove the Wallabies back 15 metres: 'That decided the Test. They weren't worried about the ball, they just wanted to drive. They came at us like mad dogs'. Of the twelve matches on the tour up to the final Test the Wallabies had lost five. Worse than this, though, was the fact that after being a competitive team in the first Test the side's form had slipped so badly that a former All Black coach, John Stewart, was called in to give advice about rucking, mauling and lineout techniques. Coincidentally with this help from the enemy the Wallaby coach, Daryl Harberecht, had a heart attack and could not coach the team for the rest of the tour.

Chris Handy was brought in as prop for the third Test (his first cap). He tells in *Well I'll be Ruggered* how he was grabbed by two Sydney journalists on the evening of the Test, as he was pacing the corridors, and taken into a hotel room where the three men drank a bottle of Kahlua and milk. The next morning, after 'a very deep and peaceful sleep', Handy attended a team meeting in which the manager, Ross Turnbull, told the players that Australia's rugby future depended on the outcome of the Test. Turnbull sent the backs out of the room. Then he told the forwards: 'Look, these Phantom-comic-swoopers and Mintie-eaters, these blond-headed flyweights, are one thing, and we'll need them after the hard work's done. But the real stuff's got to be done right here by you blokes'. He identified the lineout jumping of the All Blacks giant, Andy Haden, as the key to the New Zealand game. Haden had to be 'attended to'. Turnbull then turned to Handy: 'Now, Buddha, we think you're the man'.

The oratory seems to have worked. For the Wallabies rescued their tour—and the Test careers of a number of players—with a conclusive 30–16 victory. The Australian journalist Adrian McGregor, analysing the outcome of the Test for the *National Times*, felt impelled to quote the 19th century poet Robert Southey in 'The Battle of Blenheim':

> 'But what good cause came of it at last?'
> Quoth little Peterkin.
> 'Why that I cannot tell,' said he,
> 'But t'was a famous victory.'

Yes, a famous victory—and close run, despite the winning margin. Greg Cornelsen, who created the record with his four tries of being the highest individual points-scorer against the All Blacks in a Test, told McGregor that as the All Blacks clawed their way back into the match from 18–3 down to 18–13 in the second half with a try by Stu Wilson, he thought: 'Here we go again. It shouldn't just happen. We switched off'. Tony Shaw, the Wallaby captain, a hard and aggressive Queenslander, now showed his leadership qualities. He called the dejected Wallabies together and told them they'd bloody well lose if they bloody well didn't commit everything to the game: 'We haven't come this far to throw it away, have we? Look around you. Look at each of us. Look at your mates. You'd do anything for them, wouldn't you? Well do it now. Give your guts'.

Successful penalties were kicked by both teams and then, with sixteen minutes left to play, John Hipwell burst down the blindside from a scrum. His pass in-field was knocked down by the All Blacks cover. Cornelsen, Harberecht's 'fastest forward' in the up-the-jumper tactic, won the race for the ball to score his fourth try.

THE MYTH OF ALL BLACKS INVINCIBILITY IS BROKEN FOREVER

Greg Cornelsen's four tries represented the largest number of tries scored against the All Blacks in a Test. As already noted, he became, too, the highest individual points-scorer in a Test against the All Blacks—displacing Okey Geffin with his 15 points (all penalty goals) in the first Test in 1949 between New Zealand and South Africa. The five tries scored by the Wallabies equalled the record number of tries scored against the All Blacks in a Test, recorded by the 1937 Springboks in the third Test of that series. And the 30 points scored by the Wallabies was the highest total put up in a Test against the All Blacks.

These records highlight the drama of that 1978 victory. Its real magnitude, though, was that for the first time since anyone could remember the All Blacks had started to overhaul the Wallabies' lead and were decisively repulsed. In the past, there was a sense of inevitability that once the All Blacks started to unleash their Panzer-like attacks, as they did at Brisbane in 1968, the attacks would succeed. But the inevitable did not occur in Cornelsen's Match.

From 1950 (the year after the Bledisloe Cup was won in New Zealand) to the second Test in the 1978 series against the All Blacks, the Wallabies played 111 Tests: winning 33, drawing 5 and losing 73. Against New Zealand the statistics for the Wallabies were: played 32, won 4, drew 2 and lost 26.

Then, including the last Test in 1978 and running up to the last Test in 1994, the Wallabies played 112 Tests: losing 36, drawing 3 and winning 73—an almost exact reversal of the record up to 1978. Against New Zealand the statistics for the Wallabies during this period were: played 32, won 15, drew 1 and lost 16.

The myth of invincibility cannot be restored. Like the fact of virginity, once it is broken it is lost forever. This truth burst into the consciousness of New Zealanders when the New Zealand administrators generously—and foolishly—agreed to the All Blacks' playing a one-off Test at Sydney in 1979.

BROCKHOFF: AUSTRALIAN RUGBY'S CHURCHILL

Marxist historians tell us that personality plays no part in the great thrust of history. Events happen because there is, to quote a line or two from *Julius Caesar*, 'a tide in the affairs of men which, taken at the flood,' forces change, forces the pace of history. Yet the English historian H. A. L. Fisher, in the preface to his massive *History of Europe*, conceded that he could find no pattern in the events he laid out before his readers. A somewhat different position is taken by Pascal, the French philosopher. 'If Cleopatra's nose had been a quarter of an inch longer', he suggested in a famous aphorism, 'the course of history would have been different.' Much the same point is made by A. J. P. Taylor, the controversial English historian, who argued that the railway timetables were an important factor in the causes of the First World War. The events of our own lives suggest that, while the great forces of history do exist as the marxists insist, the great man theory, too, must be accorded recognition in trying to understand what happened and why it happened.

Personality and coincidence play their part, often importantly, in the outcome of a great event. Would the outcome of the Second World War have been different if Winston Churchill had died from overdrinking in the 1930s? Even the most dedicated advocate of the 'tide in affairs' theory of history has to concede that Churchill's oratory, his sense of history, his vision and energy and his aristocratic cussedness determined to a great extent that the war would be waged mercilessly to a successful conclusion against Nazi Germany.

David Brockhoff was Australian rugby's Churchill. The man and the moment fitted each other. Australian rugby had a chance with the flukey but inspiring victory at Eden Park in 1978 to push on to some sort of equal position with New Zealand rugby—or to regress as it had in the past, notably after the 1929 blackout series against the All Blacks. Like Churchill, Brockhoff did not believe in surrender as an option. He was a 'no prisoners' advocate. He believed, in the world of rugby at least, in the doctrine of 'blood, toil, tears and sweat'. As a breakaway for the 1949 Wallabies in New Zealand, he had earned the ire of spectators who nicknamed him 'Offside Brockhoff' for the way he played at and often over the advantage line. The New Zealand newspapers called him 'impetuous'. But he was ruthless more than daring. Time after time he smashed the New Zealand five-eighth, Ben Couch, into the ground with punishing tackles in the manner (ironically) of a traditional New Zealand loose forward. The theory behind what he was doing he learnt from long conversations with Vic Cavanagh, the Otago coach of the 1940s and 1950s—the creator of the modern rugby system of keeping the ball over the advantage line at all times, of quick rucks, of driving hard into the middle of the field with a big inside centre and then playing the side of the ruck where the opposition had the fewer men. On defence, the Cavanagh method called for relentless pressure. The ball was to be contested at all times. Tackles had to be hard and surely made. Cover had to be deep and intensive. And every player had to realise that his individual effort could be crucial to the performance of the whole: the power of 15 was dependent on the power of all the ones.

For many years Brockhoff misunderstood some of these principles when he coached the oldest rugby club in the world, Sydney University, although the club won the Sydney first grade premiership under him in 1968, 1970 and 1972. His teams kicked the leather off the ball. The point of this method was to keep the ball in front of the forwards, to get field position and to apply pressure on the opposition. But, while kicking for position was part of the Cavanagh pattern (he had developed a neat five-eighth, Jim Kearney, to implement this aspect of the Otago game), the—Cavanagh—principle was that the kick was always the last and not the first—Brockhoff—resort. The ball was, or should be, kept in hand as much as possible. The theory behind this is that if a team maintains possession it is more likely to score tries than the team without the ball. Cavanagh's teams scored most of their tries, as a successful consequence of their pressured, ball-in-hand rucking game, on the wings.

Brockhoff's Wallaby sides in his first coming as the national coach were inclined to become too carried away with his fiery oratory. After the spiteful first Test against England in 1975, when boots and fists flew from the kickoff, Vivian Jenkins, the former Welsh international and rugby writer for the *Sunday Times*, wrote: 'Brockhoff may not have committed the actual offences in the field at Brisbane but when a team starts kicking its opponents from the word "go", as the Australians did, the man in charge is bound to be identified with it in the minds of his opponents'. But this thuggishness, provoked to a large extent by even more thuggish England players, was not part of the Cavanagh method. That method recognised that rugby was a body contact sport. The contact, though, had to be made legally, if brutally.

It took Brockhoff many years to fully comprehend the Cavanagh (and New Zealand) pattern. But by 1979, when he was the Wallaby coach for the second time, he had mastered it intellectually. He had grasped the mantra, for instance, that the speed of the backs was the speed of the slowest back and the speed of the forwards was the speed of the fastest forward. This message came home to him when he saw the All Blacks play their—losing—second Test (24–19) in 1979 against France at Eden Park. 'The variety in the French back play and their forward speed', he marvelled, 'was incredible. The All Blacks did not have a counter—they won the scrums and jumped higher in the lineouts but could not use their possession properly.' He decided that the Wallabies needed a flier on the side of the scrum, a tackling machine somewhat in the same mould of himself as a player. Sydney University, his old club, had just the player—Andy Stewart—to cause the havoc wrecked by Jean-Paul Rives on the New Zealand inside backs at Eden Park, and by himself at Athletic Park and Eden Park in 1949.

With a game plan based on speed around the field, domination of possession and toughness in every aspect of play, Brockhoff's last task was to beat the mental disadvantage that Wallabies teams endured when they played the All Blacks. There was a vicious circle at work here: the Wallabies wouldn't win Bledisloe Cup Tests until they believed they could win but they wouldn't believe they could win until they won. We don't know what Brockhoff told his players before the one-off Bledisloe Cup Test at Sydney in 1979, but in *Nicks and Cuts* Nick Farr-Jones records this flourish of oratory before a Sydney University match:

> You have to be everywhere breakaways. Everywhere! No excuses . . . Cause havoc at the breakdown like sharks in a school of mullets. As for the tight-five, all day like wind through wheat. Not a scattered rock here and there, but like wind through wheat. And when you're through the other side we're like crows through the Opera House window. Get in, loot the joint and get out. And remember, no height in the lineout is no excuse, we must have the fruit of every lineout dockyard brawl! Except in our own 22—row of ministers—no easy penalties.

Something along these lines, we can be sure, in a passionate and stentorian voice filled the ears of the Wallabies as they waited to run on to the Sydney Cricket Ground and their fateful match.

Whether it was the Brockhoff oratory at work, or a slipping of standards on the part of the All Blacks, in one period of the Test the Wallabies inflicted the unprecedented humiliation on the New Zealanders of winning eleven rucks and mauls in succession. Sharks in a school of mullets couldn't have caused more havoc. With the tackling machine Andy Stewart, a tough Queensland front row of Stan Pilecki, Peter Horton and Chris Handy to dominate the mauls, the hard man Tony Shaw in the middle of the lineout, Mark Loane with power runs to unsettle the All Blacks on the edge of the rucks and Tony Melrose to bang the ball inside the New Zealand 22 from any part of the field, Australia forced mistakes on the rattled, lacklustre New Zealanders. Paul McLean, with three penalties out of five attempts and Melrose with a dropped goal, turned these mistakes into points.

Evan Whitton, in the *Sydney Morning Herald,* was in no doubt about the quality of the victory:

> Australia's stunning victory in yesterday's international was possibly the most remarkable of the 15 we have managed in 76 years against the All Blacks. Sent out with, on the face of it, the wrong team and the wrong tactics, the Australians overcame all odds. This argues, at the very least, great character, and the 15 players are entitled to every tribute for that.

The turning point in the match came, according to Whitton, with fifteen minutes of play remaining and Australia holding a lead of 9–6 and everyone at the ground and on the field knowing that the team that scored next were the certain winners:

> At this point, with some of the Australians starting to clutch feebly at All Black arms, Stewart, whom I had heretofore judged to be of the headless fowl type of breakaway, brought off in quick succession two bone-jarringly decisive tackles at close quarters, and the charge petered out . . . Instructed, one assumes by his captain, Mark Loane, to shut the gate, Melrose took complete charge, and his superbly placed kicks kept the All Blacks penned in their half for much of the rest of the match. While, on their record, no All Black team is a bad one, it must be said that this one was at times surprisingly inept.

Andy Haden, the streetwise All Blacks secondrower, came up to Brockhoff after the Test and told him: 'I've never been so tired in a match as in this one. No Australian pack has taken so much ball in my memory off the All Blacks'. He stripped off his jersey and handed it across to Brockhoff in a tribute to a coach who had successfully imposed the All Blacks pattern on the All Blacks. Then, with tears in his eyes ('my cup was running over because we'd finally played a forward game at the Sydney Cricket Ground the way I wanted it played'), Brockhoff joined the jubilant Wallaby team as it made a lap of honour with the Bledisloe Cup held aloft.

Seven of the Wallaby forwards who played the 1979 one-off Bledisloe Cup Test the way David Brockhoff wanted them to play were Queenslanders. Evan Whitton, a Queenslander himself, saw—correctly—a significance in this fact. 'It's lately been remarked in a national weekly', he wrote in his match report, 'that the bananabenders' commitment is total inside a maroon jersey, but less so in the jersey of a foreign country. On this occasion there was no doubting their devotion to the Australian cause.'

The weekly publication Whitton referred to was the *National Times*. The weekly ran a series of articles that foreshadowed the Bledisloe Cup Test. David Hickie in a provocative analysis called 'The Politics of Rugby' argued that 'at the national level, Australian Rugby Union is being strangled by poor administrators, more interested in advancing their own factional self-interests than the general interests of their game'. The intense rivalry, on and off the field, between Queensland and New South Wales was reflected, according to Hickie, in the way that Queensland's dominance in the annual series against New South Wales (the 1976 42–4 victory against that State has a similar significance for Queenslanders as the Battle of the Boyne has for Ulster Unionists) 'became more important than the national team effort'.

The point that was lost on New South Wales administrators—but never on Queensland administrators—is that when Queensland rugby is strong Australian rugby is strong. The truth of this assertion can be verified from as far back as the 19th century when on 15 August 1896 Queensland, according to Gordon Slater in *The Centennial Book of New Zealand Rugby*, played 'the only Test match Queensland has ever played in New Zealand'. This 'Test', though, which was played at Athletic Park, Wellington, was not acknowledged as a true international match by either the New Zealand or the Australian authorities. However, the New Zealand team was a representative side with players from Canterbury, Wellington, Taranaki, Wanganui, Auckland, Wairarapa and Southland. The New Zealand side won the toss, took the wind (a beast of a gale) and started play with such enthusiasm that, as Slater reports, 'F. Surman of Auckland enthusiastically chased the ball over the Queensland line, running full tilt into the wire rope that was keeping spectators back'. Surman left the field as did W. D. Watson, the winger from Wairarapa, and the New Zealanders with two short 'were facing the wind, yet they kept Queensland penned in their own twenty-five for most of the spell. W. McKenzie of Wellington dodged through for the third try and time was called with New Zealand winning 9–0'.

The 1897 New Zealand representative team played two matches against Queensland, winning them 16–5 and 24–6 in front of 11 000 spectators in the second match. For this match, players wore numbers on their backs ('as an experiment to assist those watching') for the first time in Australia. Up to the First World War rugby flourished throughout Queensland, notably in Charters Towers (then the State's second city) and Toowoomba, as well as in Brisbane where rugby had the support of Brisbane's GPS schools. Then—unfortunately—the Queensland Rugby Union, in the words of the historian of Australian rugby, Jack Pollard, 'simply abandoned rugby for the duration' of the First World War and 'it then disappeared for 10 years'.

The GPS schools started playing rugby again in 1928. The Queensland Rugby Union was re-formed in 1929 and five Queenslanders, including the immortal Tommy Lawton, were selected for the successful (for the Wallabies) Test series against the All Blacks in that year.

The QRU, slow learners, suspended rugby once again on the outbreak of the Second World War. This time around, though, the QRU resumed rugby competitions as soon as the war was over. But the code struggled to make up the ground lost to Rugby League during the war years. It was not until 1964, for instance, that a fulltime secretary was appointed. This appointment marked the beginning of an administrative and playing resurgence for Queensland rugby. Ballymore, now a splendid rugby ground, was purchased when it was two undeveloped grounds. The Queensland Rugby Club was developed and the State side, the Maroons, instituted a number of annual matches with New Zealand provincial sides in order to assimilate their hard, uncompromising play. Chris Handy in *Well I'll Be Ruggered* points this trans-Tasman link into a correct perspective:

> What really changed the quality of rugby in Australia was the opportunity of playing often against the All Blacks at international level, and against the best of their provincial sides at the state level. Being matched against these great teams provided us with the opportunity to learn, and subsequently to develop the things that we discovered from them to a level where we were able to match, and ultimately conquer, them.

Two decades after the war Queensland entered what became known as 'the successful seventies', beating New South Wales ten times in the decade including the famous 42–4 victory of 1976. Frank O'Callaghan, the doyen of Queensland rugby writers, reported this victory in the *Courier Mail* with these cockadoodledoo opening words: 'Queensland Rugby Union went into orbit at Ballymore yesterday crushing New South Wales by 38 points—42–4. Never has Queensland beaten the Blues by such a margin, and never has Ballymore so exploded as the partisan crowd feasted on six slashing home tries.'

The days in the 1950s and 1960s when New South Wales administrators resented Queensland players in the Wallabies were avenged in this crushing victory. But the resentment remains. Queensland officials still talk darkly about how their players were not met at Central Station when coming down to Sydney for a Test. But by 1992 there were eight Queenslanders in the Wallabies and six in the seven reserves. The bitterness has sometimes been challenged on the grounds of being excessive parochialism. And there is something in this criticism. The *Courier Mail* in 1968 ran this headline: ALL BLACKS WIN 34–3 BUT QUEENSLAND SCORED FIRST. And, after a recent Queensland v New South Wales State of the Union match, the victorious Queensland captain Peter Slattery trumpeted: 'It's great to be an Australian but it's better to be a Queenslander'.

Queensland players got too carried away with this parochialism in 1982 when a number of senior Wallabies turned down the first tour of New Zealand by Bob Dwyer as the Wallaby coach. But on balance the toughminded approach of the Queensland forwards, especially, gave the Wallabies the hard edge they lacked when Australian teams were dominated by New South Wales players. The psychology of this was that the Queenslanders had a chip on their shoulder about New South Wales rugby. Matches against New South Wales were played with an intensity that surprised the Test-hardened New South Wales players. This intensity was then transformed to the Wallabies. The more successful Queensland became, therefore, the more successful the Wallabies became. Mark Ella summarised the difference between the New South Wales approach and the Queensland approach when he asserted: 'Queenslanders look at rugby like the All Blacks. They have to win'. Queensland rugby from the 1970s, with its New Zealand approach, provided the necessary fist for the Wallabies, metaphorically—and literally.

TONY SHAW: THE EPITOME OF THE QUEENSLAND PLAYER

Everything about Tony Shaw looks hard. The balding head, the narrow intense eyes (giving rise to his nickname 'Crazy Eyes'), the taut line of his lips and the wiry angular body. He played his Test rugby (36 Tests) in the same hard and uncompromising style. There is a photograph of Shaw being held aloft by beaming team-mates after captaining the Wallabies in a successful defence of the Bledisloe Cup at the Sydney Cricket Ground in 1980. Shaw is characteristically tightlipped; a mighty left arm, with sinews exposed, is grasping the huge Bledisloe Cup. The look on his face reflects the grim satisfaction that comes to a hard player when a hard task is achieved.

There was a quality of indestructibility that marked him as a player. Between 1975 and 1981 he played 29 consecutive Tests, an achievement rarely equalled by a Wallaby. He captained the Wallabies in the 1978 Eden Park Test, the one-off Test against the All Blacks in 1979, and in the three Tests in the successful Bledisloe Cup defence against the All Blacks in 1980. This is a success rate against the All Blacks that has rarely been equalled by a Wallaby captain. In fifteen years of representative rugby Shaw suffered only one major injury, a broken jaw in 1983 in a club final. He did not leave the field. The highest compliment that can be paid to Shaw is to record that as the epitome of the Queensland player of the 1970s—the enforcer so fundamental to ensuring the newfound success of the Wallabies—he played in the tradition of the great All Blacks hard men over the decades.

WERE THE ALL BLACKS POISONED IN 1980?

A 90-metre try by the All Blacks, one of the great tries in the history of the Bledisloe Cup, rescued the second Test for them at Brisbane in 1980. The try rested on the lunging fingers of the Wallaby centre Michael O'Connor grasping and then failing to secure the sock of his opposite Bruce Robertson as he dashed past him. Robertson made his break from inside the New Zealand 22. O'Connor's fingers, as he went in to make the tackle, only succeeded in pulling Robertson's sock down to his ankle. The All Black raced downfield and linked up with his supports. Player after player exchanged passes, all of them timed perfectly, so that the ball was transferred just as the passer was being tackled. The final transfer to Hika Reid, the hooker who had started the try by putting Robertson into a gap, saw him cross near the posts with no Wallabies to stop him planting the ball down for the try.

As the Wallabies had won the first Test 13–9 the third Test of the series, at Sydney, decided the fate of the Bledisloe Cup. Geraldine Brooks, a young journalist on the *Sydney Morning Herald* and later a distinguished reporter in the United States, was sent to cover the emotions and actions of supporters on the infamous (and now extinct) Sydney Cricket Ground Hill. Brooks herself decided to support the All Blacks:

> Within 10 minutes, I realised I was backing the underdog. From a distance, the scrambling scrums looked like the last death agonies of a semi-squashed cockroach . . . As the extent of the massacre became obvious, towards halftime, the chants of 'Blacks, Blacks, Blacks' changed to a torrent of abuse from the New Zealand supporters. 'This isn't happening,' one black-capped man behind me kept muttering. 'This is positively spewable,' another Kiwi wailed. 'Carn ya morons, move!' yelled another, followed by the ultimate macho-man insult: 'What are ya, a team of girls?'

With the Wallabies winning comfortably 26–10, the last picture that Brooks took away in her mind was of a lonely New Zealander taking off his black cap and scarf and dropping them on the shardy carpet of squashed cans and other rubbish.

What happened? How could the All Blacks play so listlessly in such a crucial Test? The New Zealand captain, the brilliant winger Stu Wilson claimed in his rugbiography written with his wing partner Bernie Fraser, *Ebony and Ivory*, that the All Blacks were poisoned: 'Not one guy in the team believes it was other than a deliberately induced infection'. On the eve of the Test, according to Wilson, 25 out of the 28 players were poisoned. The reason for the poisoning? 'A big betting plunge on the Wallabies organised by a Sydney gambler . . . If the bettor had seen our boys agonising their way through the night, queuing up to use two receptacles at once . . . he'd have gone out and doubled his bet.'

This allegation has never been proved. What is accepted, though, is that many of the All Blacks were ill before and during the Test. The suspect potion was a batch of Bluff oysters flown from New Zealand by a wellwisher and served to the All Blacks at a function hosted by the New Zealand High Commissioner. The irony is clear: the Bluff oysters, such a potent weapon against touring Wallaby teams in the south of New Zealand, now biting the All Blacks stomachs feeding on them.

A New Zealand tragedy

The first New Zealand player to be struck hard by the food poisoning was the young five-eighth, Nick Allen. Those watching the Test, though, would not have known this for Allen gave a silky, fluent display, marked by quick passing and precise running that presaged his future as New Zealand's long-awaited answer to Mark Ella. Some months after the Sydney Test Allen confirmed his promise of becoming New Zealand's greatest five-eighth in the modern era with a magical display in the one-off Centenary Test at Cardiff Arms Park when an inspired All Blacks side, with Allen making devastating breaks and providing quick ball to his centres, exuberantly trounced Wales 23–3. But this was to be Allen's last Test.

He next made headlines in the newspapers four years later when playing in a New South Wales competition—for Port Kembla against Kiama in the Illawarra grand final at the Wollongong Showground. During the match he struck his head heavily against the ground after being tackled. He lost consciousness and was taken to hospital. Doctors operated to remove a large blood clot on his brain. A week after his last rugby match, with his father, mother, sister and three brothers by his bedside, he was taken off a life support system and shortly afterwards died. His funeral five days later at St Mary's In Holy Trinity Church in the Auckland suburb of Parnell was attended by the entire 1980 All Blacks side, ten of his Port Kembla team-mates, one representative of the Kiama team and over 1000 mourners.

Greek mythology has it that Achilles was offered by the gods the possibility of a long but boring life or a short and dazzling life. He chose the short and dazzling life. Nick Allen seems to have made a similar choice. Playing for the New Zealand Colts in 1978, he was heavily concussed. A specialist doctor warned him to give rugby away because he risked permanent brain damage if he continued to play. He stopped playing rugby for the remainder of the season but returned the following year and was selected, as a late tour replacement, to play in the third Test against Australia at Sydney. He performed so well he was selected again for the Centenary Test against Wales.

A knee injury then put him out of rugby for three years. He tore the tissue away from the bottom of the femur bone near the knee while attempting a sidestep during a match for the London Harlequins club. With his rugby career seemingly over, Allen decided to live in his favourite city, Sydney. He took up a job with a long-time friend and when the friend, Mike Beveridge, became the rugby coach at Port Kembla Allen could not resist the urge to make a comeback on the rugby field. By 1984, after a few games of lower grade rugby, Allen was confident that he was the player he had been. He was asked to make himself available for the All Blacks in their series against the Lions. In New Zealand, however, he broke the scaphoid bone in his wrist and missed the all-important All Blacks selection trials. He came back to Australia and made himself available for selection for the Wallabies. 'I love Australian rugby and how it's played. I love running and stepping with the ball, just like you people do', he told an Australian reporter. Playing with David Campese in April 1984 for Country at Wagga, he led the backline to a 43–0 massacre of the touring Fijian side. The next week Country played Sydney, with Allen facing Mark Ella in what he saw as a showdown contest for Wallaby selection: 'Mark and I have played against each other three times and I reckon the honours are about even'. The president of the Australian Rugby Union, Sir Nicholas Shehadie, confirmed before the match that Allen and the Argentinian prop, Enrique Rodriquez had gained clearance to play for Australia: 'We certainly wouldn't consider them ahead of the home-grown product. But we regard them as genuine cases who are now settled in Australia'.

Ella was retained as the Wallaby five-eighth for the 1984 Bledisloe Cup Tests and later in the year for the Grand Slam tour of the United Kingdom, where he scored a try in each of the Tests. Rodriquez became a Wallaby and made a Bledisloe Cup series–saving tackle in the third Test in 1986 at Eden Park. And Allen, confident in his talents and in love with the joy of rugby to the last, went on to play his fateful final match at Wollongong.

The Test from Hell

On 12 September 1981, the fourth anniversary of the murder of Steve Biko, the All Blacks and the Springboks played rugby's most bizarre Test at Eden Park, Auckland. The Springboks had been taken from their hotel in Auckland on the eve of the Test and spirited into the changing rooms under the main Eden Park grandstand. They spent a sleepless night lying on concrete and listening to chants of protesters. During the Test, while the players charged into each other, a Cessna 172 aircraft repeatedly buzzed the ground dropping flour bombs. Play was halted at one point when a bomb landed on the back of the All Blacks front row forward and former Commonwealth Games wrestler, Gary Knight. Knight sank to the ground like a crippled buffalo. The atmosphere was like the last act in a Wagner opera. The field was marked, as if showing wounds, with long white streaks from the flour bombs. Acrid pink smoke from flares thrown by protesters curled into the air. And time after time, from out of the pewter-coloured sky, the Cessna flew almost into the ground like a mechanical Nemesis. With seconds left to play, the score stood at 22–22. The Springboks were penalised for not retiring ten metres from a quick tap. Alan Hewson, playing in his first Test, from 45 metres out made a lovely, relaxed swing of his left boot, peered into the gathering dusk as the ball soared, and then punched the air in jubilation as the touch judges raised their flags.

After the melodrama of the Test, it was clear that the Springboks would not tour New Zealand again until—and this seemed to be decades away—the apartheid rules were dropped in South Africa. Rugby players still hankered for further confrontations with the Springboks. And in 1986 (with a disastrous impact to the playing capacity of the All Blacks) a rebel players tour, with a Cavaliers team, was organised. The New Zealand public, though, has lost its stomach for the old and bitter confrontation.

This meant that another object of hate, another national side that had to be defeated by the All Blacks, had to be found. New Zealand rugby has flourished on a determination to establish the All Blacks as world champions. Pretenders to this title have been subjected to a furious attack on and off the field. Wales was the first rugby nation to be confronted with this fury. The 1905 All Blacks lost one match on their tour of the United Kingdom, a 3–0 defeat at the hands of a brilliant Welsh side. This humiliation was avenged in 1924 by the Invincibles, 19–0. Although the All Blacks lost the next two Tests against Wales in 1935 and 1953, no more Tests have been lost to the Dragons. This mastery over Wales has taken the heat out of that particular rivalry for New Zealanders.

The Welsh, anyway, were supplanted as pretenders to the world championship by the real thing, the South African Springboks. After drawing two series in 1921 and 1928 the All Blacks were defeated in 1937 and 1949 (horrors of horrors, four Tests to nil!). After that each side won its home series and lost its touring series. The strength of the New Zealand passion for the rugby contests against South Africa was summed up by Colin Meads, regarded as the greatest All Black of the modern era and later the All Blacks manager, with this comment quoted in his 1973 rugbiography, *Meads*, written by Alex Veysey:

> Meads does not think only of Test players when he expresses his despair over the possible demise of Springbok–New Zealand rugby. What of the players who are the very heart of rugby? What of the country union players who keep the game going in areas like North Otago, South Canterbury, East Coast and, yes, King Country? To them, a match against a touring South African team is a lifetime's reward for everything they have given rugby. It is an experience to linger on over a pipe when playing days are done. No New Zealander, says Meads, would fail to be stirred

> by an epitaph which said, 'He Played Against The Springboks 1937'—nor would it cause undue surprise. But 'He Played Against Australia 1974'? . . .

Without the Springboks challenge after the 1981 tour there was nothing—seemingly—to really challenge the supremacy of New Zealand rugby. Even the series lost in 1971 to the British Lions had been avenged with (an almost) Grand Slam the following year. Luckily for New Zealand and Australian rugby, the Wallabies emerged as a compelling competitor at precisely the time the Springboks disappeared, swallowed up in the dark underworld of South African politics and international indignation over apartheid.

Throughout the 1980s a generation of New Zealand supporters and players looked naturally, inevitably—and finally—to the Wallabies as the new threat to the nation's rugby supremacy that had to be extinguished. When the talented inside centre, Lee Stensness, was brought into the All Blacks in 1992 against the Lions, he nominated as his favourite rugby memory: 'Playing for the New Zealand Colts side that thrashed Australia 61–9 in 1991'. This memory, in a sociological sense, was created back in 1982 when the All Blacks and the Wallabies in the deciding Test of the series filled Eden Park for the first time in a Bledisloe Cup Test—with 52 000 people, one of the biggest crowds to watch a rugby Test in New Zealand.

THE BATTLE BETWEEN MOURIE AND ELLA

After an invitation rugby match at Darwin at the beginning of the 1982 season the All Blacks captain, Graham Mourie, as shrewd off the field as he was on it, picked up the information from conversations over a beer with Brendan Moon, the Queensland winger, and Simon Poidevin, the New South Wales flanker, that all was not well with the Wallabies after their difficult tour of the United Kingdom some months earlier. Mourie felt sure that a number of Queensland players would drop out of the tour of New Zealand. And this was what happened. Eight or nine Queensland players (depending on the version of the story you read) made themselves 'unavailable' for the tour. The brilliant Queensland centre and later a distinguished Rugby League player, Michael O'Connor, in his rugbiography *The Best of Both Worlds* claims that there 'was talk that the Queenslanders were boycotting the tour because of the coach, Bob Dwyer, but most simply could not afford time away from work and study'.

The boycott theory, with due respect to O'Connor, makes more sense. Mourie believed that Australia's biggest loss from this defection was Brendan Moon, in his opinion 'among the world's best in the previous two years'. But with Moon unavailable the selectors cast their eyes wide across the talent in Australian rugby and came up with a teenager who had devastated the New Zealand Colts at the Sydney Cricket Ground some weeks before the touring team was selected. This teenager's performance was so electrifying with broken field running that took the breath away with its audacity and success that people like myself who saw the performance have never forgotten it. This was the day, on the curtain-raiser to the Australia v Scotland Test, that the incomparable David Ian Campese created the first of his many lasting impressions during an international rugby match. 'When someone told me I was in the touring party', Campese writes in his account of his career, *On a Wing and a Prayer*, 'I rubbished them, thinking they were having me on. Even when I read it in the newspaper, it took some time to persuade me that it wasn't a misprint.'

The defection of the Queenslanders, then, proved a benefit for Australian rugby by opening up positions to players who might not have got their chance for some years. A similar outcome occurred for New Zealand rugby in 1986 when the rebel All Blacks coming back from their tour of South Africa as Cavaliers had to stand down for two Tests. The success of the 'Baby All Blacks' against France revealed Sean Fitzpatrick, Mike Brewer, Joe Stanley and David Kirk as players of immediate Test quality.

The youngster Campese played all the 1982 Bledisloe Cup Tests (and virtually every Test for the Wallabies since), scored eight tries in nine matches and kicked four conversions and two penalties. The team itself (in an early manifestation of Bob Dwyer's gifts as a coach) scored 316 points in fourteen matches, compared with the previous best of 299 points in thirteen matches scored by the 1972 side. Although he was only 19 and without even the experience of playing in the Sydney grade competition, Campese began his Test career as he finished it—as a fearless and confident player who threw the All Blacks backline into a panic whenever he touched the ball. Dwyer likes to tell of Campese's first touch of a ball in a Test match. Campese had no support near him, so the safe thing to do was to kick for touch. Instead, he chose to take on his opposite winger Stu Wilson, a veteran of 26 Tests and at that time the leading try-scorer in Tests for the All Blacks. With a brilliant change of pace, he left Wilson stranded. In the second Test, Campese made a startling break, beating three All Blacks including that ferocious tackler Bill Osborne with, according to Evan Whitton, the most 'prodigious' sidesteps 'since Prince Obolensky, cutting back

from the right wing, spreadeagled the All Blacks at Twickenham in 1935'. The overweight Scottish referee Alan Hosie, who was left metres behind along with twelve All Blacks, ruled that Campese's pass to Andrew Slack was forward, thereby preventing the Wallabies from pulling off a famous victory.

The Test series, though, which the Wallabies lost two Tests to one, hinged on the battle between the minds and bodies of two talented and intelligent players—the All Blacks captain and openside breakaway, Graham Mourie, and the Wallabies captain and five-eighth, Mark Ella.

This account of the crucial battle of the captains is taken from Mourie's excellent rugbiography, *Captain*. Early on their tour the Wallabies played Taranaki, Mourie's provincial side. Taranaki had the Wallabies well beaten 'until a final try against the run of play by the mercurial Mark Ella'. But all was not lost for Mourie. During the game Mourie used tactics 'which confounded Ella so completely that we caught him three or four times, an absurdity given the rules of the game'.

What was Mourie's method? In *Captain* he gives a rigorous exposition of his general method as a breakaway:

> To me, the loose forward game is both an art and a science . . . The pressure which I tried to put on the first-five was extended only to the point where I was still able to remain in play should he pass the ball. If

I wanted him to pass the ball I would remain on his inside, forcing him to move the ball further out yet at the same time ensuring that I was able to take up the same position on the next ball carrier, hopefully until the centre. The basic aim of this positioning was to ensure that the backs in my side would only have one tackle to make, the easiest type, side on with the opposition going for an outside break. After the ball moved to the wing my angle of approach would alter to get me between the ball carrier and the goal-line as quickly as possible.

Mark Ella did not stay confused for long. 'While playing for an international side against New South Wales', Mourie notes laconically, 'I explained this system to a team-mate and was overheard by the Australian hooker, Bruce Malouf, who at that stage was recovering from another of his unfortunate injuries.' Malouf told Ella. Ella worked out the weakness in the Mourie system in the last minute of the game against Taranaki and scored the vital try.

Malouf now told Mourie that he had told Ella about the Mourie system. 'The next move', Mourie writes, 'was mine.'

Going into the first Test at Christchurch, I had a long talk with Murray Mexted and Mark Shaw. If as in Taranaki Ella was going to watch me and pass once he was sure of our position then we would not try and place as much direct pressure on him. We hoped he would delay his pass for a second or two to assess who was where and thus allow our backs that extra second to get up on their opposites . . . It appeared to work and we said nothing to Malouf.

In the second Test, won by the Wallabies 19–16, the Australian forwards played well and Ella was able to make some breaks. For the deciding third Test, though, after Mourie opted to play with the wind, the All Blacks had a comfortable victory, 33–18. The Wallabies scored two tries towards the end of the Test and one from Roger Gould sprinting 22 metres to the tryline outside the winger from the fullback position, into the wind, the first time the Wallaby backs handled the ball in the Test. Alan Hewson, the erratically brilliant All Blacks fullback, scored almost immediately after this, converted the try and went on to score a world record 26 points. According to Mourie the forward play of the All Blacks that day was magnificent: 'No All Blacks team which I had been associated with had played in New Zealand like that before . . . It was a satisfying and fitting end to the tour—a satisfying and fitting end to a Test career'. Mourie's satisfaction was justified. Mark Ella, who two years later scored in every Test on the 1984 Grand Slam tour, was kept tryless and the All Blacks (probably as a consequence of this victory of the loose forward captain against the five-eighth captain) won back the Bledisloe Cup from the Wallabies.

1983, AND CAMPESE KICKS HIMSELF

Should brilliant ball runners ever be given the task of kicking goals for their side? The question arises from the failure of David Campese to kick the Wallabies to victory in the one-off Bledisloe Cup Test at the Sydney Cricket Ground in 1983. The Wallabies lost 18–8 but scored two tries to one. Campese, however, kicked one penalty only from five shots at goal, most of them from handy positions. Alan Hewson, the New Zealand fullback, converted the try scored by the All Blacks and kicked four penalties. Although the All Blacks were outplayed by the Wallaby backs, with Campese at fullback in sensational form, the New Zealanders tackled tenaciously and forced penalties which Hewson converted into points.

The Wallabies' experience with Campese replicated the All Blacks' experience in the 1970s when the winger Bryan Williams, a devastating runner, and Sid Going, New Zealand's greatest running halfback, were occasionally required to be the main goal kickers in Tests. Throughout the history of the All Blacks brilliant players like Williams and Going rarely proved to be even adequate kickers in Test matches. In 1993, too, Jeff Wilson, a winger of excessive talents and the New Zealand player most likely to become New Zealand's Campese, scored three tries in his Test debut as a 20-year-old against Scotland and banged over a conversion from the sideline for good measure when the regular kicker Matthew Cooper had to leave the field. The next Saturday against England, though, when the kicking responsibilities were squarely on his shoulders, he missed kicks that should have been booted over. He was blamed, as was Campese, for 'losing' the Test.

In the early days of Test rugby the inability of brilliant players to kick goals did not matter very much. Penalties were rare. Billy Wallace, for instance, nicknamed 'Carbine' for his classy running, the first All Black to score in a Test with his opening penalty in the 1903 Test against Australia, played 51 matches for New Zealand scoring 36 tries, 114 conversions, two goals from marks, two drop goals—and nine penalties. Don Clarke, the prodigious kicker of the 1950s and 1960s for the All Blacks, a man who frequently kicked penalties from inside his own half, played 89 games for New Zealand scoring eight tries,

173 conversions, 120 penalties, 15 drop goals and two goals from a mark. Fifty or so years after Wallace, then, kickers were still kicking more conversions than penalties. But, in the 1990s, penalties have become king hits. Michael Lynagh in thirteen Tests against the All Blacks up to 1994 scored 76 points with two drop goals, nine conversions and 28 penalties, an average of 5.8 points for each Bledisloe Cup Test. Grant Fox, the game's greatest goal kicker, played twelve Tests for New Zealand against Australia scoring 112 points with four drop goals, 20 conversions and 30 penalties.

The best goal kickers, and Lynagh and Fox undoubtedly fall into this category, tend to be players who are shrewd and calm; they are backline generals who tend to kick too much in general play rather than dashing cavalry types like Campese and Wilson. Anyone who watched Fox kicking for goal realised that this pragmatic discipline required a certain nervelessness, method, steadiness, accuracy in procedure and technique. Anyone watching Campese or Wilson running with the ball will realise, as well, that the effectiveness of the running art comes from a nervy unpredictability, exuberance, the unexpected swerve or step, inspiration rather than the practised move. This generalisation is given greater authority from the experience of Lynagh who gave up goal kicking in 1993 for a while and transformed himself from a kicking five-eighth into an exuberant passing and running player. Perhaps this experience might have reversed itself for Campese if he had become a successful goal kicker. The dashing Campese might have been transmogrified into a boring kicking Campese. Fortunately, this never eventuated. As Campese remarked, boot in cheek, about his ill-fated 1983 kicking performance against the All Blacks: 'I felt like kicking myself, but I would probably have missed!'.

A Greek wrestler tells the Wallabies how to play

A few days before the third Bledisloe Cup Test between the Wallabies and the All Blacks in 1984, and not long after the second Test in which Australia squandered a 12–0 lead at Ballymore to finally lose 19–15, Jim Webster, the *Sydney Morning Herald*'s rugby writer, came up to my desk and put a tape cassette on it. 'You should listen to this, mate', he said. The tape was a recording of a press conference given that morning by the new Wallabies coach, Alan Jones. Towards the end of the conference one of the journalists asked Jones: 'Have you read that article in the *Sydney Morning Herald* about the Wallabies blowing the second Test?'. Jones has been a schoolteacher, has academic qualifications from Oxford University, was a highly-rated tennis player as a youngster, and was a speechwriter for Malcolm Fraser when he was prime minister of Australia (and is credited with giving his boss the line from G. B. Shaw's *Man and Superman*, 'Life isn't meant to be easy'). He had coached the Manly club side to a premiership victory over the dominant Randwick club in 1983 and later became a controversial and popular radio broadcaster, glorying in the reputation of chopping opponents off at the knees with the sharpness of his tongue. There was a moment's silence on the tape and then Jones's clipped reply: 'That fellow with a name like a Russian wrestler? We don't take any notice of people like him'.

The Greek 'Russian wrestler' had written a long and analytical piece pointing out that Jones was embarking on an historic mission to change the traditional Australian approach to rugby strategy:

> Alan Jones's attitude runs counter to the traditional Australian approach of letting the backs have their heads . . . For he is determined on a profound reorientation of the Australian style, making it more international (more like the British and New Zealand styles) and less Australian . . . The All Blacks at Sydney in the first Test were startled when Australia, unexpectedly, took them on in the forwards. On the day, Australia were clearly superior and better coached, using short lineouts to devastating effect. There is nothing intrinsically new in this. Des Connor almost stole a Test in Brisbane in 1968 with short lineouts. But it is a trick that cannot be played often. At Ballymore the All Blacks used short lineouts themselves and crushed the Australian ones quite easily.

The article then went on to make the point that the safety-first rugby propounded by Jones was 'paradoxically, a high risk way of winning . . . In Sydney, although Australia were overwhelmingly on top most of the game, the match was not sewn up until Brendan Moon's last-minute try. Theoretically, the outplayed All Blacks could have won, if luck had turned for them, until that moment'.

I made the point, too, that in the Ballymore Test the All Blacks were twelve points down early on in the match, six of the points coming from a drop goal attempt by Mark Ella in which the ball hit the post and bounced allowing him to run on, catch it and score an easy try. Instead of the Wallabies trying to extend this huge margin the backs, particularly Michael Hawker at inside centre, repeatedly kicked the ball downfield. Jones's only criticism of this tactic was that the kicks should have been directed to the corners and not down the middle of the field. He supported the kicking tactics even though the All Blacks, with Robbie Deans at fullback and Mike Clamp and Craig

Green on the wings, began to run the ball back at the Wallabies with some success. This was in marked contrast to the Australian backs who, under Jones's 'evangelical coaching style', looked to be scared of making a mistake. My article finished with this comment: 'When Jones sent out a message towards the end of the Ballymore Test to "run it from anywhere," the lack of confidence developed under Jones's fierce devotion to disciplined play saw Andrew Slack throw a panicky pass along his goal-line, thereby setting up the All Blacks try'.

A critic was described by the 18th century poet Alexander Pope as a 'man without legs who teaches others how to run'. But sometimes a critic does see things that the practitioner either does not see, will not see or does not want others to see. There is no doubt that Jones's safety-first pattern, reinforced with zealous oratory, contributed to the Wallabies' losing the Bledisloe Cup series in 1984 two Tests to one (16–9, 15–19, 24–25), when they should have won the series after the second Test. Two years later, though, the Jones Method of big forwards, pressure, playing for position, rehearsed moves inside the opposition's 22 and Michael Lynagh kicking the goals gave the side an historic Bledisloe Cup triumph in New Zealand—the sweetest of all victories for a Wallabies team and its coach. Not even a Russian wrestler could quibble about such a victory.

One point in it

Before most Tests the television commentators give their assessment of how the match will work out. When they are asked 'Who will win?' (a stupid question as the Test is being played to find this fact out, surely) the commentators invariably take the easy and understandable option and talk about a 'close match' with only 'a point or so in it'. The television commentators aren't to be blamed.

Predictions about rugby matches can be perilous to the reputation. Greg Growden, the *Sydney Morning Herald*'s rugby writer, likes to give an exact points prediction. Before the Australia v Manu Samoa Test in 1994 he suggested an Australian victory by 'three points'. The final score was 73–3. He reminded his readers that his call was only out by 70 points when two weeks later he predicted in the *Herald*, almost exactly, that the Wallabies would defeat the All Blacks by three points.

A 'one point in it' call for the 1985 one-off Bledisloe Cup Test at Eden Park would have been vindicated. Before the Test there was an ominous incident. The NZRU had announced that the All Blacks would tour South Africa the next month. Legal action, on the grounds that the tour was 'against the best interests of rugby', was initiated. The action proved to be successful but this was not known at the time of the Test. Before the kickoff, a spectator rushed out on to the field and was arrested, kicking and heaving in the grasp of the police. During the first half of the match, too, spectators were asked to remain calm while police blew up several suspicious objects behind the main stand.

On the field, the game was not quite as explosive. Hard, relentless Test match rugby was being played between two well-coached (Brian Lochore and Alan Jones) and talented teams. The Wallabies, trying to exploit Steve Cutler's wonderful jumping ability in the lineout and Tommy Lawton's accurate throwing, tended to kick deep down the field and force the New Zealanders to kick for touch and give away the lineout throw. In his account of the Test Phil Wilkins described the opening minute of the second half, with New Zealand leading 6–3, in this way:

> Australia began the second half furiously when Mexted, New Zealand's number 8, failed to clear the ball from within his own 22. Farr-Jones made two breaks, one of which almost led to Steve Cutler plunging over for a try. Then when Farr-Jones knocked the ball behind him, he managed to retrieve the ball, which swept along the backline until James Black surged over in a mass of tacklers for the first try. Lynagh converted from the right and Australia led 9–6 after 41 minutes.

With about fifteen minutes left for play, the All Blacks were awarded a penalty inside their half. The Wallabies wandered back into their own half to where they thought a lineout, following the penalty kick, would be taken. But what's this? David Kirk, the clever New Zealand halfback, quickly tapkicks the ball and rushes downfield. He passes to Jock Hobbs, the alert openside flanker, who draws the fullback and passes to the winger Craig Green who cruises towards the Wallaby tryline to score an unexpected, inventive, crushing and matchwinning try. Kieran Crowley, the New Zealand fullback, who missed six out of eight shots at goal, several of them from handy positions, missed the conversion. Near the end of the Test David Codey won a lineout for the Wallabies inside the New Zealand 22 and Michael Lynagh, trying to capitalise on the possession and win the Test, just missed with his dropkick at goal.

For the second successive Test the All Blacks had managed to retain the Bledisloe Cup with a one-point winning margin. The first one-point Test in New Zealand–Australia matches was in 1929, the clean-sweep series for the Wallabies, with an Australian victory at the Sydney Cricket Ground of 9–8. The famous 'Penalty Try Test' at Ballymore in 1968 resulted in a 19–18 victory to the All Blacks. The first Test at Wellington in 1978 saw the All Blacks winning 13–12, with Ken Wright missing a penalty attempt from near touch right on time. Then, from the third Test in 1984 through to the second Test in 1986, four successive Bledisloe Cup Tests were decided by a one-point margin (25–24 and 10–9 to New Zealand, 13–12 to Australia, 13–12 to New Zealand). One point separated the two teams once more in the first Test of the pulsating 1992 series, with the Wallabies winning 16–15.

The Wallaby coach, Alan Jones, always voluble, put the 1985 one-point defeat down to an apparent Wallabies death wish in the face of the All Blacks. 'We surrendered the opportunities to win', he fumed. He was horrified at the poor tactical kicking, the erratic goal-kicking and the 'inexcusable' lapse which allowed Craig Green to score the matchwinning try.

'NOW I CAN LIVE IN PEACE'

In his study of New Zealand's search for national identity, *A Destiny Apart*, Auckland historian the late Professor Keith Sinclair summed up the ambivalent feelings New Zealanders have for Australians in this way: 'There is a wry blend of rivalry and inferiority as well as a compensatory superiority, strongly sibling'. By 1986, though, in the rugby context, the wryness had turned to an intense, parochial and unforgiving hostility. Greg Growden, who covered the 1986 tour of New Zealand by Alan Jones's Wallabies for the *Sydney Morning Herald*, was struck during the tour by the persistence of the anti-Australia jokes on radio talkback programs. He felt that, although he was only an Australian journalist doing his job, a certain loathing was directed even at him because he was in some way connected with the Wallabies and, anyway, because he was an Australian. On one occasion in a small New Zealand town he approached a female bank teller and was asked: 'You an Aussie?'. Growden said: 'That's right'. 'I'm not serving you', she replied. 'I'm going to take my lunch now.'

The Wallabies reacted to this intense and unremitting hostility by retreating to the community of the team and dreaming of making up for the unpleasantness they were being subjected to by defeating the All Blacks. Against the 'Baby All Blacks' (a team selected with none of the players who had just returned from the Cavaliers tour to South Africa in it) the Wallabies struggled (unexpectedly) in the forwards, but held on to a one-point margin for the last ten minutes of the Test into a stiff Wellington wind. The young New Zealand pack, after competing successfully for possession for 70 minutes, lacked the strength, expertise and experience to win a couple of lineouts so that field position deep inside the Wallaby half could be established.

With the Cavalier All Blacks available for the second and third Tests, the Wallabies believed that their best hope of winning their first Bledisloe Cup series in New Zealand since 1949 lay in overcoming the full-strength All Blacks in the next Test at the Carisbrook ground, Dunedin. Again it was a 13–12 result. But this time the All Blacks were the side that clung like men on flotsam after a shipwreck to the slenderest of leads.

The Wallabies' changing room after the Test resounded to cries and tears of rage, frustration and bitterness. Alan Jones publicly identified David Campese (the tryscoring master) as playing a 'horror of a game'. There was no public criticism, though, of Michael Lynagh, a Jones favourite, even though pressure from the All Blacks flanker Jock Hobbs had made him uncertain whether to pass or kick. The result of this indecision was that the Wallaby backs, all of them—and not just Campese—played horribly. Lynagh also missed a relatively easy penalty goal kick just before halftime which would have made the score 13–6 to New Zealand.

The Wallabies were convinced that the referee, Derek Bevan of Wales, had cost them the game when he disallowed a 'try' by Steve Tuynman which would have levelled the score and allowed Lynagh a conversion attempt on a spot from which minutes later he kicked a penalty goal. Evan Whitton in the *Sydney Morning Herald*, though, provided a characteristically acute analysis of the incident which put the Wallaby whining into a proper context:

> A frame-by-frame examination of the tape indicates that Mr Bevan was certainly in error, but not for the reasons stated. Before Tuynman got to the line, he handed the ball to Jeff Miller, who was in front of him, and then took it back. The play should have been stopped there, for the forward pass. As for the 'try' itself, the Australians would have done more for their reputations as sportsmen if, instead of whinging, they had applauded All Black winger Craig Green for a piece of in-goal play so wonderfully clever that one has to go back to the 50s for its equivalent. Nick Shehadie, in South Africa in 1953, and Muncher Hughes in Brisbane in 1956, calmly plucked the ball out of the hands of a Springbok in the act of placing a try, and placed it themselves for a five-yard scrum. Marvellous reflexes, those lads. On this occasion, the frames clearly show

that Green, wrestling Tuynman as they went over the line, managed to get his right hand on the ball. Tuynman thus placed the ball on the palm of Green's hand, and not on the turf.

One Test all, then, and the decider at Eden Park. Whitton, observant as ever, told his readers before this Test that he fancied the Wallabies to win 'because for the first time on tour they have generated a bit of momentum. They also appear to have the advantage at the lineout, and they finished stronger in the second Test'. By contrast, the 1982 Wallabies, who also had a Bledisloe Cup series-decider in a third Test at Eden Park, had lost on the Saturday and Wednesday before this match to Counties (15–9) and Bay of Plenty (40–16). Whitton was also encouraged by the recall to the All Blacks of Mark 'Cowboy' Shaw, to the blindside of the scrum:

> His return hints at a degree of desperation, as if the All Blacks take the view that coming the knuckle and the slipper may be their only hope. The eight Australian survivors of the 1982 tour will recall that it was the Cowboy who lost the Wellington Test by inadvertently breaking a bone in Duncan Hall's back. With Hall off the field the All Blacks risked, for once, a backline movement but this resulted, after one of the great counter-attacks in international history, in a try to Campese.

Greg Growden in an interview with Alan Jones on the eve of the Test found the Wallaby coach, who was reading David Stockman's *The Triumph of Politics*, confident of victory. 'There is an element of arrogance in the team now', he told Growden. 'There is a deep reservoir of resentment and they felt denied after the second Test. It haunts them and this has to be purged. Still, they are so relaxed about it. We have spoken so often. There is nothing left to do but win.'

With journalists, like historians (and coaches), inclined to be prophets of the past, these comments of Jones and Whitton—before the Test—were remarkably perceptive. At a lunch before the 1994 Bledisloe Cup Test—Alan Jones deconstructed the Wallabies' victory in the 1986 Eden Park Test in much the same way as Whitton's prematch analysis. The All Blacks, he said, played a whirlwind, almost maniacal ball-in-hand game in the opening half hour. But with Mark Shaw mainly effective close to the line from lineouts, Jones knew that what breaks would be made by the All Blacks would not be completed with a try. His coaching instructions to the Wallabies, therefore, were for them to expect and endure an opening onslaught and then to strike when they established field position inside the New Zealand quarter. This game plan almost came unstuck when a ferocious New Zealand attack set the powerful hooker Hika Reid storming towards the Wallabies line only to be stopped in his tracks by a shoulder-driving tackle by Enrique Rodriquez. Jones, enjoying the memory of that moment and not knowing what was to come later that day with George Gregan's famous tackle, peered into the dimmed lighting of the dining room from his speaker's podium and said: 'Stand up Enrique . . . He's somewhere here today'. And when the still burly, smiling Rodriquez stood up and raised his arms in triumph to the applause of the audience, Jones called out: 'The man who made the tackle that saved the Bledisloe Cup for the Wallabies!'.

Touring is a fantasy world where young men are thrown together to pursue the magnificent nonsense of beating another group of young men in a game of chasing a ball around a big field in front of tens of thousands of spectators. A claustrophobic atmosphere within the team is developed where the Holy Grail of a Test series victory becomes the only important matter in a person's life. Small things, if they are related to rugby, become matters of life and death. Life-and-death matters, if they are not related to rugby, become irrelevancies. Simon Poidevin, a player of passion and commitment, has given a vivid account of how dominating the emotions can be for a touring player when a Bledisloe Cup series victory—sweet, sweet victory—has been achieved in New Zealand. In his autobiography (written with Jim Webster), *For Love Not Money*, he says:

> I remember that very day before we ran out onto Eden park. The walls of the dressing-rooms have louvre windows between the players and the public outside. The locals know that, and the rude and barbed jibes that drifted through as we prepared for that deciding Test worked better than a blow-torch to the stomach to get us stirred up for that conflict. As I recall, there wasn't much noise coming from outside those windows about 4.45 that afternoon.
>
> Then again, we probably wouldn't have heard it. The dressing-room was packed with people, there were television lights and photographic flashes, Jonesy was running around shouting hoarsely (who ever thought he'd be hoarse) that this was '. . . bigger than Quo Vadis,' we had our arms around each other, singing and congratulating ourselves, and every now and again you'd be passed the massive Bledisloe Cup, take a swig of champers from it, and pass it on. Here we were deep in enemy territory, and we were the champions. We were absolutely racked with exhaustion, but it's remarkable what that euphoria did for all those aches and pains . . . Amidst all the dressing-room din, in walked Brian Lochore, the All Black coach. This was akin to Rommel suddenly appearing in the doorway of Monty's headquarters at El Alamein. But Brian's big in humility as well as size. The noise quietened in his presence. Then, choosing his words carefully, he warmly congratulated Australia on the way they had played . . . As Brian spoke, I could see the great sadness in his eyes and I felt very sorry for him, for it was [only] the fourth time

Simon Poidevin

> this century the All Blacks had lost a series at home and he was going to bear the brunt of that humiliation . . . A tour of New Zealand is where the commitment to the game of Rugby is more intense and the basic principles of winning and losing are honed more sharply than anywhere else on earth. Therefore, winning a series there is the ultimate in terms of pure footballing satisfaction. I remember Greg Growden from the *Sydney Morning Herald* asking me that afternoon in the Eden Park dressing-room what winning that 1986 series meant. I replied: 'Now I can live in peace.' It meant that much to me.

Later that evening, the Wallabies were at an Auckland club indulging in a happy-hour before the official dinner. Then it was time to move the huge Bledisloe Cup into the dining room. One of the players looked at the Cup and said to Greg Growden: 'After that game you've gotta be kidding. I wouldn't be able to lift it'. Other players told Growden how they felt like collapsing at halftime, so frenetic had been the pace of the game. One player began retching after a few lineouts. A reserve, Greg Burrows, took the wooden base of the Bledisloe Cup, another player took the silver top and, as Growden reported on the Monday for the *Sydney Morning Herald*, 'since there was no one left, I had to carry the Cup. It was an eerie moment . . . walking through the club, cheered by hundreds of New Zealanders, when the Cup came into view, shaking it above my head in triumph, with everyone wondering who this unknown prima donna was in spectacles and a speckled suit. I wasn't about to admit anything, relishing the moment while it lasted'.

For Growden (in a small way), but especially for the players and officials who made up the wonderful 1986 Wallabies, the experience of winning the Bledisloe Cup in a dramatic match, in New Zealand, after the heartbreak of a Test loss they felt shouldn't have been recorded, produced the vast sense of relief and accomplishment expressed by Simon Poidevin. Demons had been expelled, something extraordinary had been achieved, they knew they had been touched with greatness: 'Now I can live in peace'.

1987: Fitzpatrick's Match

A general rule about great players, no matter what sport they play, is that they always have plenty of time to do what they want to do. They make what they are doing look so simple that a spectator watching them thinks: 'I can do that'. The Roman poet Virgil summed up this characteristic, of great players or practitioners having space and time and 'vision' while all the players around them appear to be stressed and harassed, in the aphorism *Arts celare artem* (True art is to hide art). With great rugby players, this seeming artlessness is utilised to have a dynamic impact on the flow of a game. A great rugby player makes his position the key position on the field. And this is what Sean Fitzpatrick, a relatively young international player and the son of an All Black, did in the one-off Bledisloe Cup Test in Sydney in 1987.

Ron Palenski, an informed New Zealand journalist, made Fitzpatrick's devastating play from the unlikely position of hooker in this Test the lead in his match report:

> All Blacks hookers are supposed to keep their heads down and their other parts up and grind away in a rugby match so the fancy loose forwards or backs score tries. But Sean Fitzpatrick, the 24-year-old Aucklander, who has grabbed every chance offered in the game, spurned the traditions but delighted New Zealanders when he scored the first and last tries in their 30–16 Bledisloe Cup win over Australia in Sydney on Saturday . . . He became the first hooker to score two tries in a Test for the All Blacks and in doing so also scored more tries for his country than his father,

> midfielder Brian, managed as an All Black . . . It was Wallaby desperation that led to Fitzpatrick's first try. The Wallabies won a lineout ball but it was slightly spoiled by the All Blacks and Nick Farr-Jones did well to scramble it away to Stephen James. His inexperience—on this and other occasions—told and he sliced his defensive kick to touch so badly that it lobbed into the long arms of Murray Pierce, from whom Fitzpatrick took it and scored . . . A similar Australian mistake on defence led to a kick ahead from David Kirk going astray. Wayne Shelford drove on as he did all day and Fitzpatrick out on the right wing picked up the pass for the final try that made it 30–16.

THE GREATEST RUGBY TEAM OF ALL TIME

Sean Fitzpatrick's tries were no accident. With the loss of the Bledisloe Cup and then a thrashing and a whacking for the All Blacks from a clenched-fisted French side at Nantes, 1986 was another *annus horribilis* for New Zealand rugby. At the end of that year the New Zealand selectors (chairman and coach Brian Lochore, John Hart, the creator of the formidable Auckland machine, and Alex Wyllie, the creator of an excellent Canterbury side which in 1986 defeated Alan Jones's Wallabies 30–10) sat down and decided that the future for the All Blacks lay in playing an aggressive, skilful and fast game in the forwards and an intelligent pacy game in the backs. With this blueprint in mind, they selected a side not necessarily of the best players in their positions but of the best players in New Zealand to play the expansive game they had decided on playing.

John Gallagher, an Englishman who had come to New Zealand as a centre, was selected as fullback; John Kirwan and Terry Wright, one a physical and determined close-range tryscorer and the other a whippet-fast finisher, were the wingers; Joe Stanley, a player of strength in the tackle and on the tackle and with exquisite timing in his passing, and John Schuster, a stepper and darter, were the centres; Grant Fox, brainy, cool and a winner, was the backline organiser (and a world-class goal kicker) at five-eighth; Bruce Deans was a tough and hardworking link between the forwards and the backs at halfback. The front row of Steve McDowell, Richard Loe and Sean Fitzpatrick was powerful, bloodyminded and fast around the field; Gary Whetton was the best number two lineout jumper in the world and dynamic in the loose with the ball in his hand, while Murray Pierce was a strong spoiler in the middle of the lineout: Alan Whetton developed the blindside breakaway position to levels of jumping, covering, tackling

Wayne Shelford

and taking the ball up that had not been expressed before; Michael Jones on the openside was rated by the English rugby writer, John Reason, as the finest rugby player he'd seen in 30 years of reporting on the game; at number eight was Wayne Shelford forever slamming the ball shoulder-hunched across the advantage line and being inspirational as a captain. There is a wonderful Maori word mana (meaning pride, achievement, standing, leadership and success) that sums up Shelford's position as captain. In big and little things he had mana. The All Blacks under him expressed the team's mana, too, by doing the haka in the authentic manner.

From the beginning of 1987 through to the end of 1990 the heart of this marvellous team, the greatest rugby team of all time, put together to win the inaugural Rugby World Cup (which it did easily), was undefeated for 50 matches and for over 20 Tests, a record that surpasses the previous record of 16 undefeated Tests achieved by Fred Allen's All Blacks in the late 1960s. The team's two Test victories against Wales in 1988 provided remarkable evidence of its capacity to destroy opponents. In beating Wales 52–3 the All Blacks scored ten tries. To put this into perspective, this was only the second time that ten tries had been scored in a major Test. The last time was in 1912 when the Grand Slam Springboks defeated Ireland. The All Blacks' second Test victory against Wales, 54–9, represented the highest score ever recorded up to that time against a major rugby nation in a Test. Simon Poidevin, in *For Love Not Money*, put Shelford's team into the perspective of someone who had had to play against the side:

> When I'm talking rugby with my grandkids 40 years from now I will more than likely suggest that this was the finest national Rugby team of my time . . . This was a truly great team, immensely powerful in set pieces and at the ruck and maul, with Grant Fox one of the deadliest goalkickers in the game's history, and a backline with much more incisiveness than the All Blacks had ever had before . . . this particular team that won the inaugural World Cup simply couldn't be faulted on any count. It came as close to Rugby perfection as anything I've ever seen . . .

Poidevin came up against this perfect team for the first time in a remarkable game of the 1988 tour of Australia when the All Blacks played Randwick, the famous Galloping Greens, the perennial premiership winners in the Sydney club competition. The atmosphere that afternoon at Coogee Oval, Randwick's home ground, was like that in one of those intense Welsh mining towns on rugby day. The crowd surrounded the field. People took vantage points ('the Mark Ella Stand') in the apartments overlooking the ends of the ground and even in the steep street that provided views from the city end. There was a fervour among the onlookers, a sense that their team might beat the great All Blacks. A spectator jammed in beside me, though, exclaimed involuntarily when the All Blacks ran out on to the field: 'Jeez, they're huge'.

But Randwick was not overawed by the occasion. Almost from the kickoff David Campese was brought into the backline from fullback on one of Randwick's trademark intricate moves involving dummy runs and switch passing—and suddenly there was Campese swooping through a gap to be tackled only metres away from the tryline. 'When Lloyd Walker scored our first try wide out early in the game', Poidevin remembers, 'the crowd went beserk.'

> I thought I was dreaming. But then Grant Fox knocked over a field goal and some penalty goals and the All Blacks slowly pushed ahead. Yet we were really frustrating and angering them, and that was never more evident than when I infiltrated their side of a maul and grabbed the ball. Well, their skipper Wayne Shelford went beserk, grabbed me in a vicious headlock and tried to reef my head off while my arms were pinned. He held on for so long that I lost my breath and almost passed out. When the maul finally broke up I'd even temporarily lost my voice . . . In the end we were beaten 25–9 but it was one of the most courageous contests I've been associated with in my whole Rugby career. A team of virtual unknowns challenging the All Blacks and taking them right to the wire.

Randwick did so well against the All Blacks—being more competitive than the Wallabies were in the first Test (32–7) and the third Test (30–9) but not the second at Ballymore where the All Blacks had to come back from being well behind to force a 19–19 draw—that Shelford insisted that never again, never ever again, would the All Blacks play Randwick or any other club side during a tour of Australia.

On this tour of Australia the 1988 All Blacks in all their matches scored 476 points and had only 96 points scored against them. Driving the team, particularly in the forwards, was Shelford—'Buck'—a nickname that came from his schooldays ironically when he was 'as skinny as a buck'. The forwards, particularly, were relentless, clever and cruel. Peter FitzSimons, a successful journalist even when he was playing for the Wallabies as a robust secondrower, gave this vivid description of what it was like playing against them in representative sides that conceded 126 points in two matches:

> In an upright position and pushing against the New Zealanders in the rucks and maul one sees their feet whirring around, spitting the mud out behind them. Fall into that maelstrom and it feels like you were caught tying your shoelaces when the bulls of Pamplona passed through . . . The All Black forwards might often be described as 'a machine' but there's always a lot of communication going on between them. Not only the fairly standard 'Drive it!' and 'Take it up!' but often the more specific calls of 'Here's the ball,' 'Rip his hands off it,' 'Roll it left,' and 'Get him!' . . . Overall, a unique experience, if not altogether as pleasant as taking tea in the sun. With plenty of milk in it.

An observer with an obvious interest in the way these All Blacks played was Bob Dwyer. Dwyer's greatness as a coach lies in his razorsharp mind, the wealth of rugby information in it (over 1000 pieces of specific intelligence about such matters as how a lineout jumper should place his feet for, say, a short hard catch, he has reckoned) and his penchant for pointed, unromantic analysis of his own team and the opposition. This ability to read the game is highlighted in his excellent rugbiography, *The Winning Way*, where he has a profound section on the way the All Blacks play:

> Another great feature . . . is their ability to apply pressure at their opponents' most vulnerable point. They are very quick to identify a weakness in their opposition, and thereafter they will attack that weakness remorselessly. It's rather like a crack in the dam wall. The pressure becomes more and more intense until the dam bursts. This is what the All Blacks do—they burst through the crack in the opposition's defences with an enormous surge of manpower. My recollection of this goes back to Fred Allen's great All Blacks teams of the 1960s. I can see in my memory a black avalanche descending on some hapless player, and at the front of

the avalanche is Waka Nathan, the 'Black Panther.' Conversely, the All Blacks are more adept at hiding and protecting their own weaknesses than any team I know. Often we have identified a New Zealand player we considered not quite up to standard, but invariably supported by his team-mates, he has played well. Kieran Crowley is a good example. We have looked at Crowley and agreed among ourselves that he was a little on the slow side and that we should be able to take advantage of this, but invariably he has come out and played a fine game. In fact, I believe he played an important part in New Zealand's two victories against us in 1990.

With Evan Whitton retired and teaching journalism in Queensland, I offered myself (while continuing to write editorials) as his successor as the *Sydney Morning Herald*'s expert rugby analyst. My selling point to the Sports Editor was that all New Zealanders (I am a New Zealander) know, as if by instinct, the best practice and the best theory of rugby. My offer was accepted and my first Test analysis for the paper was on the first Bledisloe Cup Test at Sydney in 1988.

Bob Dwyer, returned as the Wallaby coach after the high achievements of Alan Jones's regime turned sour in Argentina, laid some of the blame for his team's overwhelming defeat on the rotund referee Fred Howard. After noting that the five-tries-to-one margin to the All Blacks was as decisive as any Test can be, I added: 'Bringing Howard into the discussion is a bit like Michael Spinks blaming the referee for Mike Tyson hitting him too hard'. The problem with the Wallabies, along with having to confront a mighty team, was that they 'played too closely to the old Alan Jones style of obsessive reliance on field position by use of the kick into touch'. I went on:

> The Randwick game of running the ball at the All Blacks' inside backs was, for some inexplicable reason, never utilised . . . It was noticeable that Fox kicked for touch only within his own 22. His other kicks (even penalties) were offensive in intention, high and in the field of play to force the maul and the next attack.

The technical excellence of the New Zealand team, which when matched with its intensity to win made it unbeatable, was revealed by the lineout statistics I compiled: 'On my reckoning, the All Blacks won the lineouts 21–9. But more importantly, whereas Australia won only two lineouts of the 18 the New Zealanders threw in, the All Blacks won five of the 12 Australian throws'.

After the third Test, which ended with John Kirwan (who had played all over and through David Campese in the series) scoring a galloping tearaway try after a lightning-strike run from the side of the maul by Michael Jones, the Wallaby coach Bob Dwyer appeared to be mentally and physically exhausted. But he told Greg Growden that he was not all that pessimistic: 'The dawn will definitely be brighter in a couple of months'.

BLACK IS NOT ALWAYS BEAUTIFUL

One of the curious aspects of the 1988 All Blacks, who were unbeaten on their tour of Australia, was the remarkable number of penalties they conceded. Take these statistics, for instance:

Score: All Blacks 60 – Western Australia 3
Rucks and mauls: All Blacks 39 – Western Australia 7
Tightheads: All Blacks 10 – Western Australia 0
Penalties: All Blacks 6 – Western Australia 7

And what about these penalty statistics?

Australia B 12 – All Blacks 6 (match score NZ 28–4)
New South Wales Country 15 – All Blacks 5 (match score NZ 29–4)
Wallabies 14 – All Blacks 6 (match score NZ 32–7)

When the All Blacks actually won the penalty count against Queensland 12–9 (match score NZ 27–12), Evan Whitton in the *Sydney Morning Herald* felt that the referee 'all but blew the Queenslanders off the field'. The puzzle is how can a side be so dominant in every phase of a match and still lose so many penalty counts? Australia wasn't the only country where the penalty jinx worked against the All Blacks. In 1983 when they toured the United Kingdom they were penalised 165 times in eight games. Their opponents were penalised 75 times.

Why were the All Blacks winning everything except the penalties?

One explanation is that the penalty counts tend to favour the home side. This is true in Tests also, even in the days of neutral referees. During 1988 a former Welsh international referee, Corris Thomas examined every international rugby match that had been played in the previous 40 years. He found that when the away team has scored fewer tries it has won through penalties only eight times in more than 700 matches. This explains, perhaps, adverse penalty counts against the All Blacks on tour. But the curious matter of the adverse penalty count against the All Blacks is made curiouser by the fact that, even when playing in New Zealand, the All Blacks tend to give up more penalties than they are granted. Why is this? Given the discipline that the All Blacks traditionally play with there is no logical answer to the question. Perhaps there is an 'illogical answer'.

A New Zealand journalist, Joseph Romanos, investigated this matter and discovered what could be the explanation. Romanos cited research done in the United States by two psychologists, Thomas Gilovich and Mark Frank, at Cornell University. They studied penalty counts from 1970 and 1985 of five American Football teams and five professional hockey teams whose uniforms were predominantly black. They found that these teams—like the All Blacks—were penalty-prone. They also found, however, that when two of the hockey teams, the Pittsburg Penguins and the Vancouver Canucks, changed their jerseys from white to black their penalty counts jumped by 50 per cent.

The colour bar theory may make sense. When the All Blacks (30) played Scotland (3) in the World Cup quarter-final in 1987 at Eden Park, wearing white jerseys as the home side in deference to Scotland's traditional dark blue, the penalty count was 14–14, one of the better penalty results achieved by an All Blacks side.

Gilovich and Frank explained, according to Romanos, that 'bad guys wear black'. This is certainly true of the hired killer of the Wild West and Darth Vader. Referees, the two psychologists say, 'are more likely to characterise aggressive players as malicious when players wear black'. Hence the adverse penalty counts against the All Blacks, perhaps?

Balancing this out, though, is the other finding that 'after a while black aggressiveness has an effect on the opposition'. The All Blacks, therefore, wear black and retain an intimidating image which wins them many games even before they go on to the field. The disadvantage, which history suggests has been absorbed without too much impact on the flow of victories, is that All Blacks sides, just because of their all black outfit, will have to cop the adverse penalty counts.

THE ROTTWEILERS

After the All Blacks destroyed Wales in the 1988 season Clem Thomas, the respected rugby writer, described the two-Test annihilation this way: 'It was like chihuahuas against rottweilers'. As the overwhelming Test victories mounted up, awed journalists began to see a divinity about Wayne Shelford's All Blacks. Writing for *The Australian*, for example, Jeff Wells claimed:

> They are not, as a band of the fanatics who worship them suggested in a banner, 15 BLACK GODS. Mostly white men known as All Blacks, they are only the chosen high priests of the religion of rugby union as it is practised by our southern neighbours . . . Before the game I had asked the ayatollah himself, the New Zealand coach, Alex Wyllie, about the religious tag that New Zealand rugby has been given in explanation of the fact that an island nation of 3.5 million people can put on to a paddock a 15-man combination of eerie invincibility. The question had to be asked because there have been reverential whispers that this particular team, which so recently humiliated and crucified the proud Welsh, may be the mightiest which, over a span of a century, any of the world's 100-odd rugby playing nations has been able to let loose to pillage and plunder. 'I wouldn't say it was a religion,' Wyllie said, nodding his great, wise head, 'but I would say that in New Zealand more people play rugby than go to church.'

The mark of the greatness of the All Blacks of this era is that when the Wallabies were defeated (24–12) by the large margin of 12 points in the 1989 one-off Bledisloe Cup Test at Eden Park, the headline in the Sydney *Sun-Herald* was: HEROIC AUSSIES. Bob Dwyer, in a stroke of genius, introduced into the Wallabies a teenager from the Queensland B team, the centre Tim Horan; a converted flanker and at the time obscure frontrower, Tony Daly; and the Randwick second-grade hooker Phil Kearns. All three newcomers played with passion and effectiveness. Joe Stanley went into the Wallabies dressing room after the Test and gave his All Blacks jersey to Tim Horan as a gesture of respect for the quality of the game played by the youngster. Daly, according to the match report of Phil Wilkins, had 'exceptional mobility and began driving in and scrummaging far more virulently through the second half'. And Kearns was 'all heart and action.' Nursing a black eye and a broken hand, Kearns said after the match: 'It was every bit as hard as I imagined'.

The Wallabies had run into a strong wind in the first half and, with the score 12–6 to the All Blacks at halftime, there were hopes in the Australian camp of a stunning upset when they played with the wind. But Grant Fox with four penalty goals and two conversions from two tries registered his 300th point for the All Blacks in Test rugby, the fastest ever achieved, and made sure that the lead was always in the comfort zone. The All Blacks with four minutes left in the Test won a lineout near the Australian line and swung the ball wide towards the left wing. From there it was driven towards the Australian posts in a series of ramlike runs before the prop Richard Loe with his Manchu emperor moustache crashed over for a try, his arm raised in triumph.

Rottweilers insist on having the last bite.

There comes a time for every team, especially a great side, when the essential characteristics on which its strength is built are turned into caricatures that make it vulnerable. The strengths are perverted into weaknesses. The physicality of the great All Blacks side had by 1990 turned into a surly viciousness. Peter FitzSimons found the New Zealand pack too eager to become involved in altercations: 'Playing the All Blacks is like being in an out-of-control washing machine with 100 football boots'. The patterned play in the backs, the slick moves that cut opposition backlines to pieces, became predictable. The team began to play its rugby by numbers. So predictable were the moves, in fact, that the Wallabies were able to call them out before the All Blacks put them on. And the leadership of the team, so vibrant and forthright when Wayne Shelford was unchallenged as the captain, became a source of weakness when he was replaced by Gary Whetton. Whetton was a great player but he was not regarded as a man of mana as Shelford had been. The coach Alex Wyllie, too, seemed to be unable to reinvigorate the All Blacks with new ideas or new personnel.

The great side was going through the motions of being a great, dominating team. For the first two Tests in the 1990 Bledisloe Cup series this was enough. In the second Test at Auckland, after a 21–6 win at Christchurch, the All Blacks virtually strolled through to a 27–17 victory. The Wallabies did not believe they could defeat the All Blacks and because of this allowed themselves to be beaten. In the 48th minute of the Test the All Blacks forced a five-metre scrum near the Australian tryline. The Wallabies expected the All Blacks to use a move called 'Butcher', which sees the ball being passed to John Kirwan who then takes the tackle and offloads to the halfback doubling around him. A try was scored in the Bledisloe Cup Test in Dunedin in 1986 using this move, which is designed to utilise the strength of Kirwan whose family ran several butcher shops. Tim Gavin, the Wallaby number eight, disengaged as soon as the ball was fed into the scrum so that he could cover Kirwan and wrap him up in a ball-and-all tackle. The All Blacks, sensing a weakened Wallaby shove, kept the ball in their scrum and drove over for a pushover try. This was one occasion on which the Wallabies failed to anticipate an All Blacks move.

After the Test, even though the victory meant that the Bledisloe Cup had been retained, Greg Growden reported in the *Sydney Morning Herald* that the New Zealand coach Alex Wyllie and the captain Gary

Whetton 'received little recognition of their triumph from the large media contingent during a lengthy press conference. It was as if there could be no other conclusion, and Australia were just the latest forgotten dancing partner'. There was a desultory acknowledgment by Wyllie that the All Blacks had to consolidate their scrum and reduce the lost ball in the rucks. But winning had become a bad habit. The team had played at three-quarter pace. Grant Fox, who converted all three tries, kicked two penalties from two shots and dropped a goal from his only attempt, had added a flattering gloss to the score. The All Blacks were ripe for the taking, if an opponent was prepared to take the game to them.

The All Blacks, then, were creating a crisis for themselves without realising what was happening. The crisis of the Wallabies, though, was only too obvious. The Bledisloe Cup series was over after only two Tests. The Wallabies were facing a 3–0 thrashing in the series, a humiliation that was last suffered by the Woeful Wallabies of 1972. The New Zealanders apparently had their measure even though they were not playing well. There was a belief in Australian rugby circles that the second coming of Bob Dwyer as the Wallaby coach was going to be as unsuccessful as his first manifestation. The third Test, a dead game in the series, would have to be Dwyer's last stand.

This dark hour in Dwyer's career was documented by the relentless Evan Whitton, who insisted that the 1990 Test results raised a number of questions the answers to which 'will be of compelling interest', Whitton's questions were:

- Will coach Bob Dwyer re-start the campaign with rather different personnel here and there?
- Will Farr-Jones and Lynagh, with heroic self-abnegation, suggest that Peter Slattery and Tim Horan be tested as halves in coming matches and in the furnace of the Athletic Park international?
- If so, will the captaincy go to the senior man, Campese, who seems at any rate a great reader of the game?
- And will the Australian Rugby Football Union cut and deal again in December and appoint new selectors and a new coach?

As this trenchant analysis made clear, even if the third Test was a dead game in the series it had the potential to spell the rugby death of many of the leading Wallabies, including perhaps the captain Nick Farr-Jones and certainly the coach Bob Dwyer. We know now how the story worked out. That day in November 1991, when Farr-Jones held the William Webb Ellis trophy high above his head marking the Rugby World Championship for the Wallabies, has been described as the greatest day in Australian rugby. And so it is. But one of the most crucial days in Australian rugby was 18 August 1990, the day of the third Test in Wellington. Another defeat on a cold, windy Athletic Park for the Wallabies and the players and the coach who created the World Cup triumph a year later would have been axed. And with their departure there would have been no World Cup for Australian rugby.

On his high-rating 2UE breakfast radio program Alan Jones, the dismissed Wallaby coach who was now coaching the Balmain Rugby League club, was asked several days before the Test: 'Alan, what's wrong with the Wallabies?'. Jones made two constructive criticisms which amounted to a telling indictment of Bob Dwyer's qualities as a rugby coach. Everyone was talking about how slow the back row was, Jones said. But this was missing the point. Backs had to learn to maul when the ball went loose and not to wait for a loose forward to come and tidy things up. 'This is not something that just happens', he said. 'You've got to practise it.' Here Jones was talking from his own experience. On the 1986 tour of New Zealand Jones devised special drills to take account of the fact that it was a particularly wet winter. Dwyer, apparently, had not been so acute in his appraisal of what was required. It was not until a request was made by Michael Lynagh, the tour vice-captain, that Dwyer allowed the Wallabies to engage in opposed work at training in order to counter the All Black domination at the breakdown. Jones' second point was that the Wallabies were relying too much on rucked ball. There needed to be more emphasis on mauled ball. Rucked ball, Jones's insisted, was too 'predictable'.

Ian Williams, the dashing and intelligent winger, in his account of his career, *In Touch*, has given a touching account of emotional minutes before the crucial 1990 third Test:

> It is traditional with the Wallabies that, before each match, just before the team gets off the bus, one of the players not taking the field wishes the team the best. Normally this is the job of the duty boy of the day, who on the day of the third Test was lock Peter FitzSimons. However, he asked the injured flanker Brendan Nasser to take his place, and Nasser, who is a religious man by nature, said only a few words, finishing with 'God bless.' And so it seemed that He did, as the Australian team produced one of its proudest moments by ending New Zealand's 1,373 day, 23-match reign as the unbeaten world champions with an historic 21–9 victory.

Despite the seemingly large winning margin, it was a close-run thing for the Wallabies. The All Blacks won the lineouts 23–14 and the rucks and mauls 24–10. The fact that the game was played in rain, slush and a stiff wind helped the Wallabies. The control the All Blacks

The Wallabies' formidable front row, from left, Ewen McKenzie, Phil Kearns and Tony Daly.

usually maintained was less certain than usual. Twice Mike Brewer plunged across the line from lineouts in the first half, only to lose the ball. If one or both of these attempts had been rewarded with tries the Wallabies might not have been able to come back in the second half from being points down. But early in the second half Gary Whetton muffed a lineout catch near the New Zealand tryline. Phil Kearns stormed through on the bouncing ball and smashed his body on it for a try. Struggling to his feet, he swung his arm in a massive uppercut salute to the bewildered All Blacks. With the gale at their backs and ahead by 12–9, the Wallabies knew they had the chance to break the All Blacks ascendancy. Even then, though, they were helped by inept captaincy by Gary Whetton. With only three points separating the sides, the All Blacks forced two five-metre scrums. Both times the Wallaby scrum was immovable. Calling for pushovers, without setting up decoys in the backs such as the 'Butcher' move, was poor captaincy that lacked imagination. In the 53rd minute of play Whetton turned down the chance of drawing level when he opted for a passing rush instead of a penalty shot that Grant Fox would have kicked comfortably, despite the wind. This was captaincy that involved too much fantasy and not enough realism. Evan Whitton, noting this mistake in an article on the Test, surmised: 'Perhaps hubris was the problem'. Whatever the explanation is, Whetton allowed the Wallabies to stay in front. Ian Williams put the player's perspective on what having the lead meant to the Wallabies:

> This forced the All Blacks to do all the hard work, trying to run the ball into the wind for the last 35 minutes. Rather than continuing to run the ball at Australia in close, the All Blacks uncharacteristically tried to use a number of set moves that were disjointed and difficult to execute in the greasy conditions, which exacerbated Graeme Bachop's problems at halfback and meant that Grant Fox did not enjoy his normal armchair ride.

And in the end the lead was made comfortable for Australia by Michael Lynagh's kicking three more penalties to round out a 21–9 victory to the Wallabies.

Whetton and the All Blacks management clearly did not realise the psychology of what had happened. If they had been more thoughtful and intuitive they would have realised that the All Blacks had the chance to destroy Australia's chances of being competitive the next year in the Rugby World Cup. But, lacking imagination and a sense of the traditions of the game, they approached the third Test as a dead match, a Test that had to be played but which didn't have to be won. This mistake set in train events that four years later still had repercussions on New Zealand rugby. Just as the unlikely third Test victory to the Wallabies in 1978 marked the renaissance of Australia as a trans-Tasman rugby power, the unlikely third Test victory in 1990 marked the beginning of Australia as a world rugby power. Four years later, in 1994, after losing a one-off Bledisloe Cup Test to a Wallabies side that believed it was the best in the world, and for 40 minutes played as if it were (scoring 17 points), the All Blacks were still being punished for the stupidity of not destroying an opponent when the opportunity presented itself. The confidence the Wallabies had gained back in 1990 in defeating the All Blacks gave them the spirit to hold the 1994 All Blacks out when charges were being made from all parts of the field.

For the All Blacks, the third Test loss at Wellington in 1990, even though the Bledisloe Cup had been retained, was one of New Zealand's blackest days in rugby. For Bob Dwyer, after the Test victory Australian rugby had to have, it was the dawn of the great Wallabies era he had promised more than a year earlier.

ZENO'S 1991 BLEDISLOE CUP

The Greek philosopher, Zeno, once proposed this paradox: a second arrow (no matter how fast) can never catch a first arrow, because by the time the second arrow has halved the distance between it and the first, the first arrow has travelled further on . . . and so on into infinity. In the years following the 1987 World Cup, up to 1990, the All Blacks were Zeno's first arrow in the world of rugby. When another country made gains in its game, the All Blacks managed to stay in front. But in the first encounter of the two-match Bledisloe Cup Test series in 1991 at the Sydney Football Stadium, a well-organised and strongly motivated Wallabies side exposed Zeno's paradox for the illusion it is with a convincing 21–12 victory.

The Wallabies were better in virtually every position, from front row to the fullback. Who could have predicted this only a year before when Bob Dwyer sent the Wallabies out on to the field at Wellington with the instruction not to allow themselves to be called the new 'Woeful Wallabies' by losing all three Tests in the series. With John Eales, arguably the finest out-and-out lineout jumper in the game's history, playing his first Test against the All Blacks, the Wallabies were able to win their own ball when Phil Kearns (not a noted thrower-in) made his toss. Eales's remarkable ability to effect two-handed catches set up plays from the back of the lineout with Nick Farr-Jones running around the lineout's end like a gridiron running back turning the corner. As well, the All Blacks had to struggle to win their own lineout ball against Eales, despite Sean Fitzpatrick's accurate throwing.

It was ironic, therefore, that when Michael Jones did win a lineout in the second half he was promptly dumped on his back and turned. The Wallabies cleared the ball to Michael Lynagh who put a hopeful kick in, down the field. Rob Egerton, a useful club fullback for the Sydney University club and Oxford University, a player who liked to wear his sox around his boots because of a quaint theory that around his calves they might cause cramp, a club fullback who always ran the ball because like the incomparable J. P. R. Williams he couldn't kick the ball as far as he could throw it into a stiff wind, an optimist who enthusiastically chased every kick through—Rob Egerton, the uncommon common player, now makes his dramatic entry into the story of the Bledisloe Cup. As soon as Lynagh kicks, Egerton rushes through as automatically as one of Pavlov's dogs salivating at the sound of the bell. The conditioned reflex to chase pays off. The ball, which is being covered by John Kirwan, the All Blacks winger, instead of bouncing in a gentle loop, for no apparent reason arcs higher and higher into the air before beginning its soft fall to earth. Just as the patient Kirwan begins to extend his arms to gather the ball in, Egerton bursts past him, in his characteristic scudding run with his feet only centimetres off the ground with each pace, and rushes on towards the goalposts with the ball tucked securely high on his chest.

Egerton capped his first Test against the All Blacks in the uncustomary position of wing with a famous, match-winning try. His success reflected a remarkable turn in the fortunes of the Wallaby coach, Bob Dwyer. Now entrenched in his position following the win in the third Bledisloe Cup Test of 1990 and two devastating victories early in 1991, against Wales (63–6) and England (40–15), two of the most complete performances ever presented by a Wallabies side, Dwyer responded with some astute selections. Eales was critical in the lineouts and Egerton was brought on to the wing to cover any missed tackles by David Campese, to chase every ball kicked through and, thereby, exert pressure on opposing fullbacks and to catch the kick into the box from a maul or scrum from opposing halfbacks.

Although Dwyer had been brought back as the Australian coach to inject the spirit of the 'Randwick Game' into the Wallabies, it was noticeable that the game plan of his team in the 1991 season followed a pattern set down by Alan Jones. Under Jones the Wallabies had huge packs that dominated or tried to dominate set pieces. The leviathans were complemented by alert backs running set moves inside their opposition's 22 and a seemingly inexhaustible repertoire of back row moves (36 for the 1991 Wallabies according to some sources) when a scrum was forced near the opposing team's tryline. The difference between the Jones Wallabies and the second-Dwyer Wallabies is that the restricted tactics were played to perfection by Dwyer's side. The genius of David Campese, too, from 1991 onwards obscured the fact that the Wallabies were playing boring rugby. Against England early in 1991, for instance, the Wallabies won 16 lineouts to 12 but were content to see England run the ball across their backline more often. This was the year, too, that Campese began his trademark play of banging the ball downfield from defensive positions instead of setting up Randwick-like counter attacks.

Starved of rugby success, Australian supporters (except for the occasional journalist like Evan Whitton) were prepared to tolerate the Grinding Wallabies, just so long as they were successful. In New Zealand, though, success bred what amounted to a resentment of the methodical and ruthless style of the All Blacks. Winning was not enough. The New Zealand public wanted winning in style. And when winning in style was achieved the public wanted even more style.

With Alex Wyllie as coach, the All Blacks had won nine successive Test series. Up to the first Test against Australia in 1991 the All Blacks had played 24 Tests in that time for 22 wins, one loss and a draw. Yet the *New Zealand Rugby News* ran a cartoon showing Alex 'Grizz' Wyllie in a series of boxes holding a newspaper with 'NZ Media' on its masthead, In the first box the headline read: 'TEST 1. ALL BLACKS PUMMEL PUMAS: CRITICS GUT GRIZZ'. And then the second box: 'TEST 2. ARGIES ANNIHILATED: WASTE WYLLIE THE CRY!'. The third box showed Wyllie holding his throat and muttering: 'Cripes—what'll they do to me if we whip the Ockers?!!!'.

In the after-match media conference following the 1991 first Test loss, Wyllie managed a wry smile when he was asked if he thought the Australians had played All Blacks tactics learnt from a scrutiny of the videos of past All Blacks performances: 'Perhaps they liked what they saw', he replied cagily.

The caginess was understandable because Wyllie was moving rapidly from the position of a New Zealand cult hero to something like a wanted criminal. High-ranking officials within the New Zealand Rugby Union wanted John Hart, the charismatic and gifted coach who created the modern Auckland side and then a New Zealand selector, to have a more significant input into the coaching of the All Blacks than he had had up until then. But from the beginning of his reign Wyllie had discarded the collegial system, used (successfully) by Brian Lochore and revived in 1993 and 1994 (unsuccessfully) by Laurie Mains, in favour of a coaching panel of one—himself. When I congratulated Earle Kirton, a schoolmate, a year or so previously on his ascension to the All Blacks selection panel and suggested we should meet up in a Sydney Test, he said: 'Grizz has already made it clear to me that he's totally in charge. I'm not likely to come across'. By 1991, too, the media was obsessed with the belief that Wyllie had to go. A respected television commentator rushed across the street when he saw me in Wellington in January 1991 and regaled me for about an hour on the damage that Wyllie was doing to the credibility of the All Blacks.

This disillusionment, which was hardly justified by the results, for the All Blacks had had their most successful Test run ever, spilled into the consciousness of the public. Peter FitzSimons, the journalist and former Wallaby, appeared on an Auckland radio talkback program a day or so before the second Bledisloe Cup Test in 1991 at Eden Park (for the first time reciprocal one-off Bledisloe Cup Tests were being played) with the Wallaby captain, Nick Farr-Jones. He was stunned by what the callers were saying: 'I just want to say, Nick, that I hope you Wallabies give the All Blacks a really good thumping at the weekend'. And 'I think the only way New Zealand can win the World

Cup is if we lose on the weekend and then we can rebuild the whole team'. The 'rebuilding' theme was really a code for the desire to return Wayne 'Buck' Shelford to the All Blacks as captain. FitzSimons was with several Wallabies when they were approached by a grey-haired woman who earnestly pleaded with them to defeat the All Blacks so that her beloved Buck Shelford could force his way back into the team. 'Just promise me you'll beat them', she begged.

But the Wallabies were not quite up to the challenge. The referee, a 39-year-old fire officer from Scotland, Ken McCartney, provided an officious and meretricious display of refereeing, handing out 18 penalties to the Wallabies and 15 to the All Blacks. The New Zealanders played with two openside flankers, Michael Jones and Mark Carter. On a slippery and treacherous Eden Park pitch the gamble played off. Jones ran wide to cut down Tim Horan and Jason Little in the centres and David Campese on the wing. Carter stayed close to the rucks and mauls where he picked off the Wallaby close-in runners. And one memorable tackle in this role, after twenty minutes of play, turned the match. Lynagh saw Jones covering the centres and cut back on the angle to set up his loose forwards. Just as he gathered speed he was flattened in a devastating tackle by a Carter primed to make just this type of hit. After this, Lynagh was reluctant to run the ball at all. 'Once we got Lynagh that first time', Carter said after the Test, 'their backline didn't look threatening.' Rob Egerton on the wing received one pass in the first half. Campese had to try to make play from missed clearances by the All Blacks.

Constant forward pressure from the All Blacks forced two penalties close to the Wallaby goalposts which Grant Fox converted. This was not as easy as it sounds. The field was slippery and the goalkickers found it hard to set their non-kicking foot. As well, several of the match balls had seams on them that were as wonky as the seams on a prostitute's stockings. The balls, according to Greg Growden in his match report, 'had the powers of an amusement park trampoline'. Two of the balls apparently had been overinflated. Fox kicked his two goals with balls that were correctly inflated. (Were the ball boys cooperative?) Lynagh, though, had the misfortune to kick at goal every time with a bad ball with a seam that, in his words, 'went like a snake'. He managed to kick one goal out of six attempts when, right on time, the Wallabies forced a penalty near the sideline and just outside New Zealand's 22. With 623 Test points to his credit, the kick normally would have been an easy one for him. But, to the obvious relief of the All Blacks, he pushed his kick wide of the posts.

After the Test Farr-Jones told journalists: 'We're not really happy. I guess our biggest disappointment is that we haven't got the Cup.

Campo's now played 55 Tests and won it once'. And Bob Dwyer told the after-match press conference that he rated the Bledisloe Cup, because of the two teams involved, on a par with a World Cup final. He was disappointed with the outcome of the Test: 'How often do you get where you're 100 per cent certain you could win a Bledisloe Cup . . . and not win it? It's extremely disappointing'.

While relieved about retaining the Bledisloe Cup, Alex Wyllie revealed that his aim at the start of the season had been directed towards retaining the World Cup: 'If we win the World Cup, everything else will be forgotten'.

The 1991 World Cup

During the 1991 World Cup tournament, being played in England, Scotland, Wales, Ireland and France, I was stopped in George Street, Sydney, by a friend who said to me: 'I thought you were in Wales covering the World Cup'. Unfortunately, no. I was writing columns about the World Cup for the *Sydney Morning Herald* from our main office in Jones Street, Broadway, in Sydney. The disadvantage was that the 'colour' of being there was denied to me. Against that, though, with television one saw every match in greater detail than when being at the back of a dark grandstand on a murky day. As well, being away from the pressure of the players and officials provided a safety zone from which tough things could be written that it might not have been possible to write living close to the official entourage. What follows is—mostly—what I saw on television and wrote in my daily columns.

3 October 1991
. . . The bookmakers initially made the All Blacks favourites for the Rugby World Cup. Then they established the All Blacks and the Wallabies as joint favourites. After watching the Wallabies train, they made them favourites. But after watching the All Blacks train, the bookmakers restored them to favourite odds. The bookmakers then made the Wallabies and the All Blacks joint favourites again. Now the Wallabies are favourites. This resolute indecision seems about right to me. The WallaBlacks will win the World Cup but which half of the beast is victorious depends on who responds better during the semi-final (but the REAL final) at Dublin on 27 October.

5 October 1991
The pace of the forwards is the pace of the fastest forward. Adherence

to that fundamental principle won the nervy, mistake-strewn opening match of the World Cup tournament for the All Blacks against England. Michael Jones, singled out for praise by the New Zealand coach Alex Wyllie (an unusual occurrence given the All Blacks' commitment to the team game) and by Australia's Bob Dwyer, was yards faster to the ball than his England counterpart. When we are talking about Jones, though, we are talking about one of the great players of the modern era. Dwyer could afford to be lavish with his praise because Jones, a devout Christian, won't play on Sundays and the Dublin semi-final between the All Blacks and the Wallabies is on a Sunday . . .

New Zealand 18 – England 12

7 October 1991

After an impressive start, the Wallabies were rescued from a possible defeat against an unexpectedly resilient Argentinian side by the rugby genius of David Campese. Watching the winger beat three Argentinians to score his first try, then burst through explosively for a second and finally set up centre Tim Horan for a try after retrieving a lobbed pass from No. 8 John Eales with a searing run, I was reminded of Kenneth Tynan's tribute to the beauty of Greta Garbo: 'What men see in some women when they are drunk, they see in Garbo when they are sober'. This can be paraphrased into rugby terms along these lines: 'What good players fantasise, when they are drunk, of doing on a rugby field just once in their lifetime, David Campese does every time he plays'. It is customary to criticise Campese's reluctance to tackle. Against Argentina, for instance, his opposite player slipped inside him to continue an attack with the ease of a person going through his own front door. But the Wallabies have to adjust to Campese's defensive weakness the way Australian cricket teams reconciled themselves to the fact that Sir Donald Bradman wasn't much of a bowler . . .

Australia 32 – Argentina 19

14 October 1991

What is happening to the All Blacks? . . . They struggled in their last game against Italy, a team they scored 70 points against at Auckland in the opening match of the 1987 World Cup tournament. The All Blacks also conceded the first two tries scored against them in the tournament to the competitive Italians.

I rang up the former All Black fullback and goalkicker, Alan Hewson, in Wellington to find out how people in New Zealand were rating the prospects of the All Blacks to go on and win the World Cup tournament . . . Hewson believes the All Blacks will rethink their

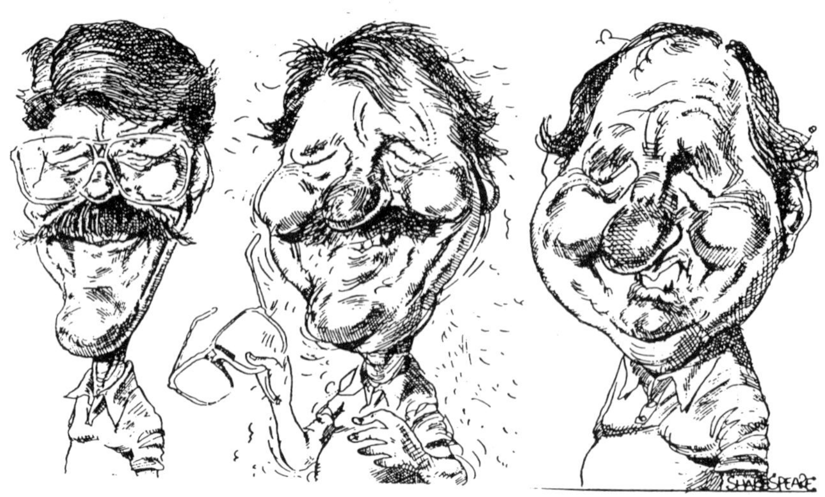

strategy of playing an expansive game: 'We've been trying to move the ball from too deep in our territory. We'll probably play the game tighter now, with more high kicks from Grant Fox. We've been doing enough to win but, now we're in the finals, the All Blacks will play with greater commitment than they've shown in their last two matches . . .

New Zealand 31 – Italy 21

15 October 1991

Wallaby coach Bob Dwyer is a Perils of Pauline expert. Just when it looks as though an onrushing train of critics is going to run over him, the Wallabies play superbly, and with one bound, Dwyer is free . . . After the first two matches in the World Cup tournament, the lacklustre forward-power-obsessed play by the Wallabies focused attention once more on the coach. But the result of the match against Wales—and, more particularly, the way the Wallabies played—has released Bob Dwyer from his critics once more . . . In the second half against Wales, the Wallabies—at last—got the balance right between driving and releasing. The result was a perfect half of rugby. The backs were able to run all the correct lines. The forwards released to set up second-phase, third-phase and (can it be believed in this tournament blighted by whistle-happy referees?) fourth-phase ball. The resulting ensemble play was marvellous, and the Wallabies can go into the finals series with a renewed confidence in their ability to win the tournament.

Australia 38 – Wales 3

23 October 1991

Are the Wallabies perhaps fated to win the World Cup tournament?

No other rugby side in the world could have come back after Ireland's spectacular try, as the Wallabies did, and score a match-winning try with only minutes left to play. The Wallabies kept their nerve (one of the toughest challenges in sport) when everything seemed lost. And just as importantly their captain, Michael Lynagh, made a series of critical decisions—all of which came off. From the kickoff, should the Wallabies kick short (and try to win the ball back) or long (and strike from the next lineout, if possible)? Lynagh kicked long knowing that a good catch and a raking kick would virtually finish off the Wallabies. Then, when the scrum was forced, Lynagh had to decide whether to keep the ball close to the scrum and play one of the now-famous back row moves, or run the ball in the backs . . . And which of the backline cut-out moves should be run, given that the simple ploy of cutting out Jason Little in the centres and passing flat and long to Marty Roebuck coming in from fullback had worked three times before? Could it work a fourth time? All these decisions had to be taken in a matter of moments with the crowd screaming and the Wallabies realising that one mistake would have them on the plane back home. An intriguing thought: would Nick Farr-Jones have come to the same decisions as the calm, confident Lynagh?

Australia 19 – Ireland 18

29 October 1991

It's the end of the All Blacks era and the beginning, perhaps, of a new world rugby order of Wallaby power. The Wallabies did the tackling and the All Blacks controlled (and often fumbled) the ball for long periods of play, but it was the rugby genius of David Campese, the outstanding player of the World Cup tournament, that turned the Dublin semi-final Australia's way again. Without Campese, the Wallabies would have struggled to find a way through a swarming and dedicated defence . . . Campese took on the All Blacks three times, scored one try, set up Tim Horan for the decisive try of the match and almost got away for another . . . A colleague has described Campese as 'the rugby incarnation of quantum physics: he's there, he's not there, he's atomic'. In three Tests against the Wallabies this year, the All Blacks managed only one try and that was a flukey one from a high kick at Sydney . . . With hindsight, we can see the All Blacks (with three defeats and one draw in 30 Tests since 1987) had been kept together a year too long.

Australia 16 – New Zealand 6

1 November 1991

A British rugby writer has made the case that it was good for rugby that the Wallabies beat the All Blacks because the All Blacks had been 'too magnificent for too long'. This is not a view shared in New Zealand where the blinds are still down . . . Scotland were saved by some bizarre refereeing. Despite being totally dominant in the scrums, for instance, to such an extent that a couple of tight heads were won and the Scots pack was occasionally marched backwards about 20 metres, the All Blacks were penalised five times to one in the first half for scrum infringements . . . As the All Blacks ran around Cardiff Arms Park acknowledging a standing ovation for winning the third place play-off, there was the feeling that we were witnessing rugby's equivalent of the last parade of Napoleon's Grand Army—after the retreat from Moscow.

New Zealand 13 – Scotland 6

2 November 1991

SIR: Who the hell is Spiro Zavos? Some world-class fly half, no doubt? The English team plays to its strengths, as does the Australian team. A wet, heavy pitch, such as encountered for most of an English season, does not lend itself to fleet, carefree play. Sure, it's not as fluent as the Australian game, and yes, England could do more to use Guscott, but that does not make England either boring or mindless or useless—it makes them sensible. I don't seem to remember Australian journalists saying after Eden Park that, hey, we lost the Bledisloe Cup, but it's OK because we played such a nice, popular running game and we're all such jolly good chaps. I probably agree that Australia will win the final (I hope I'm wrong), not because their style is inherently superior to the English style, but because the 15 Australians are collectively better than the 15 Englishmen.

Chris G. Green
Eastwood

4 November 1991

Bob Dwyer's 1991 Wallabies are now—deservedly—legends . . . What distinguished the World Champion Wallabies from the rest of the teams in the tournament is an awareness of the tryline—on attack and on defence. Fifteen of the 17 tries scored by the Wallabies in the tournament were by the backs, with David Campese and Tim Horan contributing 10 of them. Near the line, the Wallabies, of all the teams, were prepared to go for tries. Although it was the Daly–McKenzie front row machine which scored the only try of the final, the significance of the try was the ruthless way the Wallabies capitalised on the gut-wrenching run out of defence from Tim Horan. The bulky England backrowers were still trying to gather their breath after a hectic chase, and they allowed Willie Ofahengaue a free jump for the lineout ball . . . There was a memorable moment when Simon Poidevin took the ball on the burst and ran straight into a braced and ready Mike Teague. Teague wears his jersey collar tucked into his shirt like a Rugby League heavy. He is powerful and ruthless. He put his shoulder into the charging, unsuspecting Poidevin. The physical collision was tremendous and Poidevin was sent sprawling. But he retained the ball and was able to bounce to his feet immediately for the ensuing scrum . . . The victory of the Wallabies was a victory for Australian rugby: for all the players who turn out week after week, many of them in the bush travelling hundreds of kilometres for a match; for all those characters—Peter Fenton, Jeff Sayle, David Brockhoff (the list is representative of people I've come in contact with)—who have made training on a cold, wet Tuesday evening something to look forward to; for the school coaches who have spent hours of their time developing the talent in their teams so effectively that the younger members of the Wallabies are the most disciplined and mature in the side; for teams like St Joseph's First XV which set the highest standard for other schools to aspire to; for players like Peter FitzSimons who gave the Wallabies some fire and muscle when they were being intimidated and who took the cut from the World Cup squad with grace and good humour; for the players who haven't gone to Rugby League; for the officials and referees who love the game and are proud to work for it for nothing; for (dare I say it?) the journalists who have scolded, criticised, praised and kept alive the ideal of the ensemble Wallaby game; and for Bob Dwyer and his coaching staff for a brilliant preparation of a side which has achieved what no other Wallaby side can ever emulate—Australia's first rugby championship of the world.

The Australian rugby community is a tribe which has its roots in the past, and is aware of generations yet unborn. The Twickenham triumph was the tribe's greatest moment—so far.

Australia 12 – England 6

An Epiphany at Twickenham

At the blast of the final whistle of the World Cup final at Twickenham, Norbet Byrne and John Howard, two long-serving Australian rugby officials—Byrne the cerebral Cardinal Richelieu figure of Queensland rugby and the burly John Howard the quickwitted finance organiser of New South Wales rugby—embraced. 'Twenty years ago, who would have thought this could have happened', said Byrne as he surveyed the commotion going on in front of him as the Wallabies prepared to receive their World Cup medals and the gleaming William Webb Ellis trophy from the Queen. Howard, amid all the noise and congratulating, had a small epiphany. His mind unaccountedly went back to a sunny afternoon in 1975 when New South Wales played Queensland at North Sydney Oval in front of 1452 spectators—the number was so that low Howard had personally checked the figures. In despair, he had wondered after receiving the count how Australian rugby could ever survive if only a thousand or so spectators could be attracted to a glamour game. Then his mind switched back from this bleak time to the glorious moment at Twickenham. 'Who would have thought it, Norbet', he replied.

THE LAWS RULE, OK?

After the 1991 World Cup tournament the International Rugby Board revised the laws (not the rules) of Rugby Union. The two crucial changes were a 'use-it-or-lose-it' law regarding the maul and ruck. A side taking the ball into ruck and maul had to ultimately get it back to the halfback or lose the feed to the scrum. Previously, the side going forward with the ball, almost always the side in possession, retained the feed to the scrum. The point of this law was to kill off the boring, smash-through-the-middle tactics that many teams had adopted. The value of a try was increased to 5 points, to complement the new maul law's encouragement to open up rugby for players and spectators.

It took the early rugby administrators six years, from 1882 to 1888, to move the points for a try from 2 to 1. Then six years later, in 1894, the value of a try was increased to 3 points and by way of compensation for the favoured kicking game, dropped goals moved up in value from 3 to 4 points. The 3-point try remained until 1972. The increase to 5 points marked the first time since the newly formed International Rugby Board introduced an official scoring system in 1882 (try = 2 points; conversion = 3 points; other goals, including speculators, going over the crossbar = 4 points) that a converted try was worth more than two successful penalties.

The bugbear of Rugby Union remained, however—the complexity of the game. Danie Craven once told me in an interview that we would know when we had the correct laws for Rugby Union and that would be when the critical ones could be written on the back of a postage stamp, as in soccer. In the early 1920s there were already 34 ways of being penalised. The 1992 'new' laws, which aimed at clarifying the laws, detailed no fewer than 111 ways of allowing opponents the possibility of a kick at goal.

According to the Wallaby coach, Bob Dwyer, who had admittedly built up one of the biggest packs in the history of Test rugby, the 1992 laws took 'the structure' out of Rugby Union. Dwyer's Wallabies in the World Cup tournament, for instance, had 36 different back row moves. Supporting the back row drives was the law that allowed the side making the drive off the back of the scrum or a maul to retain the ball. The 1992 change meant that the drive could be stopped if the charging forward was contained by the opposition. For Auckland in 1991, under the old law, Zinzan Brooke scored 18 tries off the back of the scrum. In 1992, he did not score one try in this manner for Auckland.

A recent study done at Auckland University of ten Tests, the last five played under the pre-1992 laws and the first five under the post-1992 laws, found that under the new laws 71 per cent of all plays lasted less than 20 seconds while under the old laws the statistic was 59 per cent of plays. About 20 per cent of plays, with the new laws, lasted less than 5 seconds compared to the 13 per cent of plays under the old laws. At the other extreme, 14 per cent of plays under the new laws lasted 30 seconds, whereas the figure under the old laws was 21 per cent, with most of the time taken up with teams having a breather in tedious maul pushouts. What emerged from this analysis was that 'new-law' Rugby Union had become a staccato, energy-sapping game, with a jazzy, improvising structure rather than classical structure that Bob Dwyer espoused. For the 1994 season, the IRB adjusted the maul and ruck law to give the feed, in the case of a ruck not being cleared, to the side going forward in the ruck, almost invariably the side taking the ball into that ruck. As the rucking game encourages quick and numerous phases, which in turn create an open and often spectacular game of Rugby Union, this was a compromise made in heaven.

Slowy, but not too surely, the IRB is creating a legal regime for Rugby Union to be a running/kicking game rather than a kicking/running game. This is in line with the intention of the first lawmakers. A newspaper account of the first match played under the new Rugby Union laws of 1871, the Football Company against the Harlequins, provoked this comment from a reporter: 'This was the first match where play was under the Rugby Union rules and they worked admirably, more especially having the ball down at once, and thus preventing the long and serious mauls so often complained of in the London–Rugby game . . .'

A modest proposal is made here in this discussion of the laws of

Rugby Union. While players have become bigger and faster the field in terms of actual size has remained the same. In practice, this means that the modern team is playing on a much 'smaller' field than their counterparts did even twenty years ago. It is unlikely that the size of fields will be increased; too many modern stadiums have been built to accommodate the present requirements. The solution is to take one player out of each team and make Rugby Union a 14-player game. The first reference I have come across to this solution was in a set of laws sent by the Otago Rugby Union in 1908 to the International Rugby Board. The proposed Otago Laws—this material is taken from an excellent history of the ORU, *The Pride of Southern Rebels* written by Sean O'Hagan—argued for: no charging a kick at goal (now a law); the throw-in from touch being for a distance of five yards (now a law); the imposition of a penalty on any player who crosses an imaginary line at the back of a scrum while the ball is still in it (now a law); that a player brought to ground be allowed to pass the ball even though it has touched the ground, provided it is done immediately (almost a law); that the game be played in four quarters of 20 minutes (a proposal for the Super 10 competition); and the reduction of a side to 14 players. These proposed laws were—unfortunately—rejected by the IRB at the time, along with a proposal 'for the referee placing the ball in the scrummage in all cases', an orphan law recruited from the Australian Rules game which was still popular in parts of the Otago district among goldminers from Australia. So annoyed was the ORU at the lack of cooperation it received from the IRB, and so worried by the challenge of the Rugby League code that was beginning to make ground in the district, that a copy of the Otago Laws was sent to the New South Wales and Queensland Rugby Unions 'with a view to securing their cooperation in the formation of an Australasian Rugby Union to control the game under the revised rules'.

Given the intransigence of the British rugby establishment towards innovative and practical thinking about the laws of rugby and the great issue of professionalism that has dogged Rugby Union since 1895, it is not entirely fanciful that the ORU proposal made in 1908 for a southern hemisphere Rugby Union might come to pass. If it does, it should be with a 14-player game, with a 2–3–2 scrum.

The 1992 series was the mother of all Bledisloe Cup series. Three pulsating matches, brilliant tries being scored by both sides, games turning on a slight mistake, two kicks at goal just missing right on time, both sides scoring the same number of tries and the same number of points but the Wallabies winning the series two Tests to one (16–15, 19–17, 23–26)—this was a series to be savoured for decades; with its competiveness, flair and continual excitement it represented the epitome of Bledisloe Cup rugby. In Australia the series established a reputation for the Bledisloe Cup as an event of high quality and drama. Jane Fraser for instance, a witty Sydney columnist, began to use the event, as a metaphor for something that was memorable and of great pleasure and delight when she talked about Eastern Suburbs matrons trying to give themselves Bledisloe Cup affairs.

Ka Mate, Ka Mate! (It was death, It was death!) Like most great events it began with a great controversy. Bob Dwyer's rugbiography, *The Winning Way*, had just been published in 1992 and the media in New Zealand and Australia had picked on two paragraphs in it, on the 'ridiculous practice' of the All Blacks' haka, to create a windstorm of controversy. Dwyer's paragraphs, in fact, were tempered by psychological and coaching logic, as befitted his book which is Aristotelian in the rigour of its analysis. After reading the book, with its clear-brained and witty analysis of all aspects of rugby, it becomes obvious why Dwyer is one of the great coaches in the history of the game and the most successful coach (along with Carwyn James) against the All Blacks:

> In my view, it is just as silly for players like Grant Fox, John Kirwan and Sean Fitzpatrick to be out there doing the haka as it would be for players like Michael Lynagh, David Campese and Nick Farr-Jones to be doing an Aboriginal corroboree. My chief objection to the haka, however, is that it is an unfair distraction to the other team . . . The minutes before the kickoff are extremely important for players trying to prepare themselves mentally for the match. By doing the haka the New Zealanders can maintain their focus, but their opponents are left with a lack of focus.

Ka Ora, Ka Ora! (It is life, It is life!) The former New Zealand captain, Wayne Shelford, who has been credited with re-establishing the proper form and practice of the All Blacks haka by making it more like the challenge it is supposed to be, bought into the argument in his newspaper column: 'In my time, the haka became a strong motivation tool, a final top-up before the kickoff, so to speak'. Shelford said he had no objections to the Wallabies doing an Aboriginal war dance, 'but then the Australians don't seem to be too interested in honouring their Aboriginal culture like we do with our Maori heritage'. This barb got to the heart of the matter in defence of the haka. It has a psychological impact. Back in 1884, when a New Zealand side used a Maori warcry to introduce themselves to their Australian opponents before a match, a newspaper reported: 'The sound . . . given in good time and unison by 18 powerful lungs, was something tremendous. The New South Wales men declared it hardly fair for visitors to frighten them out of their wits before the game began'.

Whiti Te Ra! (The sun rises!) As the Shelford-led haka became more aggressive, though, opponents started to attempt to impose their own psychology on it. In 1988 the Ireland XV responded to the haka by lining up just inside their half. Shelford found that he had advanced so close that he couldn't make his climactic haka jump. For the first Test of the 1993 Bledisloe Cup series the Wallabies adopted the Irish standoff, except for David Campese who nonchalantly leant on a goalpost while the frenetic eye-balling went on 50 metres upfield. Mindful of the Shelford experience, John Timu, the All Blacks haka leader, in a break with tradition stood behind the advancing line of All Blacks.

Perhaps that was the moment the Wallabies won the Test.

For the All Blacks, anyway, it was a Test that slipped away from them, almost as if this was fated to happen. If Grant Fox had kicked one more goal . . . If Ian Jones had controlled that ball over the New Zealand line to stop David Campese's try . . . If John Kirwan had taken his time and waited for the ball to cross the line before touching down rather than knocking on in his haste to get his hands to the ball . . . If the centring kick from David Campese had not bounced so wickedly, forcing a mishandle, the offside and Michael Lynagh's nerveless winning penalty goal. 'A couple of bounces in it', was the summing up of All Blacks coach, Laurie Mains.

As I was walking out of the ground an enthusiastic Wallaby supporter came up to me and said: 'Make sure you tell your *Herald* readers that it was never in doubt'. Outlandish though this comment appeared to be at first, there was a sense in which the supporter was correct. The Wallabies played with a composure and organisation which allowed them to exploit their chances ruthlessly, and to stifle the All Blacks' chances almost as ruthlessly. The Wallabies played, in other words, as All Blacks teams in the past have played and the All Blacks, nervy, seemingly inviting bad luck or failing to impose their own good luck, played like some of the extremely good Wallaby sides of the past years. While the Wallabies kept their discipline all round the field, the All Blacks played with indiscipline. Three points were lost, for instance, for a senseless late tackle on the Australian winger, Paul Carozza. And five lineout free-kicks in the second half were conceded because the forwards reverted to habit and began using their outside arm when jumping. There were two occasions when huge clearing kicks were nullified because players ran forward before they put onside. And when the All Blacks scored their second try, one of the great ensemble tries in Test history, from breakout inside his 22 by Walter Little, everything had to be done perfectly, even though the Wallabies were outflanked, before Frank Bunce could place the ball beneath the Wallaby goalposts.

In the second Test at Ballymore, the winning of which gave the Bledisloe Cup to Australia, the Wallabies demonstrated once again what a great side they had become. Like all dominating teams they had the confidence to know that when they had to score points they would score them. Their last try in the Test to save the match, for instance, scored by Paul Carozza, was the culmination of a perfect two-handed jump in the lineout by John Eales, a metre-perfect bomb by Michael Lynagh, a fierce chase and a disciplined driving maul by the forwards that unsettled the All Blacks and led to the ball being kicked through to the Wallabies, a perfect cut-out pass by Nick Farr-Jones, and Lynagh committing the defence before making a perfect pass to Carozza who charged like a little rhino for the line.

My match report on the Test for the *Sydney Morning Herald* ended with this tribute:

> Occasionally in sport, everything comes together, the right coach, an inspiring captain, players of supreme ability in virtually every position and that indefinable team spirit that makes the whole better than the parts. This is what has happened with the Wallabies. The team is entitled to make the claim that it is now one of the great rugby sides of the modern era.

Given claims like this, it was hardly surprising that Bob Dwyer expressed great disappointment at the way the Wallabies played in the third Test, where the closeness of the scoreline flattered his side. The backline play and tackling had been poor, Dwyer told journalists. There was now pressure on the Test spots, he added grimly. And why was he so critical when the Bledisloe Cup had been captured, after all? Because he knew that the advantage of a team being perceived as unbeatable often becomes a self-fulfilling prophecy. He knew, perhaps better than any other coach in modern rugby, the importance of being thought to be invincible. For the 1992 Bledisloe Cup series, in fact, this perception in the first two Tests had been the critical difference between the two teams.

In the New Zealand dressing rooms, only metres away, there was no cheering or shouting, either. Players stood around in various states of undress, the fearsome Richard Loe as naked as a baby and looking almost as benign. There was a sense, though, of a side that believed it had turned the tide against its greatest opponents. From the deeper recesses of the dressing rooms came the soft harmonic singing of some of the Polynesian players. The embattled coach, Laurie Mains, talked softly to journalists about how 'JT', John Timu, was going to be one of the great All Black fullbacks. 'The sky's the limit for JT', Mains said. Mains also saw good things in the play of Jamie Joseph, the young, overcommitted flanker (a large part of the massive 20–10 penalty count against the All Blacks was due to his undisciplined play). Joseph, though, scored the crucial try out on the wing when he broke a weak tackle by David Campese. 'Was Joseph out of position?', Mains was asked. 'The experience of Test rugby gives you the confidence to take decisions like that', the coach replied, with the barest suggestion of a smile hovering across his face as he gave his analysis.

Hupane Kaupane, Hupane Kaupane! (Up this step, Up that step!) *Whiti Te Ra!* (The sun rises!)

THE LOWDOWN ON RICHARD LOE

During the Ballymore Test in 1992 Richard Loe was caught isolated on the blindside. Jason Little drew him and passed on to Paul Carozza who scored a try. Loe continued chasing Carozza and after the try was scored smashed his elbow across the winger's face breaking his nose. In the same series Loe stomped on Sam Scott-Young's head. Later in the year, back in New Zealand, he administered what the French call 'le cravat', a stiff-arm tackle across the neck, to Steve McDowell, his former prop partner in the All Blacks front row. Then he gouged Greg Cooper's eyes when Waikato and Otago played for the New Zealand provincial championship. Outed from rugby for nine months, Loe returned to give away penalty after penalty in the first half in the 1994 Bledisloe Cup Test in what seemed to be a maniacal attempt to pull off Ewen McKenzie's legs in the way a kid snaps a wishbone. And, back in New Zealand again, Loe was outed for another month for stomping on John Timu (a fellow All Black only a few weeks pre-

viously in Australia) in the Ranfurly Shield match between Canterbury and Otago.

The same Loe who gets into so much trouble on the rugby field once donated an All Blacks jersey to an auction to raise funds for a local player who had sustained very serious injuries playing rugby. The Appeals Tribunal hearing the gouging claim against him found the donation to be an act of 'kindness and generosity' and an example of Loe's 'sincere nature, and commitment to rugby and charity'. The tribunal, in fact, in its 32-page judgment placed a great deal of emphasis on 'the side to Richard Loe that may not be publicly known . . . there is Richard Loe, the father of young daughters and the head of a family which has been racked with publicity this matter has engendered, and the nasty anonymous telephone calls that some members of our society seem to regard as their prerogative to make.'

Early in the 1992 rugby season I sat in a restaurant on Good Friday with one of the All Blacks selectors, Earle Kirton, chatting about the series against the World XV that was to start at Lancaster Park in two days' time. It was a chilly, overcast day and Kirton chuckled as we noticed Loe walking away from the motel in a T-shirt (fitting his massive body so tightly it looked as if it were pumped up), shorts, football socks and sandshoes. Holding his hands were two skipping, blonde-haired little girls wrapped up in ski-type jackets to keep out the cold. Kirton remarked how tender Loe was with his kids: 'Just a beaut family man'.

Loe's personality, then, seems to reflect a Jekyll-and-Hyde split. The beaut family man off the field becomes an over-the-top menace to opposition players on the field. Why is this so?

Peter Gay, a professor of history at Yale University, has written an interesting survey of what he calls the 'bourgeois experience' from Queen Victoria to Sigmund Freud, called *The Cultivation of Hatred*. Athough the middle classes of the 19th century seemed to spend most of their time provoking various forms of hatred—personal, social, political, racial and sexual—Gay's argument is that many institutions were created to 'civilise' this aggressive behaviour. The cult of flogging, for example, was developed as a means of social control of the lower classes when they rioted and of upper-class students at the famous public schools such as Eton (with 'the famous but beloved flogger', John Keate). An alternative to flogging was developed at less famous public schools with the introduction of organised games. Thomas Hughes's novel *Tom Brown's School Days* was an important vehicle for broadcasting the doctrine of 'manliness' and 'muscular Christianity' that—as was noted earlier—Dr Arnold, the headmaster of Rugby School, believed was the key to sound education of young men. The legalised and acceptable aggressiveness on the playing field was to be the acceptable surrogate for illegal and unacceptable aggressiveness off the field.

Richard Loe, therefore, is the ideal mirror of the Dr Arnold method. But with his own on-the-field strongarm tactics he is a man out of his times. The 20th century sensibilities to violence on the field have become far more acute than they were in the 19th century. Our society does not accept that violence in a game is any more tolerable than violence perpetrated outside a game. There are a certain tolerances in this, admittedly. During the Wallabies' tour of Wales in 1992 they encountered what Bob Dwyer called 'bagsnatching' (gripping the player's balls rather than the match ball), in the match against Neath. The Wallabies responded with some over-vigorous and in the circumstances acceptable rucking. And few people would deny that the Wallabies were justified in their reaction. Rugby remains a tough body contact sport; one of its attractions in an effete age is that it still provides a context for exhibitions of manliness. Loe, though, tends to get his retaliation in *first*. And there is nothing manly about eye-gouging and stomping. With neutral referees, touch judges and the unwavering eye of the television camera this has meant that he gave away too many penalties in close matches and encouraged referees to referee the All Blacks (to their disadvantage on the penalty count) rather than their opponents.

The good team-man, in other words, made it difficult for his teams to win, thereby negating the purpose of the violent play.

A SHORT NOTE ON HEIGHT

At the first Bledisloe Cup Test in 1992, at the Sydney Football Stadium, I came across Peter Crittle, now the president of the New South Wales Rugby Union and in his playing days a hardworking and intelligent Wallaby forward. We had a short chat about his impressive collection of rugby books. As he moved away I murmured to my son: 'He used to play in the second row for Australia'. Zachary, who was in Year 12 at the time, sized Crittle up and replied: 'You're kidding. He's not even as big as Lawson'. Lawson Donald was a classmate who had just been selected to play openside breakaway for the Australian Schoolboys against New Zealand. The fact that the Australian Schoolboys forward flier was bigger than someone who had played in the tight five against the All Blacks in the 1960s impressed on us how huge modern rugby forwards have to be now, even at the schoolboy level.

An article I wrote making this point ('Schoolboy Giants Face a Big Task against Stylish Kiwi Rivals') in the *Sydney Morning Herald* prompted the following (tongue in cheek) reply to the editor from Peter Crittle:

> SIR: On behalf of not only myself but my fellow Wallabies of the 1960s, I must take strong exception to the disparaging comments made by your Mr Spiro Zavos in last Tuesday's article about the schoolboy giants. Mr Zavos's unfortunate attempt to portray we players of the 1960s as a team of bibliographic pygmies does us a grave injustice . . . Mr Zavos might have had the decency to point out to his son Master Zachary Zavos that my former 6ft 5in has been reduced to 6ft 2in by virtue of an unfortunate displacement of four of my lumbar vertebrae in an accident 10 years ago. This happened when I enthusiastically leaped to my feet at a book auction to make a winning bid on a remaindered copy of Mr Zavos's sycophantic history of post-war New Zealand rugby, *After The Final Whistle.* Unfortunately I fell over, fractured my spine and consequently lost not only 2 inches of height but also a chance of adding Mr Zavos's appalling tome to my collection . . . Mr Thornett, incidentally, was once 6ft 4in tall. His reduction to 6ft 1in is directly attributable to the fact that he had the simian-like Australian hooker, Mr Peter Johnson, suspended from his neck

> in something like 9,000 international scrums . . . One only hopes the same thing does not happen to the present Wallaby props, Messrs Daly and McKenzie. On present indications, they will have the dynamic Mr Kearns strung from their shoulders for many years to come. As they are both lucky to make 5ft 10in even now, one wonders where they will finish up—down with us pygmies from the 1960s perhaps?

Peter Crittle, even at this fantasy height of 6ft 5in (195cm), would be too small to play in the second row in the 1990s. So, obviously, would have been Colin Meads, who at 193cm would be considered almost too short for even the blindside breakaway position. 'If he played these days', writes Stephen Jones in an uplifting article in the *Sunday Times* of September 1994, 'the great Pinetree would be staring his opponent square in the chest. He might still win the ball, but that is another story. "That can't be him," people often say when they encounter Meads in the flesh'.

Statistics provided by Jones show that Andy Haden, who was the tallest All Black ever when he played in the 1980s, was a 200cm giant. Mark Cooksley, the All Blacks secondrower in the 1994 Bledisloe Cup Test and the current tallest All Black ever, stands—selfconsciously—at 208cm. John Eales, who won far more lineout ball in that Test than Cooksley did, is only(?) 203cm. But, even in the era of the giants, agility and athleticism are still important skills to have. Similarly with size. In 1993 Wellington produced a player claimed to be 'the biggest forward in world rugby', the tight head prop Bill Cavubati who weighed in at 146kg and wore 130cm shorts which had to be hand-made. After a strong performance against New South Wales Cavubati was encouraged to play for the Eastwood club in Sydney. He was quickly relegated to second grade because he had no scrum technique or lineout blocking skills. Big and tall is rarely enough by itself in modern rugby. Big and tall and skilful are the required elements.

In his well-argued piece of writing Jones makes the correct response to what he calls 'the burgeoning of the rugby animal':

> It is a basic human reaction, of course, to take to a physical confrontation the biggest mates you can find. Secondly, people in general are bigger. But the rate of growth of rugby players is vastly faster than the rate in the outside world . . . The real trends behind the trend lie in rugby's changed tactics, and also in advances in sports medicine and preparation culture. The desperate search for big men comes directly from the overwhelming importance in the modern game of the lineout . . . The flyhalf is no longer the focal point of the team, as he was of old. All efforts are directed into pampering, supporting, lifting and powering-up the champion of the lineout. The importance of the lineout increased significantly when measures to curb the power of the scrum came in

during the 1980s and made the lineout the primary means of re-starting the game. It is now extremely rare for any team to win a match in which it has been decisively beaten in the lineout.

To the old adage, 'You can't coach speed', modern coaches have added a rider, 'You can't coach height, either'.

WHEN IS A LOCK A SECONDROWER?

When is a lock a secondrower? When he is a New Zealander or a South African. One of the difficulties of writing about rugby between New Zealand and Australian sides, or of drawing up coaching manuals in, say, Japan where the game is exploding or China where the People's Liberation Army has made Rugby Union one of its official sports, is that the various countries have their various nomenclature of the positions.

To resolve the problem, the International Rugby Board has issued an edict setting out the international nomenclature: loose head or tight head props, hooker, left lock and right lock, left flanker and right flanker, number eight, scrum half, fly half, left centre and right centre, left wing and right wing, fullback. But what happens to the number eight if Rugby Union becomes a 14-player game? The edict, too, uses the scrum as the basis for the nomenclature. But locks (in the secondrower context) are now selected to jump at either number 2 or number 4 in the lineout. Similarly, with flankers the modern thinking is that one is picked to play on the openside of scrums and the other on the blindside. This means that on occasions the designated 'left flanker' will be playing on the right flank, and vice versa.

There is a clear need for the IRB to reconsider its designated nomenclature which has been unsuccessful so far in imposing an international order on the naming of positions. Australians, for instance, continue to call the number eight the lock—while New Zealanders continue to call the secondrower the lock.

There is a need, too, to impose an international order on other rugby words. The sixth Asian Pacific Congress Laws Workshop in 1993 nominated the following terms in the laws of rugby 'as conveying no clear meaning and therefore the translation can become inaccurate': touchline, in goal, in touch (which is the opposite of what it means), dead ball line, no side, touch judge, free kick, fair catch, ruck, maul, lineout, scrummage, unconverted try, converted try, conversion, pen-

The IRB edict	*Australia*	*Great Britain*	*New Zealand*	*South Africa*
Loose head or tight head props	Front row	Loose or tight head props	Loose or tight head props	Loose or tight head props
Hooker	Hooker	Hooker	Hooker	Hooker
Left lock, right lock	Second row	Second row	Lock	Lock
Left flanker, right flanker	Breakaway	Wing forward	Flanker	Flanker
Number eight	Lock	Lock	No 8	No 8
Scrum half	Halfback	Scrum half, Inside half, Stand off half	Halfback	Scrum half
Fly half	Five-eighth	Outside half, Fly half	First five-eighth	Fly half
Left centre	Inside centre	Inside centre	Second five-eighth	Inside centre
Right centre	Outside centre	Outside centre	Centre	Outside centre
Left wing, right wing	Wing	Wing	Wing	Wing
Fullback	Fullback	Fullback	Fullback	Fullback

alty, a try, a dropped goal, touch down, drop out, knock on, throw forward and mark.

DIARY OF THE DUNEDIN AMBUSH

Saturday, Dunedin, 4.45pm, 17 July 1993

Phil Kearns, the Wallaby captain, patiently points out to the New Zealand rugby writers in the cramped media room in the main stand at Carisbrook that the Wallabies needed a match or two more to get the rust out of their game. And Bob Dwyer says: 'It went from a two-Test series to one Test and instead of being played after our series with South Africa, it went before. Also, instead of being played in Australia, it was played in New Zealand'. This was Dwyer's comment about the notion of the Wallabies' being 'ambushed' at Dunedin. But the problem with the scheduling of the one-off Test at Dunedin was that the French had insisted on touring South Africa early, and not late, in the southern hemisphere's rugby season. Thanks to the negotiations over new schedules drafted to accommodate the French, the Wallabies had somehow found themselves defending the Bledisloe Cup in New Zealand—and in a one-off Test.

Shades of Sydney 1979. Had Australian rugby ambushed itself?

The bare recital of the facts about schedules, though, suggests several pointed questions. How did the New Zealanders manage to exploit the schedules? Why did the Australian Rugby Union acquiesce in an arrangement that clearly was against the interests of the Wallabies and, therefore, Australian rugby? As someone said to me at Sydney Airport on the way to catching the plane to Dunedin: 'We're the world champions, why aren't they playing us here?'. And, knowing the magnitude of the task of defeating the All Blacks in New Zealand, why wasn't a better preparation organised for the Wallabies?

Saturday, Dunedin, 2.35 pm, 17 July

Minutes after the start of the Test, Grant Fox demonstrates that he is not just the finest goalkicker in rugby history. The Wallabies have mounted an attack. The ball is chipped through. Tim Kelaher, the Wallaby fullback, chases the ball through. Fox runs the ball over the deadball line and sees that it is Kelaher who is following up. He quickly takes a long drop out. It goes back well into the Wallaby half. Pat Howard, a first Test player with a confidence in his ability to beat players with a sharp sidestep, fields the ball. Frank Bunce and Michael Jones bear down on him. The All Blacks have been practising all week to take David Campese in broken play from long drop outs and this practice is put into action as Jones and Bunce hunt down Howard. Howard tries to sidestep Jones and is grabbed. Bunce finishes off the tackle. Isolated, Howard clings to the ball and gives away a penalty.

Pat Howard's dropkick to begin the game after Grant Fox has kicked the penalty for the All Blacks doesn't go the required ten metres and the Wallaby forwards trudge back for a scrum on the halfway mark. This was a predictable mistake from a young, inexperienced player in his first Test. This was where Michael Lynagh's absence was most greatly felt by the Wallabies. For over a decade, Lynagh like Grant Fox has been putting the ball up high enough and far enough for the forwards to win back or crash the opponents to the ground. But hardly one Australian kickoff today gave an advantage to the Wallabies.

Thursday, Sydney Airport, 11.30 am, 15 July

The flight carrying the Wallabies to Dunedin is supposed to have left. The fog lifts to allow the plane to take off at 12.15. It's nearly five o'clock New Zealand time when we arrive at Christchurch and there is another flight of about 40 minutes before the Wallabies—finally—arrive in Dunedin. The whole of Thursday, basically, is wasted for the Wallabies. While they're trapped in the boredom and discomfort (for players with sore backs and stiff legs) of a long distance flight, the All Blacks have a long, detailed training session and then a boat excursion around Dunedin harbour.

Wednesday, Sydney, 6 pm, 14 July
'The team could be heading for the abattoir'. Three days before the Test, this is the assessment of an influential Australian rugby man who rings me up in some anguish.

Saturday, Dunedin, 3.40 pm, 17 July
Six minutes into the second half, the Wallaby forwards who had outjumped and outshoved the All Blacks in the first half inexplicably go to sleep. Mark Cooksley, the All Blacks' giant jumper, ineffectual for most of the match, won several lineouts and the All Blacks threw charge after charge to their left before moving the ball to the right. Sean Fitzpatrick lowered his head like a charging bull and not even Tim Horan's tackle could prevent the try. Moments later, from the kickoff, the All Blacks charged again. The impressive centre, Lee Stensness, chipped through. David Campese calmly (too calmly?) waited for the bounce, which turned back into the hands of the massive Va'aiga Tuigamala. The All Blacks winger carried Campese and the Wallaby fullback Tim Kelaher on his back like annoying but useless crabs, before passing to Frank Bunce to score.

The try gave the All Blacks the comfort zone of a 16-point lead, which Grant Fox, the kicking machine (no passes to his centres from set play in the second half) stretched to 19 with a neatly taken penalty. The Wallabies looked set for a massive defeat. But Pat Howard sent a steepling kick towards the New Zealand goalposts. Tim Horan raced through, leapt high over John Timu and skidded across for a breath-taking try. Jason Little then made a snaking break when the centres were finally given the chance to run the ball. But the Wallaby back row wasn't at the breakdown to back him up.

Saturday, Dunedin, 6.30 pm, 17 July
Groups of men and women students, many of them with English-style long scarfs draped around their necks—the 'scarfies'—stand outside the pubs that cluster around the Carisbrook rugby ground, beers in hand. Their cup is running over as they chant: 'We've got the Bledisloe Cup, we've got the Bledisloe Cuuuuuup'.

THE BATTLE FOR THE BLEDISLOE IS FOUGHT ON STORMY GROUND . . .

Of the hundreds of international rugby matches that have been played over the last 100 years or so, the 1994 Bledisloe Cup Test at the Sydney Football Stadium, under lights for the first time, has the strongest of claims for the title 'The Great Test'. The spectators at the ground were roaring from before the Wallabies ran on to the ground and for minutes after the match. It was one of those occasions where the spectators were so uplifted by the spectacle and thrilled with what they had seen that they didn't want to leave the ground.

At a pre-Test lunch the Australian songwriter Mike McClellan delighted his large audience with his 'Run Wallaby Run' song. As McClellan was singing the chorus a Maori haka party chanted in the background and when the song reached its climax they started to make their foot-stamping challenge closer and closer to the host of the lunch, the former Wallaby coach Alan Jones. By the end of the song the Maori leader had his face only centimetres away from that of Jones, who took the grimacing, the chanting, the tongue-swivelling and the eye-rolling in good, if somewhat bewildered, grace.

> Upon New Zealand's hallowed fields their packs are rarely tamed
> But the tide has turned, the Wallabies learned the power of the running game
> And though we share a common bond the Tasman cannot drown
> The battle for the Bledisloe is fought on stormy ground . . .

The excitement was intense, too, for people who stayed at home and watched the Test on television. The game peaked at a rating of 35 on Channel 10 in Sydney. It rated 41 in New Zealand. In Napier police were called to a house about 10.30 pm where a domestic dispute was reported. Neighbours claimed they had heard screaming. The police discovered this was true, but the dispute was over the fact that the All Blacks secondrower Ian Jones was ruled offside at the back of the lineout. Middle New Zealand was indulging in a primal scream of despair over the impending loss by the All Blacks. David Knox kicked the penalty which took the Wallabies out to a four-point lead.

Peter Roebuck, the brilliant cricket writer, watched the Test in a dressing room somewhere in Somerset where he was captaining the county's second XI. He was so moved by the experience that he wrote a salute to brilliance for the *Sydney Morning Herald:*

> The match between the Wallabies and the All Blacks was one of the most thrilling contests it has been my privilege to watch. Rivals spring to mind, Ali against Frazier, Crisp, the great Australian chaser, at Aintree, Laver and Pele any time anywhere, Kingston Town, Balesteros, Borg v McEnroe at Wimbledon, they roll off the pen and there are plenty more . . . None, surely, outshines the breathtaking struggle seen in Sydney on Wednesday night. Two mighty teams hurled themselves at each other and the thud could be heard around the world, or so it seemed. In those dying minutes, it was as if a raging sea was hammering at a wall, mountainous wave after wave, hammering and not a stone turning. So well matched were the teams, and so spirited their approach, that one hardly dared blink for fear of missing something heroic. They say life is a search for nobility. It's the same with sport. Mostly it inhabits a humdrum world, occasionally it rises and brings joy, once in a blue moon it soars as it did in Sydney . . . Seeing Kiwis and Aussies playing with such fury was to recall the famous remark by a noted cleric that 'a nation is a society united by a delusion about its ancestry and by a common hatred of its neighbours.'

Another appraisal that captured some of the magic of the match was in the *Sunday Telegraph's* 'Mr Walker' column: 'It should be a clear warning to the New South Wales Rugby League. That breathtaking Bledisloe Cup epic at the SFS on Wednesday night proved the rah rahs have really got their act together. As a promotion and as a spectacle, it was 10 out of 10 stuff. Chain passing, brutal defence . . .'

After the Test, which finished some time after 9 pm, I went (or tried to go) to a secluded part of the Sydney Football Stadium to phone my match comment through to the *Sydney Morning Herald*. It quickly became clear to me, though, that there was no quiet place within the stadium. People were refusing to leave. Great knots of people were gathered chattering excitedly about the match. I made my way back to the media room. The place was crowded as journalists frantically phoned their stories through and others used their laptops plugged into the telephone sockets. The rumour was transferred to me that Laurie Mains was going to announce his retirement at the after-match press conference. Heads nodded when this rumour was announced. Peter FitzSimons came up to me in an agitated manner. He couldn't find a phone and he had to get his story through for the front page: 'Could I use your phone first?'. Later I was to find out that the front page is the last page to be 'put to bed'. My copy, in other words, for the back page of the sports section, was needed more urgently. But FitzSimons and I knew nothing about newspaper production, so I handed my mobile phone across to him. And then I had the mortification of hearing him read out an opening paragraph that was going to be my opening paragraph.

When I finally got my mobile phone back I found that it was difficult to read my notes and I felt, too, a certain selfconsciousness about dictating my words with other journalists milling about, listening in occasionally and raising eyebrows at certain parts of my comment. Under these difficult circumstances, then, I dictated the following paragraphs to the copytaker back at the *Herald*.

> What a Test, one of the most pulsating in the long history of rugby matches between Australia and New Zealand which began at the Sydney Cricket Ground in 1903. It took a tackle by George Gregan coming from nowhere to knock the ball out of the hands of the All Blacks winger Jeff Wilson just as he was going to score The Try That Would Have Won The Test for the All Blacks. Wilson, who is called 'Goldie' by his team-mates for his prodigious sporting talents, beat four or five players in a run to the line, in what seemed to be a storybook ending to his controversial selection, before launching himself into a triumphant dive. And then came Gregan . . .
>
> The Wallabies kept the All Blacks waiting for some minutes before coming out on to the field. And then David Campese and David Knox nonchalantly kicked the ball to each other while the All Blacks were doing an impassioned haka. The point of all this, it seemed, was to give the impression that the Wallabies were supremely confident. The opening seconds of the match confirmed this approach. Knox kicked-off high, the Wallaby forwards recovered the ball, Knox then kicked a monstrously high ball to the All Blacks tryline and Jason Little, in the manner of Tim Horan, soared like an Australian Rules footballer, caught the ball and fell across the line. For the All Blacks, who were under intense pressure and criticism, this was the worst of all possible starts.
>
> As the first half proceeded, the All Blacks knocked the ball on, missed passes, gave away penalties and generally played like a side that did not

expect to win. When the Wallabies produced a well-rehearsed and unstoppable move from the back of the scrum to score their second try, it looked as if the All Blacks were being prepared for the sort of massacre that was inflicted on Manu Samoa. Knox's kicking from re-starts and general play had the ball hanging agonisingly in the air for the All Blacks, and with John Eales charging through to put pressure on the catcher, the All Blacks spent the half being pushed and shoved towards their tryline.

At halftime I came across an All Black from the 1970s, Joe Karam. I asked him what he thought was happening out on the field. 'They're playing with no confidence', Karam said. 'Too many players have been played out of position. Senior players like John Kirwan should be in the team.' But in the second half the All Blacks reached back to that New Zealand genius for rugby and played a magnificent 40 minutes. The bounce of the ball which had gone against them in the first half started to turn their way. They began to win a sequence of lineouts. I wrote in my notes: 'The All Blacks are getting on top but do they have enough time to win the game?'. A certain try was lost when Zinzan Brooke passed forward to an unmarked Michael Jones who crossed for a try—disallowed. The errant pass had followed a sustained series of attacks by the All Blacks from one side of the field to the other, time after time, until there were no Wallabies left to defend. Series after series of similar attacks were launched but the Wallabies' tackling was as secure and thorough, and often pile-driving in its effects, as the handling and running had been in the first half.

Shane Howarth scored the try that had to come and the All Blacks were finally within a score of winning the Test. Howarth then missed a penalty. Knox kicked a penalty. And then Wilson made the wonderful run into the same corner that John Kirwan had fumbled a ball in two years ago and lost a try that would have probably won the Test for the All Blacks. The corner has become Hell's Corner for the New Zealanders. And in a finish that a master of melodrama might have concocted, the All Blacks ran the ball from behind their goal line with holes opening up in the Wallaby defence all over the field. People beside me were standing on their seats and screaming out 'Tackle Wallabies, tackle, tackle!' and the desperation off the field was matched with a similar desperation on the field . . .

THE GOLD AND THE BLACK

The first rugby Test between Australia and New Zealand in 1903 proved that there was a thirst, a demand and a need for such encounters. The robustness and manliness of rugby suited the raw colonial lifestyle. Jim Webster's humorous but true definition basically explains why rugby had this attraction to young men on the edge of the world: 'RUGBY: a pastime of delirious enjoyment, much story-telling, plentiful drinking and occasional singing disturbed only by 80 minutes of often pointless endeavour on a strip of barren earth'. By 1907, the Tests between New Zealand and Australia drew huge crowds. The first Test of that year at the Sydney Cricket Ground saw a crowd of over 47 000 in attendance, still one of the largest crowds to watch a Test between the All Blacks and the Wallabies.

But the momentum of enthusiasm that great competitions require was lost with the Great Split, the consequent weakening of Australian rugby with the brawn drain to Rugby League, and then the patriotic but foolish decision by Australian rugby officials to stop playing rugby during the duration of the First World War. Rugby in Queensland collapsed and was not revived officially until 1929, when the first Test series between the Wallabies and All Blacks in fifteen years was played. Meanwhile, in New Zealand the taste for intense, high quality rugby was sated with the Ranfurly Shield challenge matches, tours of the United Kingdom by the All Blacks and, from 1921, a series of Tests with the South African Springboks that were regarded—rightly—as rugby battles for the title of World Champion. As the words and music (written by P. W. Gregory) of a popular song of the 1920s, 'The All Blacks Football Song', had it:

> From the Cape of Northland to the Plains of Southland hear the cry
> Come a-way Black! Play it hard! Play it fast! Play it to their line
> Bury their line with our Silver Fern.

The Bledisloe Cup for Australia–New Zealand rugby competition was inaugurated in 1931 in an attempt to give life to the trans-Tasman rivalry. But the rugby competition between the All Blacks and the Wallabies, even with the trophy at stake, initially lacked credibility because it was not competitive. The Wallabies had a small golden fluke of victories in the 1930s. But the Bledisloe Cup was not regained by an Australian side once it was lost in 1936 until 1949 when a New Zealand Third XV (the All Blacks were touring South Africa at the time; the Third XV included a handful of first-class Maori players) lost the cup to a Wallabies side captained by Trevor Allen. Australian rugby then went into the rugby wilderness for 30 years, until a surprise victory to the Wallabies in a one-off Test at the Sydney Cricket Ground in 1979 revived it. The Bledisloe Cup, a trophy that New Zealanders had taken for granted, no longer resided in New Zealand. The natives, consequently, got restless.

Regaining that which has been lost in the face of what is assumed to be the natural order of things often provokes an inspired interest where apathy previously reigned. Regaining and retaining the Bledisloe Cup became as consuming a New Zealand rugby passion as beating the Springboks had been. And when rugby against South Africa in the 1980s was marred by controversy and geopolitical considerations the desire to beat the Australians intensified. This intensity coincided with a renaissance in Australian rugby. Peter Fenton's inspiring poem, 'The Spirit of the Wallabies', which is sometimes read out in the dressing room before a Test, is a sign of that renaissance:

There's a spirit in the Wallabies
Mere words can not describe,
It's as if they had descended
From some legendary tribe.
There's kinship, a tradition,
As in days so long since past,
Of crusades, of knights in armour,
And of men before the mast . . .
But it isn't just the winning,
Nor the scoring, nor the cheers,
It's the friendships and the memories
That last you through the years.
It's the camaraderie
That's born of valour not of fame,
It's the sheer exhilaration
When you play the running game.

What physicists call a critical mass was achieved—finally—in the Bledisloe Cup competition. From the 1980s onwards the rugby battles between the Wallabies and New Zealand became true contests between the Gold and the Black. The shining play and optimistic tactics of the Wallabies by 1991 produced one of rugby's historically great teams. The Australian rugby community, too, was becoming increasingly inclusive, assertive and demanding of success. Against this was the Black of New Zealand rugby, powerful, rooted in the tradition of winning, resilient—and when Wayne Shelford was captain between 1988 and 1990 majestic in its domination of its opponents and the breathtaking efficiency and ruthlessness of its play. Rugby people in both countries became increasingly obsessed with the significance of the emblematic trophy. The days of easy victories to the New Zealanders were over. With Bledisloe Cup Tests scheduled for every year in the 1980s (at last), the final ingredient, the attraction of annual testing and Tests, was added to the mix that now makes up the world's finest rugby competition between two countries. Dr Mark Loane, the devastating Wallaby loose forward of the 1970s, has stated that 'rugby is a disease for which there is no known cure'. As the best of everything about rugby the Bledisloe Cup has become an even more virulent form of that disease.

Competitions thrive when the participants believe they have a chance of winning. That blessed state of affairs has now been attained with the Bledisloe Cup. The All Blacks and the Wallabies now play on stormy ground. The Wallabies lost the Bledisloe Cup (this wording is used because of the remarkable achievement of New Zealand rugby in remaining competitive at the Test level from 1903 onwards) in 1982. The Wallabies regained the Bledisloe Cup, with Alan Jones as coach, in 1986. The All Blacks won it back in their Rugby World Cup year, an *annus mirabilis* for New Zealand rugby, in 1987. A marvellous series in 1992 saw the Wallabies hold the Bledisloe Cup again, only to lose it in the Dunedin ambush the next year. And in 1994 the Wallabies regained the Bledisloe Cup in a pulsating and dramatic match that has already become the stuff of legends, the Great Test.

As with the cricket Ashes between England and Australia, there is now a history to the Bledisloe Cup that gives each individual match played for it a resonance. The current players are emulating the deeds of a long line of peerless performers: from the future stars like Jeff Wilson and George Gregan, their great contemporaries David Campese and Sean Fitzpatrick, down through Tony Shaw and Graham Mourie to Colin Meads and Ken Catchpole, through to Fred Allen and Cyril Towers and all their fellow players of the 1930s and 1940s—and back to those original Test players whose deeds live in photographs and words and the accumulated mystique that the years have added like a patina to their names, the first great players like Billy Wallace and Dally Messenger of so long ago. May their memory never die and may the Bledisloe Cup competition never end.

Ake Ake Kia Kaha! (Forever, forever be strong!)

Appendix 1: Record of tests between Australia and New Zealand

Year	Venue	Winners	Score
1903	Sydney	New Zealand	22–3
1905	Dunedin	New Zealand	14–3
1907	Sydney	New Zealand	26–6
	Brisbane	New Zealand	14–5
	Sydney	draw	5–5
1910	Sydney	New Zealand	6–0
	Sydney	Australia	11–0
	Sydney	New Zealand	28–13
1913	Wellington	New Zealand	30–5
	Dunedin	New Zealand	25–13
	Christchurch	Australia	16–5
1914	Sydney	New Zealand	5–0
	Brisbane	New Zealand	17–0
	Sydney	New Zealand	22–7
1929	Sydney	Australia	9–8
	Brisbane	Australia	17–9
	Sydney	Australia	15–13
1931	Auckland	New Zealand	20–13 (first Bledisloe Cup)
1932	Sydney	Australia	22–17
	Brisbane	New Zealand	21–3
	Sydney	New Zealand	21–13
1934	Sydney	Australia	25–11
	Sydney	draw	3–3
1936	Wellington	New Zealand	11–6
	Dunedin	New Zealand	38–13
1938	Sydney	New Zealand	24–9
	Brisbane	New Zealand	20–14
	Sydney	New Zealand	14–6
1946	Dunedin	New Zealand	31–8
	Auckland	New Zealand	14–10
1947	Brisbane	New Zealand	13–5
	Sydney	New Zealand	27–14
1949	Wellington	Australia	11–6
	Auckland	Australia	16–9
1951	Sydney	New Zealand	8–0
	Sydney	New Zealand	17–11
	Brisbane	New Zealand	16–6
1952	Christchurch	Australia	14–9
	Wellington	New Zealand	15–8
1955	Wellington	New Zealand	16–8
	Dunedin	New Zealand	8–0
	Auckland	Australia	8–3
1957	Sydney	New Zealand	25–11
	Brisbane	New Zealand	22–9
1958	Wellington	New Zealand	25–3
	Christchurch	Australia	6–3
	Auckland	New Zealand	17–8
1962	Brisbane	New Zealand	20–6

	Sydney	New Zealand	14–5
	Wellington	draw	9–9
	Dunedin	New Zealand	3–0
	Auckland	New Zealand	16–8
1964	Dunedin	New Zealand	14–9
	Christchurch	New Zealand	18–3
	Wellington	Australia	20–5
1967	Wellington	New Zealand	29–9
1968	Sydney	New Zealand	27–11
	Brisbane	New Zealand	19–18
1972	Wellington	New Zealand	29–6
	Christchurch	New Zealand	30–17
	Auckland	New Zealand	38–3
1974	Sydney	New Zealand	11–6
	Brisbane	Draw	16–16
	Sydney	New Zealand	16–6
1978	Wellington	New Zealand	13–12
	Christchurch	New Zealand	22–6
	Auckland	Australia	30–16
1979	Sydney	Australia	12–6
1980	Sydney	Australia	13–9
	Brisbane	New Zealand	12–9
	Sydney	Australia	26–10
1982	Christchurch	New Zealand	23–16
	Wellington	Australia	19–16
	Auckland	New Zealand	33–18
1983	Sydney	New Zealand	18–8
1984	Sydney	Australia	16–9
	Brisbane	New Zealand	19–15
	Sydney	New Zealand	25–24
1985	Auckland	New Zealand	10–9
1986	Wellington	Australia	13–12
	Dunedin	New Zealand	13–12
	Auckland	Australia	22–9
1987	Sydney	New Zealand	30–16
1988	Sydney	New Zealand	32–7
	Brisbane	draw	19–19
	Sydney	New Zealand	30–9
1989	Auckland	New Zealand	24–12
1990	Christchurch	New Zealand	21–6
	Auckland	New Zealand	27–17
	Wellington	Australia	21–9
1991	Sydney	Australia	21–12
	Auckland	New Zealand	6–3
	Dublin	Australia	16–9 (World Cup)
1992	Sydney	Australia	16–15
	Brisbane	Australia	19–17
	Sydney	New Zealand	26–23
1993	Dunedin	New Zealand	25–10
1994	Sydney	Australia	20–16

APPENDIX 2: REPORT ON THE INQUIRY INTO STANDARDS OF RUGBY IN AUSTRALIA

'In October, 1972, the Australian Rugby Football Union decided to appoint a Committee to investigate the Standard of Rugby in Australia. This decision followed the unsuccessful tour of New Zealand culminating in the loss in the Third Test by 38–3 . . .

It is wrong to view the position of Rugby in Australia with complete gloom. Many large gains have been made, although it is surprising how many of the code's followers do not understand its growth. Some of these features are:

1 In 1958, the number of non-first-grade teams in Sydney was approximately 24. In 1973, the number will have grown to about 235.
2 The number of juniors playing in New South Wales in 1958 was about 1200–1500. There are now almost 30 000 registered players . . .
5 It is estimated that approximately 25 teams of all ages and levels left Australia last year on Overseas Tours . . . It is further estimated that a further 45 teams of all ages and levels left New South Wales on Interstate Tours . . .
8 Queensland is developing a superb sports complex at Ballymore. A sub-district competition in Brisbane and the development of Queensland and Country are two areas that were virtually non-existent 10 years ago.
9 In 1967, the first 'Australia only' tour from a country other than New Zealand took place when Ireland paid us a visit. Previously, matches were played in Australia as an addendum to matches in New Zealand.

New Zealand Tour

Post mortems are only useful for what they can tell us for the future. The performance of the recent team in New Zealand is therefore important for the lessons that can be learnt, rather than for seeking the 'sacrificial scapegoat.'

Some of the reasons put forward for our failure . . . are as follows:

- Lack of experienced Test players. Many players who toured France 9 months previously were not available . . . The strength of our teams during 1963–1966 was due in part to a continuity of personnel. In contrast, only 6 of the 30 players who went to South Africa in 1969 toured New Zealand in 1972 . . .

There is a need for more concentration on rucks and mauls. These phases should be more constructive. No point received greater comment than the superiority of the New Zealand teams in these spheres . . . Here lies the main challenge to improving the game in Australia. The physique of the All Blacks forwards, most of whom come from rural areas, is superior to ours. In contrast, most of our forwards are in less demanding occupations. While not denying that one's normal occupation is quite important for the maintenance of general all-round fitness and therefore the All Blacks have an edge on us here, it is interesting to consider the occupations of the South African forwards who toured Australia in 1971: student, sales rep, air force officer, sports dealer, teacher, sports dealer, former university lecturer, clerk, quality controller, aircraft assembler, sales rep, architect and student . . .

Past and present players commented on the need to prepare programmes that should be followed in the off-season to develop techniques and player strength . . . These pre-season sessions must be open-ended. Many a player commented that the selection of a squad did have a detrimental effect on a player's incentive when he was not invited to join . . .

The agreement of the ARFU to playing the first match against Otago was strongly criticised and the loss of this match put the tour off to a bad start. Conditions in Dunedin were unfamiliar, for rarely do matches take place in Australia on grounds as heavy as was experienced here . . . More thought must be given to starting tours in New Zealand in the North Islands in more familiar conditions and against less formidable opponents as a major province . . . Players pointed out that they travelled all day on the Sunday after the match against Otago . . . By the end of the tour, most of the players were exhausted because of the state of the tour. It is reasonable to suggest that the reason was psychological rather than physical. In both the second and the third Test, many of the points against us were scored in a very brief period. For those in Australia who have been harshly critical of the team's performance, it is interesting to speculate on their reaction if we had scored in the first few minutes of the second Test and thereupon reversed the whole state of the game . . .

Coaching

All groups agreed that greater attention must be given to the teaching of fundamentals. Problems are apparent at all senior levels of the game and some players proceed to the national level deficient in the basic skills . . . One of New Zealand's most successful coaches, Fred Allen, worried intensively over the fundamentals and each fundamental skill was coached in considerable detail . . .

Representative football

Early in the inquiry a most interesting comment was made by a former All Black about the need to create and maintain incentive in players. This player told us that from his final year in school he had regular goals at which to aim, each one just within his grasp. There were a series of representative matches that acted as stepping stones, up to All Black status. Each level acted as a spur to improve and try for the next one. Each provided valuable match practice with other players of similar above-average ability . . .

Recommendation: That consideration be given to the introduction of a match between New South Wales and Queensland on an annual basis at the Under-23 years level.

Statistics

Although it has been stated by many of us that the new knock-on law has resulted in fewer scrums, the difference appears to be marginal. It has been suggested that play is moving across field more than in the past, but then a maul develops from which the ball does not emerge, and another scrum is ordered. The average number of penalties per game has been increasing steadily over the four-year period . . . It is understood that the leading New South Wales first grade goalkicker in 1972, John Maxwell of Gordon, has succeeded in about 51 per cent of all attempts. The rate of rucks killed (about a third of all opportunities) is alarming . . .

Ex-Internationals

. . . It is interesting to note how many former Wallabies are vitally interested in maintaining liaison with their colleagues. Many said there was no incentive from 'up top' for them to assist in the game in the national area where they are best suited . . .

Public relations

. . . Our relations with the media are quite good. However, members of the media have complained that at times they have been unable to obtain information through prescribed channels. Opportunities for publicity have therefore been lost . . . We would be less than honest with ourselves if we believed that our communications with affiliated unions were all they should be . . .

Junior rugby

Recommendations:

1 That inter-district championships for children under the age of 11 years be abolished.
2 That teams be reduced to 9 or 10 a side and matches played on half the regular sized field.
3 That the Laws of the Game be relaxed in certain situations for children of this age group to handle the ball and recognise that the game is to be enjoyed.
4 The Junior authorities introduce lectures at the start of the season for all parents/coaches and managers and advise these people of their obligations and responsibilities to the game. This form of rugby, known as Mini-Rugby, is already played in Wales.

Selection

. . . To represent Australia is the highest honour any player can achieve. Where a player is chosen for 'blooding,' this concept is eroded. All players chosen for a tour must be the best available. Players also thought that some representatives were virtually given a privileged run into a touring team. No one is entitled to this concession . . .

Suggestions made to the inquiry

- Coaches at all levels should gather under the direction of the ARU to discuss areas of technique in Australian Rugby that are presently frail.
- A flying squad of past international players should be formed in Sydney and invited to visit each first division club and country zone for one evening during the season.
- Any announcement of pre-season training squads has a detrimental effect on the representative ambitions of players not nominated.
- Players selected for overseas tours should be the best players

Statistics from a Sydney First Division club for period 1969–1972

	Average no. games	*1969*		*1970*		*1971*		*1972*		*Total*	*Average per match*
Matches per year		22		22		19		19			
Tightheads	82	150	6.82	144	6.35	136	7.16	128	6.74	558	6.80
Scrums	82	779	35.41	702	31.91	670	35.26	658	34.63	2809	34.26
Penalties	82	364	16.55	397	18.05	407	21.42	418	22.00	1586	19.34
Lineouts	82	935	42.5	832	37.82	721	37.95	685	36.05	3173	38.70
Incorrect throwing	82	66	3.00	67	3.05	65	3.42	72	3.79	270	3.29
Rucks	82	517	23.50	555	25.23	390	20.53	386	20.34	1848	22.54
Rucks killed	58	–	–	95	4.75	141	7.42	178	9.37	414	7.14
Percentage rucks killed to rucks	–	–	–	–	18.83	–	36.14	–	44.96	–	31.68
Tries scored	81	120	5.71	123	5.59	109	5.74	88	4.63	440	5.43
Attempted goal kicks	81	283	12.86	262	11.91	260	13.68	244	12.84	1053	13
Successful goal kicks	81	,123	5.59	103	4.68	110	5.79	80	4.21	416	5.14
Percentage of successful kicks		–	43.46	–	39.31	–	42.31	–	32.79	39.51	
Points scored per match	82	696	31.64	688	31.27	612	32.21	575	30.26	2571	31.35

available and should not be chosen for potential or past experience.

- The Sydney first division competition should be one round only, interspersed with an intensive calendar of representative matches.
- The law presently allowing the halfback to follow the ball through the scrum has a detrimental effect on the game.
- Indiscriminate kicking and blatant brutality should not be tolerated and selectors, officials, referees and players should co-operate to rid the game of incorrigible offenders.
- Lack of uniformity of interpretation of the laws by referees causes difficulties for players.
- Referees appointments boards should be guided in part by players' attitudes in view of the . . . role of referees towards adding to the enjoyment of playing the game.
- Coaches at both higher and lower levels—unfortunately—reduce initiative and inhibit natural talent in promising players.
- Greater attention must be made to the position of captain . . .
- Aim of local competitions should follow the following order, rather than the other way around: i/ playing for enjoyment
  ii/ supply of international players
  iii/ winning of premierships
- Greater emphasis should be made of the offensive in the game rather than the defensive.

A RUGBY READING LIST

Books

Allen, Fred and McLean, Terry *Fred Allen on Rugby*, Cassell, London, 1970

Bamford, T. W. *Thomas Arnold*, The Crescent Press, London, 1960

Chester, R. H. and McMillan, N. A. C. *Men in Black*, Moa Publications, Auckland, 1981

Chester, R. H., McMillan, N. A. C. and Palenski, R. A. *The Encyclopedia of New Zealand Rugby*, Moa Publications, Auckland, 1988

Ella, Mark and Smith, Terry *Path to Victory: Wallaby power in the 1980s*, ABC Books, Sydney, 1987

Fenton, Peter *Sport: the way I speak it*, Little Hills Press, Sydney, 1992

FitzSimons, Peter *Nick Farr-Jones: the authorised biography*, Random House, Sydney, 1993

Gallaher, Dave and Stead, Billy *The Complete Rugby Footballer*, Methuen, London, 1906

Heads, Ian *True Blue: the story of the NSW Rugby League*, Ironbark Press, Sydney, 1992

Hickie, Thomas V. *They Ran with the Ball*, Longman Cheshire, Melbourne, 1993

Howitt, Bob *New Zealand Rugby Greats*, vols 1 and 2, Moa Publications, Auckland, 1975 and 1982

Keating, Frank *The Great Number Tens*, Partridge Press, London, 1993

King, Michael *Pakeha: the quest for identity in New Zealand*, Penguin, Auckland, 1990

Laidlaw, Chris *Mud in Your Eyes*, Reeds, Auckland, 1971

McLean, Terry *Great Days in New Zealand Rugby*, Reeds, Auckland, 1959

—— *All Black Power*, Reeds, Auckland, 1968

—— *The All Blacks*, Sidgwick & Jackson, London, 1991

Macory, Jennifer *Running with the Ball: the birth of rugby football*, Collins Willow, 1991

Mossop, Rex and Writer, Larry *The Moose that Roared*, Ironbark Press, Sydney, 1991

Mulgan, John *Report on Experience*, Blackwood, Auckland, 1967

O'Hagan, Sean *The Pride of the Southern Rebels*, Pilgrims South Press, Dunedin, 1981

Palenski, Ron *Graham Mourie: Captain*, Moa Publications, Auckland, 1982

—— ed. *Between the Posts*, Hodder & Stoughton, Auckland, 1989

Phillips, Jock *A Man's Country?*, Penguin, Auckland, 1987

Pollard, Jack *Australian Rugby: the game and the players*, Ironbark Press, Sydney, 1994

Quinn, Keith *The Encyclopedia of World Rugby*, ABC Books, Sydney, 1993

Reason, John and James, Carwyn *The World of Rugby*, BBC Books, London, 1979

Reid, J. C., and Cape, Peter *The Book of New Zealand*, Collins, Auckland, 1971

Roger, Warwick *Old Heroes*, Hodder & Stoughton, Auckland, 1989
Ryan, Greg *The Forerunners of the All Blacks*, Canterbury University Press, Christchurch, 1993
Slater, Gordon *On the Ball*, Whitcombe and Tombs, Wellington, 1970
Smith, Godfrey ed. *Take the Ball and Run*, Pavilion, London, 1991
Stoddart, Brian *Saturday Afternoon Fever*, Angus & Robertson, Sydney, 1986
Veysey, Alex *Colin Meads*, Collins, Auckland, 1974
Wilkins, Phil *The Highlanders*, Gordon Rugby Club Limited, Sydney, 1986
Williams, Ian *In Touch*, The Kingswood Press, Sydney, 1991

Magazines and newspapers

Evening Post (Wellington)
New Zealand Free Lance (Wellington)
New Zealand Herald (Auckland)
New Zealand Weekly News (Auckland)
Sports Digest (Wellington)
Sun-Herald (Sydney)
The Sydney Mail
Sydney Morning Herald

Acknowledgements

The author would like to thank the following individuals and organisations for permission to reproduce material used in this book:

Rod Clement (pp. 50, 67); Rocco Fazzari (p. 34, 85); Eric Heath (p. i); Mrs Lodge (p. 73); Alan Moir (pp. 37, 98, 128); The *New Zealand Herald* (p. 53–5); Simon Poidevin (p. 139); Keith Quin (p. 75); Shakespeare (pp. 139, 142, 152, 160); The *Sydney Morning Herald* for material from the *Sydney Mail* (pp. 10, 19, 20, 21, 52, 57, 59, 61, 64); Garrick Tremain (pp. 171, 178); Wilson & Horton/*Weekly News* (p. 42).

Every effort has been made to contact the copyright holders of material used in this book. Where an omission has occurred, the author and publisher will gladly include acknowledgement in any future edition.